The Challenge of Human Rights

Dedicated to the memory of my brother, Bernard

The Challenge of Human Rights

Origin, Development, and Significance

Jack Mahoney

Blackwell
Publishing

© 2007 by Jack Mahoney

BLACKWELL PUBLISHING
350 Main Street, Malden, MA 02148-5020, USA
9600 Garsington Road, Oxford OX4 2DQ, UK
550 Swanston Street, Carlton, Victoria 3053, Australia

The right of Jack Mahoney to be identified as the Author of this Work has been asserted in accordance with the UK Copyright, Designs, and Patents Act 1988.

First published 2007 by Blackwell Publishing Ltd

1   2007

Library of Congress Cataloging-in-Publication Data

Mahoney, John, 1931–
    The challenge of human rights : origin, development, and significance / Jack Mahoney.
        p. cm.
    Includes bibliographical references and index.
    ISBN-13: 978-1-4051-5240-2 (hardback : alk. paper)
    ISBN-10: 1-4051-5240-0 (hardback : alk. paper)
    ISBN-13: 978-1-4051-5241-9 (pbk. : alk. paper)
    ISBN-10: 1-4051-5241-9 (pbk. : alk. paper)
    1. Human rights.   2. Human rights – History.   3. Human rights
 – Philosophy.   I. Title.
JC571.M25   2006
323–dc22
                                                    2006002736

A catalogue record for this title is available from the British Library.

Set in 10 on 12 pt Sabon
by SNP Best-set Typesetter Ltd, Hong Kong
Printed and bound in Singapore
by COS Printers Pte Ltd

The publisher's policy is to use permanent paper from mills that operate a sustainable forestry policy, and which has been manufactured from pulp processed using acid-free and elementary chlorine-free practices. Furthermore, the publisher ensures that the text paper and cover board used have met acceptable environmental accreditation standards.

For further information on
Blackwell Publishing, visit our website:
www.blackwellpublishing.com

Contents

Acknowledgments

As I complete this study, the fruit of several years of reading and reflection, I am happy to acknowledge my indebtedness to innumerable colleagues, students, and friends who have helped me form my views on human rights over the years, and especially to Dr. Gerard J. Hughes and Dr. Peter Gallagher for their valued comments and suggestions on an early version of the work. I also wish to record my thanks to the community of St. Mary's Hall, Boston College, Massachusetts, for their friendly welcome and their warm interest and encouragement during the final stage of writing, and particularly to Dr. Oduke Charles Onyango for generously, and patiently, sharing his computing expertise. I am indebted also to Blackwell's Commissioning Editor Dr. Nick Bellorini for his interest and his encouragement; and to the publisher's reviewers for their valuable comments and suggestions. In the final event, then, whatever merits this work may contain will reflect the contributions of many people. The faults are entirely my own.

Introduction

The emergence of human rights into human ethical consciousness and their development and now worldwide recognition constitute a moral phenomenon of astonishing scale and unparalleled significance, well meriting the remark of Henkin (1990: p. xvii) that "Ours is the age of rights. Human rights is the idea of our time." Fifty years after the historic promulgation of the Universal Declaration of Human Rights in 1948, the UN Secretary-General, Kofi Annan (1998: 18) noted that "it is the universality of human rights that gives them their strength. It endows them with the power to cross any border, climb any wall, defy any force." On the same occasion, the former President of Ireland and newly appointed UN High Commissioner for Human Rights, Mary Robinson (1998: 253), declared that "we must learn that human rights, in their essence, are empowering."

Timely, universal, and empowering. These three characteristics of human rights identified above have inspired and shaped this study which is aimed at examining, and commending, their challenge today. We begin in chapter 1 by tracing the roots of natural rights and the growth of the theory from the ancient and medieval worlds through the revolutionary ages of Britain, America, and France to the eve of the Second World War. This is followed in chapter 2 by examining the development of the modern human rights movement which emerged as a consequence of that war, and by chronicling its international expansion to the present time. Attention is then given, in chapter 3, to clarifying how the many complexities of human rights can be understood, and to responding to the criticisms which are raised against them. In chapter 4 we then expound and assess the varied arguments which are invoked to establish the existence and the validity of human rights, and suggest which of these might be most popularly acceptable today. Finally, we devote the fifth chapter to the topic of how human rights relate to the most significant and pervading feature of modern life, globalization in its many manifestations. We examine their role in a world which is in some respects increasingly interconnected and yet in other respects increasingly divided; and we indicate how some human rights have acquired a globalized application, especially those which appeal to economic justice, to environmental justice, and to HIV/AIDS justice.

We suggest finally that respect for human rights must logically culminate in some form of cosmopolitanism, or a more consciously united world, manifesting what the French in their Revolution termed *fraternité*, and what today we might prefer to term *human solidarity*. The UN Secretary-General, Boutros-Ghali (*The UN and Human Rights* 1995: p. 442), observed that humankind constitutes "a single human community." Our conclusion is a richer one, to propose that what human rights reveal is that humanity forms a single moral family, all of whose members are united in human solidarity and thus owe to each other a mutual moral respect based on their shared dignity as awe-inspiring human beings.

The canvas covered by human rights is thus a very large one indeed, and our attempt to capture at least the broad picture has inevitably meant that some details of the subject have not received the justice they would otherwise deserve. We have singled out three human rights as especially significant in illustrating the way in which rights are acquiring a global dimension today. A great deal more can be said of each of them, and about other particular rights, including the rights of particular groups in every society and rights arising within different areas of human life and activity. Our hope, however, is that the picture presented here will be recognized as a faithful, if general, one of the subject as a whole, and that it will stimulate and encourage further reading and research in the area.

The extensive reach and moral leverage of human rights appear indisputable, as the record of history shows. Yet that record also sadly acknowledges that there have been, and remain, massive defaults in recognizing and respecting these moral claims. As McGrew noted (1998: 194–5), "The twentieth century has witnessed an unprecedented global diffusion of the idea of rights . . . But whereas the idea of rights has spread, this has not necessarily been accompanied by greater universal observance of rights." Henkin (1990: 28–9), however, offers some wry encouragement: "No doubt the commitment of many countries to human rights is less than authentic and whole-hearted. Yet . . . even hypocrisy may sometimes deserve one cheer for it confirms the value of the idea, and limits the scope and blatancy of violations."

Coupled, then, with a conviction of the significance of human rights for the gradual advancement of human society worldwide must come the continual awareness of the need for vigilance to work for their recognition and implementation in every corner of that society. At the close of the study we observe that the uncovering and emerging consciousness and recognition of human rights has immeasurably enriched the human race's ethical resources. Our hope is that this work will have contributed to accepting the challenge of those human rights, which is to identify, confront, and where possible to eliminate what the Scots poet Robert Burns (1995) described feelingly as "man's inhumanity to man." Accordingly, the aim of all concerned to meet the challenge of human rights must be, as expressed by one UN Secretary-General (*The UN and Human Rights* 1995: p. 533), to "continue to mobilize [our] efforts, so that human rights may one day emerge at last as the common language of humanity."

References

Annan, K. (1998), Message of the United Nations Secretary-General, in Barend van der Heijden and Bahiaq Tahzib-Lie (eds.), *Reflections on the Universal Declaration of Human Rights: A Fiftieth Anniversary Anthology*, The Hague: Martin Nijhoff.

Burns, R. (1995), Man was Made to Mourn, *Complete Poems and Songs*, London: HarperCollins.

Henkin, L. (1990), *The Age of Rights*, New York: Columbia University Press.

McGrew, A. G. (1998), Human Rights in a Global Age: Coming to Terms with Globalization, in Tony Evans (ed.), *Human Rights Fifty Years On: A Reappraisal*, Manchester: Manchester University Press.

Robinson, M. (1998), The Universal Declaration of Human Rights: the International Keystone of Human Dignity, in Barend van der Heijden and Bahiaq Tahzib-Lie (eds.), *Reflections on the Universal Declaration of Human Rights: A Fiftieth Anniversary Anthology*, The Hague: Martin Nijhoff.

The United Nations and Human Rights 1945–1995 (1995), intro. by Boutros Boutros-Ghali, Secretary-General of the United Nations, New York: Department of Public Information, United Nations.

Chapter ①

Human Rights in History

Human rights as we understand them today are largely the product of seventeenth- to eighteenth-century Western thought, and as such find no substantial place in ethical or political reflection in Europe before the twelfth century. However, the earliest stage of Western ethical reflection contains two deeply significant features which contributed to the eventual emergence of human rights: the centering of human morality on the idea of justice; and the recourse to human nature as a source of moral knowledge. The aim of this opening chapter is to identify the source of the idea of human rights in Western thought and to trace its historical development as far as the middle of the twentieth century.

The Ancient Classical World

The ancient world of Greece and Rome did not have a theory of human or natural rights. In a wide-ranging and discursive history of human rights Gary B. Herbert seemed clear that the notion of subjective rights dates only from the late Middle Ages (Herbert 2002: 49, 69–71), yet in his history of Homeric society he regularly refers to subjective rights (pp. 1–18). He further claimed that Aristotle held that "a natural commensurability exists between natural abilities and natural rights; those who have greater abilities have correspondingly greater rights" (p. 29); and he alleged that Aquinas was to follow Aristotle in thus viewing "natural rights" (p. 62); all without providing any textual citations. Likewise Hayden writes of Aristotle as envisaging citizens having subjective rights to property and to political participation, commenting that he "defined rights only in a restricted legal sense"; but he offers no sources for his statement (Hayden 2005: 39). An attempt was made by Miller actually to prove that "Aristotle recognizes 'subjective' rights in the sense of rights belonging to individual subjects which can be claimed by them against other individuals" (Miller 1995: 113 n. 68). However, his textual argument is tenuous and not persuasive in itself; nor does he explain why Aristotle's contemporaries and successors did not pick up or develop the theme if it did indeed form part of his political or moral philosophy. Nor does Stoic thought contain the idea of human rights, in spite of several popular presumptions to the contrary, including that of Cranston (1973: 10), who refers to the concept of natural rights as elaborated by the Stoics of the Hellenistic period.

However, although we cannot find any language or theory of human rights in ancient Greek thought, nevertheless the basis of human rights, the concept of justice, is strongly present there. Thus, Aristotle recognized a clear distinction between two types of justice, one which is legal or conventional (*nomikon*) and which can change according to circumstances in society, and the other which is natural (*phusikon*) and more fundamental, "which everywhere has the same force and does not exist by people's thinking this or that" (Grant 1885: bk. V, ch. 7, sect. 1; vol. 2, p. 126). In addition, Aristotle's reference to "natural justice" invokes another major idea, the idea of nature (*phusis*), which was to provide a highly significant resource for ethical standards by acting as the basis of a moral law of human nature, or a "natural law," and eventually of "natural" rights as the historical precursor of human rights. As Weinreb observes, "from the first, the idea of a normative order immanent in nature was a fundamental element of classical Greek speculation" (Weinreb 1987: 150).

Moreover, some awareness in Greek culture of a court of moral appeal superior to all civil law or convention is to be found in the much quoted passage in the *Antigone* of Sophocles, in which the daughter of Oedipus justified her action of burying her slain brother against the ruling of the victorious ruler Creon by appealing to "the unwritten and unshakeable usages (*nomima*) of the gods" (Sophocles 1998: ll. 454–5). Yet, although this may be seen as dramatic evidence of a Greek belief in a transcendent ethical structure of reality in the light of which human constructs could be judged, it is not evidence, as some have claimed, of Antigone "claiming a right" (Warnock 1998: 62), nor of "rights bestowed by the higher law" (Cranston 1973: 10). Antigone's phrase itself, as Elaine Pagels (1979: 1) pointed out, proves "little – if anything – for the idea of human rights."

The idea of a *nomos*, or "law," of nature, however, establishing different ways of behaving as in harmony with, or at odds with, the divine *Logos*, or Reason, which was believed to permeate nature was central in Stoic ethical thought (Copleston 1944: 396–400). As Weinreb noted

(1987: 36), "Stoicism . . . transformed classical Greek speculation into a theory unmistakably identifiable as natural law." The same applied in ancient Roman writing, as we find in the *Meditations* of the Stoic philosopher-emperor Marcus Aurelius, who recalls with gratitude "to have pictured to myself clearly and repeatedly what life in obedience to Nature really is . . . though I still come somewhat short of this by my own fault and by not observing the reminders and almost the instructions of the gods" (Marcus Aurelius 1961: 1. 17).

In the legal and philosophical tradition of ancient Rome, it was this concept of a normative human nature which was to provide Roman ethical theory with a systematic basis for exploring universal moral obligations and duties as expressed in the concept of "natural law," or *ius naturale*. As explained by Buckland (1966: 53) in his study of Roman law, the notion of natural law "originated in Greek philosophy; it was a system of moral rules implanted in man, not necessarily in other living things, by nature – an intuitionist morality."

Marcus Tullius Cicero (106–43 BCE), well described as "the plain man's interpreter of ancient thought" (Grant 1971: 35), explains this law of human nature with his usual lucidity and elegance; and "his writings contain the first clear statements of natural law as a distinct philosophical doctrine" (Weinreb 1987: 39). As Cicero (1960: II. 22. 65; pp. 228–30) observes, "the origin of law appears to be drawn from nature . . . There seems to be . . . a law of nature which comes to us not from opinion but from a kind of inborn power." Elsewhere he expands on this:

> There is a true law which is right reason congruent with nature, wide-spread within everyone, constant and everlasting, which calls to duty by its bidding and deters from wrongdoing by its forbidding . . . We cannot be released from this law either by the Senate or by the People, nor need we look to anyone else to explain or interpret it to us. Nor will there be one law in Rome and another in Athens, one law now and another later on, but one law, eternal and unchangeable, will encompass all peoples at the same time. And there will be one common teacher and ruler of all, god, who is the origin, arbitrator and maker of this law. Whoever does not obey will be running away from himself and denying the nature of mankind.   (Cicero 1928: bk. III, ch. 22, sect. 33; p. 210)

The World of the Bible

As the classical tradition of ancient Greece and Rome, so also the other major contributor to Western ethical thought, the religious traditions of

Judaism and Christianity, have no theory of natural or human rights. The Hebrew Bible and the Christian New Testament have a profound interest in how God's human creatures behave, of course, but the morality is distinctly theonomous, or as legislated by God, as is indicated by the title the *Torah*, or Law, given to the Hebrew Bible, and by the title of a new "covenant" with God which is given to the Christian writings. One writer on the subject (Sugden 1996: 4) has claimed that "human rights are clearly set down in the law of Moses," but the statement is simply false, for neither the Hebrew Bible nor the Christian New Testament makes any reference to the subject of human rights. There is a great deal about justice, of course, in the Judeo-Christian tradition, mainly about God's justice in dealing with the Jewish people, but also by extension about their justice towards their God and towards each other. And it is possible on the basis of biblical teaching, particularly in its concern for the economic and social lot of the poor, to construct an argument to produce a theory of human rights. But such a logical train of thought is not to be found in the Bible itself. The point is well made by Jones (1994: 37) when he follows others in describing the Ten Commandments as "rightless rules," that is, rules which prescribe duties laid down by God from which human beings will clearly benefit, such as "Thou shalt not kill" or "Thou shalt not steal." Such conduct is not, however, Jones maintains, conceived as owed to those other human beings. The moral demands contained in the Ten Commandments are grounded in the will of God and not in a set of titles which God has given to his human creatures. As Tierney (1997: 1) expressed it succinctly, "Moses gave commandments to the children of Israel, not a code of rights." Indeed, as Habgood has noted (1993: 97), there is a "strong sense of unease among Christians about the concept of rights." The Judeo-Christian situation is, then, well described in his conclusion that "it may be possible to *deduce* some rights from biblical teaching; but it is a mistake to say that the Bible is about human rights, because that implies commitment to a concept and a way of thinking which did not then exist" (p. 96).

By contrast, however, in Christian thinking influenced by Hellenistic thought the idea of human nature as a resource from which to derive ethical obligations became accepted largely as a result of the teaching and authority of the early writer, Paul, and the distinction which he drew between the written moral law, or *Torah*, which was believed to have been revealed by God to the Jewish people through Moses, and the way in which other nations who had not received this Mosaic law nevertheless knew in their conscience by "nature" (*phusei*) how they ought to behave. In this way, Paul explained (Rom. 2: 14–15), such non-Jews were a "law unto themselves," not in the modern relativist sense of deciding for themselves what was right and wrong behavior, but in the sense of their possessing an interior conscience, or a "natural" personal consciousness, of how God wished them to behave. This Pauline doctrine would readily become the "natural law" of the medieval Schoolmen.

The Medieval World

It was only gradually that the idea of personal rights, or the application of *ius* (justice) in a subjective sense of something possessed by the individual, took shape in the course of the Middle Ages. To start with, the idea of the universal moral law emerging from human nature which was developed from classical and Christian sources became a central component of medieval ethical thought; and a systematic expression of this source of moral knowledge and duties based on the natural constitution of the human creature was developed and articulated in the thirteenth century by its greatest thinker, Thomas Aquinas (*c.*1225–74; see Mahoney 1987: 77–80). Yet Aquinas accords no place in his system to the idea of rights entitling a person to make moral claims on others; and indeed it was only gradually during the medieval period that the subjective understanding of *ius*, as a right, became accepted and widespread. Finnis (1980: 206–7) infers a "watershed" in the history of the understanding of the term *ius*, pointing out that in the thirteenth century Aquinas's explicit analysis of the word contains no reference to a subjective right, whereas Suarez's seventeenth-century analysis presents subjective right as the first meaning given to the term.

Until recently the historical approach to the origin of subjective human rights has been dominated by the French historian, Michel Villey (1962), who argued for and popularized the view that the origin and systematic development of the idea of subjective human rights is to be ascribed to the radically minded English Franciscan theologian William of Ockham (*c.*1280–1349). The conclusions of Villey were followed by Tuck (1993: 11–30) and others in the field, so much so that Ockham has become widely viewed as the originator of personal rights. There is an obvious attraction in viewing the idea of subjective moral demands as a natural outcropping of the fourteenth-century worldview which stressed the unique significance of individuals as contrasted with universals, and which considered freedom the outstanding characteristic of human beings, a worldview of which Ockham was a leading and controversial exponent. However, in his detailed study of *The Idea of*

Natural Rights, Brian Tierney (1997: 3; see also pp. 27–42) dismantled this standard view promoted by Villey. Tierney recognized that Ockham was certainly "an important figure in the development of natural rights theories" (p. 8), and he acknowledged that, after Ockham, the language of rights "increasingly inhabited the realms of philosophy and theology" (p. 202). He argued, however, "that his characteristic teachings were not derived from his nominalist and voluntarist philosophy, but rather from a rationalist ethic applied to a body of juristic doctrine available to him in the canon law collections that he knew well and frequently cited" (p. 8).

To be historically accurate, and however attractive Villey's thesis is, Tierney maintains, we must recognize that as early as "the canonistic jurisprudence of the late twelfth century . . . we can find an important shift of language, a new understanding of the old term *ius naturale* [natural justice] as meaning a kind of subjective power or ability inhering in individuals" (Tierney 1997: 8). When subsequently, within the developed Franciscan tradition in the fourteenth century, Ockham came to write on subjective rights he was not, then, inaugurating what Villet claimed was a "semantic revolution" (p. 42); "he was carrying on an established tradition of juristic discourse in new and interesting ways." In point of fact, Tierney sums up, "a rich language already existed in which rights theories could be articulated. The doctrine of individual rights . . . was a characteristic product of the great age of creative jurisprudence that, in the twelfth and thirteenth centuries, established the foundations of the Western legal tradition" (p. 42; see pp. 54–69, and, on Tuck, pp. 218–20, 257).

Tierney's argument that the idea and language of subjective rights definitely precedes the age of Ockham is historically confirmed by events to which Tierney, Villet, and Tuck do not refer, which took place in Spain and in England as early as the century before Ockham. *Las Siete Partidas* was a thirteenth-century codification of civil law and custom compiled for his kingdom of Castile by Frederick the Wise. It was significant not only in its own day but also "was the fountainhead for the slave-code later to be applied to the New World" (Klein 1969: 141) in its examination of the rights of masters over their slaves, where its reference to subjective rights is clear in its treatment of a master's right (*derecho*) to the person and property of his slaves (Burns 2001: vol. 4, pt. 4, sect. 22 title; p. 981).

The same century saw occurring in England what is widely considered one of the major landmarks in the historical development of human rights, the signing of Magna Carta, or the Great Charter of liberties wrested by the barons of England from their king in the meadow of

Runnymede in June 1215, which Edmund Burke was later to attempt to turn eloquently to his own conservative ends (Burke 1988: 117–18). There is little doubt that the term *ius* occurs in the Charter in a subjective sense, typically in the rhetorical flourish of its seemingly magnanimous royal conclusion: "Wherefore we will and firmly enjoin that . . . men in our kingdom have and hold all the aforesaid liberties, rights (*iura*) and grants, well and in peace, freely and quietly, fully and entirely, for themselves and their heirs from us and our heirs, in all matters and places" (Holt 1982: 184). There is no question, however, of such rights being either termed or justified as natural, far less human, rights. The pattern of the Charter is a series of acts of royal self-limitation expressed in terms of rights and liberties and, as Holt comments (p. 40), rights and liberties are those things to which we are entitled by law, with "rights" possibly being enjoyed by custom. In any case, although the Charter included such historic decrees as national standards of weights and measures, trial by one's peers and access to justice for all, it was really much more concerned with baronial liberties than with universal human rights (pp. 178–9).

Given the early medieval usage and proliferation of the ideas of rights, it was not surprising that by the end of the medieval period, the Chancellor of Paris University, Jean Gerson (1363–1429), was able to argue that a *ius* is a personal power or ability which enables a person to behave in ways which are naturally good for that person (Tuck 1993: 25–7). As he explained, there is a natural ownership given equally to all human creatures by God by which they have a right directly from God to make use of other lower things for their survival (p. 27). In so doing, however, as Tierney (1997: 64) comments, "the subjective understanding of *ius* that Gerson took as the starting point of his rights theory, 'a faculty or power in accordance with right reason,' associated with free choice and synderesis, was no novelty of late mediaeval theology; it had already found ample expression in the glosses on the *Decretum* [of Gratian] two centuries earlier."

Renaissance and Reformation Thought

Once the idea of subjective rights, or claims, linked in some way to human nature, had entered the moral vocabulary of Europe it became a popular, and eventually a preferred, way of characterizing the moral responsibilities of justice which humans had to one another. First, however, the development of humanism and Renaissance jurisprudence through the recovery of classical learning in the following century led to a general disregard for human nature and natural law in favor of urban culture and civil law, including civil rights. There was a shift of attention away from any "prior" or antecedent natural rights pertaining to individuals, and a new concentration on the conditions of life required for humans to live together in society, or a change of focus from what was considered "a naturally brutish life to one of civility" (Tuck 1993: 32–40). When to this was added the profound religious disagreement which came to polarize Europe broadly into Protestant northern and Catholic southern states holding conflicting versions of Christianity and contrasting theologies of the human condition, then the significance of human nature and acceptance of the moral law derived from it became themselves matter for controversy.

According to the German Martin Luther (1483–1546) and his fellow Reformers, the human race soon after it was created had fatally disrupted its relationship with its divine creator, and as a consequence human nature had itself become seriously distorted and obsessed with itself. In such a Protestant theological scenario, not only was human nature, and all purely human thinking with it, thus rendered almost completely unreliable as a source of ethical knowledge; in addition, any thought or talk of natural or human rights would serve only to illustrate and to compound the pride and self-centeredness to which all human beings were now prone since their original sin and fall from grace.

By contrast, the Catholic version of Christianity continued the medieval tradition and held to a less cataclysmic view of humanity's early break with its creator. It thus maintained a more positive and optimistic, if guarded, attitude towards human nature, and was thus more disposed to give ethical credence to the natural law, and to accept and develop the idea of natural rights which was increasingly coming into prominence. It was within this latter tradition, for instance, that the Spanish Jesuit lawyer, Francisco Suarez (1548–1617), explained the term *ius* as meaning, among other things, a moral power possessed by everyone, either over their own belongings or to things which are owed to them (Tuck 1993: 54–6).

It does not appear too contrived to see the different attitudes of Protestantism and Catholicism towards natural or human rights in those days illustrated in a contrast between, on the one hand, the scathing remarks about rights contained in Luther's commentary on Paul's Letter to the Galatians and on the other hand the missionary work of Dominican friars in Spain and its American possessions to alleviate the degrading situation of Indian and African slaves. In expounding the meaning of Paul's list of the "fruits of the Spirit" in his letter to the Galatians (5: 2–3), with their stress on peace, mildness, and self-control, the German

Reformer remarked with his usual forthrightness, "In short, it is impossible to uphold the Gospel and the rights of men at the same time. Hence it is impossible for peace to exist at the same time with rights, especially in our age, where the Gospel is nothing and rights are all in all" (Luther 1964: 375–6). By contrast, around the same time in Spain, the distinguished Dominican theologian, Francisco de Vitoria, was assiduously arguing in his *Lectures on the Indians* (1539) that since the natives in Spanish colonies were true human beings they possessed the natural rights of man, including those to freedom, property, education, family, and society; and consequently they must not be treated as subhumans incapable of accepting Christianity and fit only for enslavement by their conquerors (Jover Zamora 1998: ch. 18, p. 609; Ruston 2004).

After the first wave of the European Reformation a pivotal figure in the historical development of human rights was the Dutch Protestant lawyer, Hugo Grotius (1583–1645). Disgusted by the religious disagreements and wars which had plagued Europe, especially in the cockpit of the Low Countries where he lived and for a time was imprisoned, Grotius sought in his major study, *The Law of War and Peace*, to establish rules for entering and waging a "just war" to which all human beings would subscribe; and he set out to do so not from the tenets of Christianity, which he noted were themselves the source of wars throughout the Christian world "which would shame barbarians" (Grotius 1853: *Proleg.*, par. 28; vol. 1, p. 59), but from the power of human reason as it considered the nature of law and of rights. In doing so, Grotius was at pains in good Scholastic fashion to clarify his terminology, and in the process he explained that one meaning of the ambiguous Latin term *ius* was as "a moral quality pertaining to a person to possess or do something justly." Such a subjective right in the strict sense he identified as a claim which can include both liberty as power over oneself, and authority as power over others; and as including either the full ownership of property rights, or partial ownership relating to the use of things (Grotius 1853: bk. 1, ch. 1, pp. 4–8).

Given Grotius' conviction that, as Tuck (1993: 74) comments, "disputes over rights were the prime cause of war," it is not surprising that in exploring the nature of rights Grotius singled out for attack the view that there was no such thing as a natural right (*ius naturale*), but that people had simply sanctioned rights in society as a matter of utility and that these therefore varied according to custom and had often changed. He identified the basis of these views as the principle that all animals, including the human, are impelled by nature to seek their own advantage; but against what he considered such excessive individualism he drew upon the long tradition stemming from Aristotle (Grant 1885:

VIII. 1; 2. 251) that every human being is kin and friend to every other. Among the human "natural" characteristics, then, Grotius followed Aquinas in including a desire for society as a human association which is peaceful and rationally structured with one's fellows. Conserving such society in accord with human intelligence is the origin of *ius*, or natural law, covering such behavior as respect for other people's belongings, keeping promises, making reparation for harm, and punishing transgressions (Grotius 1853: *Proleg.*, pars. 5–8; 1. 40–5).

Thus far Grotius was building upon and developing the Scholastic, or medieval, intellectual tradition which was based on the twin foundations of confidence in the power of human reason and belief in the tenets of the Christian religion. Now, however, he was to provide a basis for a break with that tradition, arising from his perception that Christian morality had failed in practice – notably in incessant warfare – and from his confidence in the power of unaided human reason to provide moral certainty. "What we have spoken about would carry some weight even if we were to suppose that God does not exist or that God takes no interest in human affairs (which cannot be supposed without great wickedness)" (Grotius 1853: *Proleg.* 11; p. 46). Commenting on this observation of Grotius that "he pioneered a new kind of 'secular' and 'rationalist' approach that freed the concept of natural law from the religious context in which it had been embedded," Tierney also argued that this was no novelty in Scholastic discourse, simply recognizing as usual that human reason complemented by divine revelation could educe moral norms governing human behavior. Thus, Herbert appears to be wide of the historical truth when he asserts that "Grotius' liberation of natural right and the law of nature from their classical theological moorings puts him with those seventeenth-century philosophers who are the true authors of the modern, subjective theory of natural rights. Grotius clearly argues that it is nature, not God, which is the basis of the law of nature" (Herbert 2002: 76). For one thing, as we shall see, "those seventeenth-century philosophers," namely, Locke, Paine, Jefferson, and Montesquieu, not to mention the American Declaration of Independence and the French Declaration of the Rights of Man and the Citizen, all shared with Grotius a religious belief in a creating deity as the ultimate source of natural rights. However, this did not involve for them, as Herbert implies, a choice between God and human nature. As was the Scholastic custom, and as Tierney explains, they conceived of God as working and communicating through the divinely created human nature. It was not without reason that the new American state referred to "the laws of nature *and* of nature's God" (see below, pp. 22–3; emphasis added).

Nevertheless, the point is worth noting that Grotius' near-parenthesis did prove of immense significance in achieving the realization that divine revelation was not just complementary to reasoned reflection, but was also "as it later proved, detachable" from such reflection (Tierney 1997: 319–20). In effect, by thus explicitly allowing for what Tierney calls the detachability of reasoning from religion in moral matters, Grotius cut loose human nature and all that could be deduced from it from its divine creator, thus bringing about what Oskar Köhler (1981: 319–20) described as "the detheologisation of natural law." Consequently, as the non-existence of the deity became later for many Europeans much more than a purely speculative possibility, the intellectual difficulties created by Grotius' apparent claims for "free-floating" human nature and for unearthed natural rights would become evident.

Hobbes and Rousseau

As European philosophizing on natural rights proceeded, it took a variety of expressions, not all in harmony with each other. For example, the traditioneal naturally sociable and communitarian view of humanity which Grotius pursued was quite at variance with that maintained around the same time by the first major English thinker who was to deal with human rights, Thomas Hobbes (1588–1679), with whom, indeed, Grotius and many contemporaries explicitly disagreed (Tuck 1993: 81). As David Raphael (1967: 59) observed, "Hobbes's idea of natural right is an aberration from the tradition that led to the concept of human rights." To help explain this it might be suggested that, whereas Grotius' reductionist rationalism can be seen as a reaction from his weariness of war and European religious controversy, the views of Hobbes may be best appreciated against his personal background of Protestant Puritanism and of the social instability arising from the English Civil War through which Hobbes lived and which was to culminate in the execution by Parliament of King Charles I – all factors which contributed to what one commentator has called Hobbes's "ingrained desire for security" (Macpherson 1974: 17). Profoundly influenced by the rigorous deductive method of geometry and the astounding explanatory power of the contemporary physical sciences, Hobbes "saw himself as the Euclid of a new science of politics" (Hill 1965: 160), in which he aimed to deduce the origin of human society from the interactions between the conjectured primary emotions and decisions of its individual human components (see Macpherson 1974: 25–30).

Basic to Hobbes's hypothesis was an innate drive for survival in all human beings; and when to this was added his conviction that all humans are in a state of permanent conflict and competition to survive at everyone else's expense, it was logical to conclude, as he does in a famous passage, that, left to themselves, people in this state are in a condition of "war . . . of every man against every man." There is no security to permit such peaceful sustained activities as industry, agriculture, navigation, arts, letters, or society; "and which is worst of all, continual fear and danger of violent death; and the life of man solitary, poor, nasty, brutish and short" (Hobbes 1974: bk. I, ch. 13, sect. 62). In such a state, which Hobbes posited as "the natural condition of mankind" (I. 13, title), he was of the view that there was, of course, no law. Therefore, as he explained, "nothing can be unjust. The notions of right and wrong, justice and injustice have there no place"; nor is there in such a condition any property or ownership, or "mine" and "thine," "but only that to be every man's that he can get; and for so long as he can keep it" (I. 13. 63).

"Thus much," Hobbes concludes, "for the ill condition which man by mere nature is actually placed in." Yet, strangely, in this actual or potential unremitting struggle on the part of everyone for mere survival he finds himself compelled to make room for what he calls "the right of nature," although it is a right to which he now gives a unique personal interpretation. "The right of nature, which writers commonly call *Jus Naturale*, is the liberty each man hath, to use his own power as he will himself for the preservation of his own nature; that is to say, of his own life; and consequently, of doing anything which in his own judgement and reason he shall conceive to be the aptest means thereunto" (I. 14. 64). Since all mankind is driven by nature to continue in being, then everyone has likewise a moral right conferred by that same nature to take any step which they judge necessary to secure their survival. However, almost by definition, no one is obliged to respect such a "natural right" in anyone else.

> Because the condition of man . . . is a condition of war of every one against every one; in which case everyone is governed by his own reason and there is nothing he can make use of that may not be a help unto him in preserving his life against his enemies; it followeth that in such a condition every man has a right to every thing; even to one another's body. (I. 14. 64)

From the same natural impulse in everyone to self-preservation as a first-order objective Hobbes also deduces a collection of second-order objectives as so many reasoned conditions to securing that end. Thus he argues as a matter of common sense, or "precept, or general rule of reason," that all human beings are subject to a series of what he calls laws of nature, or natural laws, forbidding them to destroy or endanger their own [*sic*] lives (I. 14. 64). The fundamental law of nature binding everyone is that, since in the struggle for survival everyone lives "without other security than what their own strength and their own invention shall furnish them with" (I. 13. 62), in the sheer interests of personal survival everyone ought to aim at seeking peace rather than war. From this is "derived" the second law of nature, "that a man be willing, when others are so too, as farforth as for peace and defence of himself he shall think necessary, to lay down this right to all things; and be contented with so much liberty against other men as he would allow other men against himself" (I. 14. 64). This all men do by entering into a pact, or covenant, to transfer to another "such rights as being retained hinder the peace of mankind" and by accepting as the third requirement of nature that such covenants must be respected (I. 15. 71). The coping stone, then, of Hobbes's political structure (I. 15. 71–2) is that in order for all this to be ensured "there must be some coercive power to compel men equally to the performance of their Covenants by the terror of some punishment greater than the benefit they expect by the breach of their Covenant."

For Hobbes, then, humans apprehensively come together in society to ensure their own physical protection by forming a social contract to obey an absolute central power which will protect them, by force if necessary:

> as if every man should say to every man, "I authorise and give up my right of governing myself to this man, or to this assembly of men, on this condition, that thou give up thy right to him and authorise all his actions in like manner" . . . This is the generation of that great Leviathan, or rather (to speak more reverently) of that mortal god to which we owe under the immortal God our peace and defence. For by this authority, given him by every particular man in the common-wealth, he hath the use of so much power and strength conferred on him, that by terror thereof he is enabled to form the wills of them all, to peace at home and mutual aid against their enemies abroad. (II. 17. 87–8)

Of course, Hobbes was not particularly interested in establishing that all societies had actually begun in this way; his political point, in first publishing his *Leviathan* two years after the execution of Charles I (Scruton 1991: 197), is to persuade his readers not to let matters degenerate in society to such an extent that people would "revert" to such a melancholy "natural state." It is as part of this overall strategy that he introduces the idea of natural rights and natural laws; and, as Macpherson (1974: 41) observes, "as he defines them, both are very different from any previously received meanings of the terms." His "natural laws" are purely self-regarding and have nothing to say about one's duties towards one's fellows: one has no fellows. "A group of human beings merely collected together as individuals – that is, in the state of nature – have no obligations of any kind towards one another and . . . each member of the group pursues his own interests exclusively" (Weinreb 1987: 72). Tierney is in agreement, echoing Raphael (1967: 59), that Hobbes is seriously out of step: "it seems that Hobbes's work [on natural rights] is best seen as an aberration from the mainstream of natural rights thinking that flowed from the mediaeval jurists through Ockham, Gerson, and Grotius to Pufendorf and Locke and writers of the Enlightenment" (Tierney 1997: 340).

In fact, all appears to spring logically from Hobbes's anthropology, both theological and political, which can be summed up as a mutual mistrust among fallen and sinful human beings. Not unfairly considered a frightened Puritan, "Hobbes is said to have prized his timidity as others prize courage" (Weinreb 1987: 68). Grotius disagreed with him, and this he did precisely in rejecting his estimate of human nature and his postulate of a "war of everyone against everyone" (Tuck 1993: 81). In his day, as in modern times, Hobbes's arguments and the ways in which he chose to interpret and understand such ideas as "nature" and "natural laws" and "rights" occasioned considerable criticism, accusations of inconsistency, and debate (Tuck 1993: 128–32). Hitherto the idea of some principle of order or reason underlying reality had provided a basis for the emergence of natural rights in human thinking. Hobbes "starts not from natural order, but from natural chaos as the human condition" (Crocker 1963: 6).

By contrast, another major figure in the developing thought on human rights was the Swiss writer, intellectual, and social misfit, Jean-Jacques Rousseau (1712–78), who, like others, faulted Hobbes's gloomy view of humanity. As he wrote:

> Above all, let us not conclude with Hobbes that man is naturally evil . . . that he is vicious . . . or that on the strength of the right he reasonably claims to the things he needs, he foolishly imagines himself to be the proprietor of the whole universe. Hobbes saw very clearly the defects of all modern definitions of natural right, but the conclusions he drew from his own definition show that his own concept of natural right is equally defective.   (Rousseau 1984: 98)

In fact, what Hobbes should have said, Rousseau contended, was that the original state of nature is the one most conducive to peace and the most suited to humankind. Yet Hobbes said exactly the opposite, because he mistakenly ascribed to humanity in its savage, that is pre-social, state those aggressive and destructive passions which are in fact, for Rousseau, "the product of society." Here we meet the famous "noble savage" postulated by Rousseau in his attempt to reconstruct the human past in detail and on no other evidence than his own romantic nostalgia and his sense not of what "might have been" so much as, in the words of his biographer, what "must have happened" (Rousseau 1984: 42). It was not, however, that in his estimate of humanity Rousseau was much less pessimistic than Hobbes; it was simply that the reason for his poor view of the current human race was directed at a different stage of its development, almost reversing the Hobbesian progress from brutish nature to moderating society by claiming a human deterioration, that is, developing "a philosophical (and necessarily speculative) anthropology to explain how human society had reached its present corrupt state from an original condition of innocence" (Cranston 1987: 243).

For Rousseau, as humans began the slow process of leaving their original solitary, "healthy, happy, good and free" way of life to develop forms of coexistence and collaboration, and to experience increasingly complex relationships among themselves, then ideas characteristic of society, such as the family, community, property, and industrial progress, began to develop in this "nascent" society. In the slow course of time, as his biographer explains, "social changes produced important moral and psychological changes in the individuals. Ceasing to be a solitary person, man not only became gentler and more affectionate in the milieu of the family, he became more egoistic and corrupt in the milieu of society" (Cranston 1987: 300). All these innovations provided increasing occasion and scope for natural differences among individuals to give rise to real and perceived inequality, ambition, competition, success, and failure; and as individuals became more sensitive to the consideration of how they were being treated by others, then, according to Rousseau, "everyone claimed a right" and viewed any hurt suffered as "an insult to his person, which was often more unbearable than the hurt itself" (Rousseau 1984: 114; see pp. 114–20). *Now* in Rousseau's stage of social anarchy we have reached the Hobbesian state of the war of all against all, and the consequent need for some form of social contract which will establish and maintain universal peace and security.

> Such was, or must have been, the origin of society and of laws, which put new fetters on the weak and gave new powers to the rich, which

irretrievably destroyed natural liberty, established for all time the law of property and inequality, transformed adroit usurpation into irrevocable right, and for the benefit of a few ambitious men subjected the human race thenceforth to labour, servitude and misery. (Rousseau 1984: 122)

Of those who were thus duped, Rousseau continued, "all ran towards their chains, believing that they were securing their liberty; for although they had reason enough to deduce the advantages of a civil order, they did not have experience enough to foresee its dangers." The consequence of such a one-sided advantage he was to describe in his other work, *The Social Contract*, in what has often been read as its challenging opening sentence, "Man is born free, and everywhere he is in chains" (Rousseau 1994: bk. I, ch. 1). Rousseau's famous sentiment has been variously explained as a revolutionary slogan, as a rhetorical contradiction, or as a "record of decision" rather than as a statement of fact (MacDonald 1970: 54–5). All this is over-imaginative, however, for, as Rousseau's most recent translator has pointed out, the French verb is in the past tense (*est né*) rather than the present (*naît*), and the sentence is therefore more accurately translated as a simple historical statement which actually sums up Rousseau's whole thinking that initially "man *was* born free but today he is everywhere in chains" (Rousseau 1994: 183). For, once one social contract of this nature, however inequitable, came into being, it was inevitable, Rousseau considered, that others would arise progressively to cover the globe.

It is true, Rousseau acknowledges (1994: I. 6), that "should the social pact be violated, each associate thereupon recovers his original rights and takes back his natural freedom, while losing the freedom of convention for which he gave it up." But the point, and ideal condition, of the social contract is precisely to render such rights unnecessary. As he argues, ominously, one might consider, "properly understood, the clauses can all be reduced to one alone, namely, the complete transfer of each association, with all his rights, to the whole community." As he continues (II. 4), "just as nature gives each man absolute power over all his limbs, the social pact gives the body politic absolute power over its members." For the power of the "general will" is so central to the constitution of Rousseauan society that "if anyone refuses to obey the general will he will be compelled to do so by the whole body; which means nothing else than that he will be forced to be free" (I. 7). As Rousseau's translator, Christopher Betts, acknowledges (Rousseau 1994: p. xx), even while trying to put a sympathetic construction on it, this position is considered one of the most notorious stumbling blocks in

Rousseau's works, attempting as it appears "to disguise an objectionable degree of constraint by a mere trick of expression." However one tries to mitigate it, it certainly appears to bear out the observation of Cranston that although Rousseau at times wrote of his political thinking being indebted to Locke, nothing could be further here from Locke's view of the role of natural rights in relation to society. Rousseau "is plainly contradicting Locke when he says that men alienate all their natural rights when they make the social contract, Locke having said that men make the social contract precisely in order to preserve their rights" (Cranston 1991: 307).

For all his social fantasizing, Rousseau remained what he would have considered a realist on the social slavery with which he claimed to find human beings everywhere actually shackled; and his theory of an alternative, utopian, social order was to be found disturbing by the powerful for being entertained at all, and the more so when propounded by Rousseau as called for. For one thing, as Betts comments (Rousseau 1994: p. xii), Rousseau's introduction of the concept of the general will as a populist alternative to the divine right of kings to rule their subjects "is a clear sign that monarchist theories of the state were beginning to give way to democratic ideas" – "to write of the sovereignty of the people was a bold stroke when monarchical government still prevailed" (p. xviii). Against such a background it is also scarcely surprising that Rousseau's piercing analysis of the origins and foundations of the inequalities which beset contemporary society, and what Cranston called his "bitter radicalism," had the effect of his being "held responsible for the French Revolution" by Burke and Napoleon among others (Cranston 1987: 248, 293). Before that was to happen, however, other developments in the understanding and application of human rights were to take place elsewhere.

Revolution in England

The year after the "Glorious Revolution" of 1688 in Britain, when the Stuart Catholic King James II was forced by his nobles to abandon his country and his throne in favor of his niece, Mary, and her Protestant husband, Prince William of Orange, the English intellectual and confidant of politicians, John Locke (1632–1704) published his anonymous work, *Two Treatises of Government*, which was to have such a profound influence on the subsequent history of human rights in Western society. Within our context of studying the evolution of human rights in history the most relevant aspect of the Revolution in England was the Bill of Rights, or more fully "An Act declaring the Rights and Liberties of the Subject and Settling the Succession of the Crown" to which the Revolution gave rise in 1689. In this piece of legislation Parliament established Britain as a constitutional monarchy and prayed of the new monarchs "that it may be declared and enacted that all and singular the rights and liberties asserted and claimed in the said declaration are the true, ancient and indubitable rights and liberties of the people of this kingdom." To which their Majesties were only too happy to agree, as a fair price to pay for the throne of Britain (Browning 1953: 122–8).

Just what was so stipulated in the Bill of Rights was, in the view of one commentator, a set of "conditions or restrictions" on the monarch which were "as mild and conservative, and in some cases as vague, as could well have been devised" (Browning 1953: 20). Nor, in the eyes of the Lords and Commons, were such rights considered, or at least presented by them, as revolutionary, being claimed, as had been the case centuries previously in Magna Carta, as "their ancient rights and liberties" (p. 123). Indeed, if it is true that in 1215 Magna Carta was more a forced recognition of rights and privileges belonging of old to the barons of England, Cranston is also correct in his judgment that in 1689 "the Bill of Rights was not a Bill of 'the Rights of Man' but of the Rights of Parliament" (Cranston 1958: 325 n. 3). In fact, the major originality of the 1689 Act lay in its "settling the Succession of the Crown" in order to prevent another Catholic king ever arising in Britain. In so doing it was countering the current of royal absolutism, based on the "divine right of kings," which was running strongly in the rest of Europe, by dislodging the hereditary right of succession in favor of the will of the nation which Parliament claimed to represent; and in the process the Bill of Rights was adopting in practice the contract theory of government. It is in this respect, then, rather than in the individual rights claimed for Parliament, that one can see the influence of the ideas which had recently been developed and eloquently expressed by Locke in his *Two Treatises of Government.*

That work was published anonymously in 1689 (Lowe 2005: 160–1) and written with the express aim, according to the Preface, of legitimating the accession to the throne of "our present King William; to make good his title, in the consent of the people . . . and to justify to the world the people of England, whose love of their just and natural rights, with their resolution to preserve them, saved the nation when it was on the very brink of slavery and ruin" (Locke 1963: 171). In point of fact, as scholars have agreed for some time, Locke had written the bulk of this work of political philosophy some years previously, in the latter years of the Stuart monarchy (Laslett 1963: 60–73). However, the expulsion of the House of Stuart in favor of the Dutch House of Orange now provided him with the occasion to exemplify his theories on human rights and on the need for consent on the part of the governed; while his theories in their turn served to justify philosophically the political revolution which had recently occurred in Britain, as well as to stimulate revolt elsewhere.

Central to Locke's political philosophy was the distinction of which Hobbes had made so much and which went back at least as far as Cicero (Tuck 1993: 33) between the "state of nature" and human "society." For Locke, unlike Hobbes, however, the state of nature is not a state of war, all against all, "however some men have confounded them." On the contrary, the state of nature is one of equality among all men and of perfect freedom to order all one's actions and dispose of one's possessions and person as one thinks fit within the bounds of the law of nature (Locke 1963: bk. II, ch. 2, sect. 4). And "were it not for the corruption, and vitiousness of degenerate Men" (II. 10. 128) – not, as for Hobbes, mankind in general – there would be no need for people to leave the state of nature and by mutual agreement found political society "to unite for the mutual Preservation of their Lives, Liberties and Estates, which I call by the general Name, Property" (II. 11. 123). The state of nature need not necessarily have ever actually existed, of course, although Locke, as well as Hobbes, appear to have thought of it as existing still in their day among primitive peoples. Lowe interestingly remarks that Rawls's hypothetical notion of "the original position" performs a similar role today to the "state of nature" (Lowe 2005: 164). He also makes the useful observation that "one of the crucial differences between Locke and Hobbes lies in the relative optimism of the former and pessimism of the latter concerning human nature" (p. 166).

In that state of nature, according to Locke, every man has the right of "self-preservation" and the right of "preserving all mankind and doing all reasonable things he can in order to that end" (Locke 1963: II. 2. 11). These reasonable means include "the right of my freedom," freedom being the "foundation" of all that belongs to me and "the fence" to my self-preservation (II. 3. 17). There is thus for him what one might call a powerful natural morality, as contrasted with a conventional social morality, so that he can observe, for example, that "Truth and keeping of Faith belong to Men, as Men, and not as Members of Society" (II. 2. 14). And his strong doctrine of natural human rights as individual moral entitlements and powers is summed up in his affirmation that

Man being born, as has been proved, with a Title to perfect Freedom, and an uncontrolled enjoyment of all the Rights and Privileges of the Law of Nature, equally with any other Man or Number of Men in the World, hath by Nature a Power ... to preserve his Property, that is, his Life, Liberty and Estate, against the injuries and Attempts of other Men.   (II. 7. 87)

When they enter by agreement into society, Locke explains (II. 10. 35), men will then proceed by common consent to introduce laws. But, far from these civil laws being a replacement of the laws and rights of nature, their purpose is in fact to apply and reinforce such natural obligations and entitlements in society. "The law of nature stands as an eternal rule to all men, legislators as well as others. The rules that they make for other men's actions must, as well as their own and other men's actions, be conformable to the law of nature, i.e., to the will of God, of which that is a declaration." The existence, then, of natural law and of natural rights is central to Locke's political philosophy; and for him natural law, as Laslett (1963: 95) comments, "was at one and the same time a command of God, a rule of reason, and a law in the very nature of things as they are." This for posterity was to create something of an intellectual difficulty. For "it is of importance to see in Locke, [who is] the recognised point of departure for liberalism, the liberal dilemma already present, the dilemma of maintaining a political faith without subscribing to a total, holistic view of the world" (p. 103).

It was these features of the Lockean doctrine which, as Melden (1970: 2) observes, made Locke the notable exponent of the natural rights movement that developed in the seventeenth century and proved "important to men of practical affairs who put them to use in the political upheavals that took place not only in England but also in America and France." Weinreb (1992: 278), however, appears to be cynical on the role of natural law and natural rights in the argumentation of the seventeenth- and eighteenth-century thinkers. He recognizes that the theorists of the seventeenth and eighteenth centuries "are aware of the natural law tradition and refer to it to support their arguments," but he then comments that "the references are little more than window-dressing" and adds that "Locke referred repeatedly to natural law in traditional terms, to shore up the weakest points in his argument." Yet, *pace* Weinreb, it is not possible to have it both ways: to appeal repeatedly to natural law, but not really to consider it very important. The point surely is that natural law and natural rights were the genuine logical basis of Locke's arguments, as indeed they proved to be for the American colonists arguing for their independence from Britain on the basis of the laws of nature and of nature's God.

American Independence

The most far-reaching appeal to natural rights in history was the 1776 Declaration of Independence issued by the British colonies in America in a movement which was powerfully influenced by the English pamphleteer, Thomas Paine (1737–1809), described by one historian as "the most prominent political thinker and writer during the Revolutionary struggle against the British" (Keane 1995: p. ix). After various unsuccessful careers in England, including those of exciseman and Methodist lay preacher, Paine emigrated to America in 1774 armed with letters of introduction from Benjamin Franklin, whom he had met as colonial agent in London. There he became a publisher and this enabled him to turn his attention and his considerable powers of rhetoric in increasingly passionate support of the colonists and what they considered their mounting grievances and rights against the British government (Keane 1995: 95). With the news that King George III had declared the American colonies to be in a state of rebellion, Paine anonymously published his first major political pamphlet, *Common Sense* (Hawke 1974: 17–51), in which with the warm sympathy of Benjamin Franklin (Keane 1995: 107) he mounted a passionate attack on the English monarchy and government, accused them of "declaring war against the natural rights of all mankind," and daringly called for a declaration for independence, based on the principle that "a government of our own is our natural right" (Paine 1989: bk. II, ch. 28).

Paine's pamphlet aroused intense public interest in America and Europe, including France (Keane 1995: 110), and "crystallized" public opinion among Americans in favor of revolution (Padover 1942: 49). At the time he was accused of plagiarizing John Locke in the development of his arguments in favor of revolution, but it is worth noting that he replaced the Lockean and earlier distinction between a state of nature and civil society with a more useful and politically relevant distinction, that between society and government, or the state; that is, what has been called "natural sociability" (civil society) as pre-existing the formation of government (Keane 1995: 116–17). As Paine (1989: 3) observed in the opening paragraph of the work, "Society is produced by our wants and government by our wickedness; the former promotes our happiness positively by uniting our affections, the latter negatively by restraining our vices." Moreover, Paine denied ever having read Locke. Yet, as Hawke (1974: 50) observes, "no one in the eighteenth century could escape from Locke; his views on natural rights were part of the intellectual landscape." In any case there is no doubt that the influence of both Locke and Paine was strongly present in the mind of Thomas Jefferson (1743–1826) when, as the leader of the five-man committee appointed by Congress for the purpose, he drafted the American Declaration of Independence in which the mind, though not the hand, of Paine appears evident (Keane 1995: 560 n. 70).

Jefferson lived a political career dominated by the idea of human rights. As a young lawyer and elected landowner he was impelled by deteriorating relations between the American colonies and Britain to read and reflect on the classic European sources of political science, and in this he was profoundly influenced by Montesquieu's *Esprit des Lois*, as his commonplace book shows (Bellof 1948: 42). A philosopher of the French Enlightenment, Charles de Sécondat, Baron Montesquieu (1689–1755) "was an enthusiast for liberty and an enemy of despotism" (Copleston 1960: 9), whose belief in some form of natural law is evident in his assertion that in a state "one must admit that there are relations of fairness [*Equité*] prior to the positive law that establishes them" (Montesquieu 1995: bk. I, ch. 1, sect. 1), and in his identification of various civil laws in history as having been "contrary to natural law" (V. 26. 3).

Finding such French philosophizing congenial to his cast of mind as well as pertinent to the current political situation relating to England, Jefferson had occasion in 1774 to put his political thoughts in order in a paper which he entitled *Instructions*, and which he submitted to the Virginia Convention. There, however, "the argument from natural rights was too bold and too much outside the ordinary range of political discussion for it to be accepted at once as the basis of the colony's claims" (Bellof 1948: 54). However, later printed as *A Summary View of the Rights of British America*, the pamphlet, described by one historian as a "landmark in American history . . . the matrix of the Declaration of Independence," had wide and effective circulation and led to its author's being proscribed by the British Parliament for forcefully expressing the colonists' grievances, as Jefferson observed, "with that freedom of language and sentiment which becomes a free people claiming their rights, as derived from the law of nature, and not as the gift of their chief magistrate" (Padover 1942: 39–41).

Jefferson's *Summary View*, as Bellof notes (1948: 58), "illustrates very clearly . . . the dominant place taken in his thinking by the theory of natural rights," a personal conviction which is used to even more powerful effect in his greatest achievement, the American Declaration of Independence, the effect of whose opening paragraphs, "in stamping upon the mind of the American nation the doctrine of natural rights, has been of the profoundest significance" (Bellof 1948: 67). Some features of the background to the Declaration are important to note, however cursorily. The North American colonies, being more egalitarian than Europe and free of all hereditary class structures, while expanding rapidly in numbers and resources, found it increasingly irksome to be governed by a well-nigh absolutist parliament in London. However, unlike previous British Parliaments, they had no ancient historical claims or precedents to which they could appeal, and therefore they took their stand on "the revolutionary principle of the rights of man" in "the most eloquent revolutionary manifesto in western history" (Hampson 1984: 179), of which Jefferson was almost sole author, and whose authority was, like that of the later American Constitution, "founded not on tradition or revelation but on nature grasped by reason" (Bloom 1990: 1).

In explaining the causes why he and his compatriots were being impelled "to assume among the powers of the earth, the separate and equal station to which the laws of nature and of nature's God entitle them," Jefferson laid down as his opening principle, "We hold these truths to be self-evident, that all men are created equal, that they are endowed by their Creator with certain unalienable Rights, that among these are Life, Liberty, and the pursuit of Happiness. That to secure these rights, Governments are instituted among Men, deriving their just powers from the consent of the governed" (Padover 1942: 54–6; Melden 1970: 138–9). The list of rights identified by Jefferson replaced the traditional Lockean concept of property with that of the pursuit of happiness, leading one historian to comment that "the assertion that the pursuit of happiness was one of the objects for which governments exist was something new in the history of political doctrine . . . and laid the foundation for a unique commonwealth of justice and freedom and security" (Padover 1942: 55–6).

Jefferson's personal conviction of the central importance of human rights continued to influence his actions after his draft Declaration was approved with few changes; and it underlay, for instance, his insistence that the Constitution now to be composed for the new American republic should make explicit provision for a Bill of Rights. As he wrote from Paris of the draft Constitution sent to him for comment, "I will add what I do not like. First, the omission of a bill of rights, clearly and without the aid of sophisms, for freedom of religion, freedom of the press, protection against standing armies, restriction against monopolies, the eternal and unremitting force of the habeas corpus laws, and trials by jury" (Padover 1942: 157). As if foreseeing the bitter controversies which lay still ahead for the infant republic, he added, "let me add that a bill of rights is what the people are entitled to against every government on earth, general or particular, and what no just government should refuse, or rest on inferences." After much agitation he had his way, when a Bill of Rights was finally added in 1789 to the Constitution as the first ten amendments (p. 158). It was fitting, therefore, and consistent with his lifelong advocacy of human rights, that years later, in 1826, as he lay on his deathbed Jefferson concluded the last letter of his life with a nunc dimittis, "all eyes are opened, or opening, to the rights of man" (p. 418). For his own contribution to what he considered this human moral advancement was immense, not only in the New World, but also in the Revolution which was shortly after to engulf France.

The French Declaration of the Rights of Man

The events which revolutionized America were followed with keen interest not just in England itself, but also elsewhere in Europe and nowhere more so than in England's old enemy, France. Commenting on the American Revolution, Hampson writes (1984: 180), "the immediate lesson of the revolt was that a people had successfully deposed its ruler, created, by what could be made to appear a new social contract, a republican government, and justified itself in the kind of language that raised an immediate echo in eighteenth-century minds and hearts." Jefferson, who had moved to France as American Ambassador and who witnessed the early stage of developments there at first hand, later described in a letter to the Marquis de Lafayette, the architect of the French Declaration, how "I had left France in the first year of its revolution, in the fervour of natural rights, and zeal for reformation. My conscientious devotion to these rights could not be heightened, but it had been aroused and excited by daily exercise" (Padover 1942: 177).

   In fact, Jefferson was not an active figure in the march of events in France, declining the official invitation to have a hand in composing a Constitution for France, but deeply sympathetic to the aspirations of his friend Lafayette and other leading figures in his social circle (Padover 1942: 165–6). He did, however, report the development of events regularly to Tom Paine, who was then in London as unofficial American ambassador. This news from France Paine faithfully passed on to Edmund Burke, an early sympathizer of the American cause with whom he had developed a friendship on his return to England (Hawke 1974: 188–94). Thus it was that, when in Paris the Third Estate, representing the bourgeoisie, seceded from the assembly of the Estates-General which had been convened by Louis XVI to avert national bankruptcy, and when it formed the self-styled National Assembly, in which it was later to be joined by the other two Estates of the French clergy and the nobility, Jefferson reported to Paine in July 1789 that the first article of the National Assembly's creed was that "Every government should have for its only end the preservation of the rights of man; whence it follows that to recall constantly the government to the end proposed, the constitution should begin by a declaration of the natural and imprescriptible rights of man" (Hawke 1974: 197).

In the following month, accordingly, the manifesto of the French Revolution proclaimed the Declaration of the Rights of Man and of Citizens:

> The representatives of the people of France, formed into a National Assembly, considering that ignorance, neglect, or contempt of human rights are the sole causes of public misfortunes and corruptions of Government, have resolved to set forth, in a solemn declaration, these natural, imprescriptible, and inalienable rights: that this declaration being constantly present to the minds of the body social, they may be ever kept attentive to their rights and duties. For these reasons, the National Assembly doth recognize and declare, in the presence of the Supreme Being, and with the hope of his blessing and favour, the following sacred rights of men and of citizens. (Paine 1984: 110–12)

In what followed, the first three articles then identified the rights of man: freedom, equality, property, security, resistance to oppression, and the nation as the source of all sovereignty; and these in turn were spelt out or applied in fourteen further rights of citizens in society, in such a way as to exemplify the basic principle of Locke as repeated by Paine (p. 165), in his *Rights of Man*, that "all the great laws of society are laws of nature."

English Resistance to Human Rights

In this sequel to *Common Sense*, described by Foner as "the finest example of political pamphleteering in the Age of Revolution" (Paine 1984: 17), Paine was strenuously defending the French appeal to the rights of man, and the Revolution which was based on their vindication, against the powerful attack of his former friend, Edmund Burke (1729–97), as this was deployed eloquently in the latter's *Reflections on the Revolution in France* (Burke 1988), which in its turn may be considered the finest rhetorical case for political conservatism constructed in that or succeeding centuries. Burke had been not unsympathetic to the plight of the transatlantic American colonists in their bid for some measure of independence. However, he was far from being an egalitarian, as shown by his reluctance to repeal the various civil and social disqualifications imposed by the Test Act on those who dissented from the Church of England – an exercise of partiality which drew from Paine the expostulation, "my idea of supporting liberty of conscience and the rights of citizens, is that of supporting those rights in *other people*, for if a man supports only his *own* rights for his *own sake*, he does no moral duty" (Hawke 1974: 204). Moreover, when revolution came considerably nearer home, just across the Channel, and when it seemed likely to spread its contagion not only in an England rumbling with social and political discontent, but also to his native restless Ireland, then Burke was not slow, although at first almost alone, to sound the alarm to the political and propertied classes of England.

In Burke's reflections on what he considered a disastrous collapse of traditional government in France he showed what one modern political analyst, Conor Cruise O'Brien (1988: 71–2), has described as "the level of the prophetic" in foreseeing what terrors still lay in wait for revolutionary France – although it should be noted that these would be partly brought about by the warring reaction of France's neighbors, including England, and by Burke's own vehement opposition to the early revolution in France. The burden of Burke's attack on recent events in France, and on the all too real possibility of the flames spreading to England, was to reject political and social revolution in favor of development and gradualism, such as, he argued, had been achieved in England by the Glorious Revolution of 1688 (Keane 1995: 287–90).

In the circumstances it was considerably less than honest of Burke to play down the enforced regime change on that occasion, as well as the conditions laid down by Parliament to ensure that the succession would remain forever Protestant, by describing all this as "a small and a temporary deviation from the strict order of a regular hereditary succession" (Burke 1988: 101). He also neglected to mention the earlier Parliamentary killing of a king of England. It was, however, part of Burke's argument to establish the liberties of England on historical tradition and on the legal concept of "entailed inheritance," such as the American colonies had lacked and had, indeed, attacked, rather than on any more philosophical basis or what he termed "any other more general or prior right" (p. 119). So much so that, although Burke dismissed any appeal to human rights derived from nature, he nevertheless appealed to "nature" in so doing; but it was to nature as he understood it, that is, to inherited social structures and to instinctive reliance upon the past. It was this understanding of nature which enabled him to attack those who "are so taken up with their theories about the rights of man, that they have totally forgotten his nature" (p. 156). Thus, trust in the previous socially, rather than naturally, ordered scheme of things enabled him blandly to take for granted both a principle of the "natural subordination" of the less fortunate in society and their assurance of some compensation for this at least in the afterlife.

> The body of the people must not find the principles of natural subordination by art rooted out of their minds. They must respect that property of which they cannot participate. They must labour to obtain what by labour can be attained; and when they find, as they commonly do, the success disproportioned to the endeavour, they must be taught their consolation in the final proportions of eternal justice. (Burke 1988: 372)

Again, those whose bid for social equality earned for them the name of "levellers" were attacked by Burke on the grounds that they

> only charge and pervert the natural order of things; they load the edifice of society, by setting up in the air what the solidity of the structure requires to be on the ground . . . The occupation of a hair-dresser, or of a working tallow-chandler, cannot be a matter of honour to any person – to say nothing of a number of other more servile employments . . . [T]he state suffers oppression, if such as they, either individually or collectively, are permitted to rule. In this you think you are combating prejudice, but you are at war with nature. (Burke 1988: 138)

It was entirely in keeping with such patrician sentiments uttered from the heady summit of English society that, in the course of a famous passage eulogizing the aristocratic femininity of Marie Antoinette, Burke should eloquently lament that, with the French Revolution,

> the age of chivalry has gone. That of sophisters, oeconomists, and calculators, has succeeded; and the glory of Europe is extinguished for ever. Never, never more, shall we behold that generous loyalty to rank and sex, that proud submission, that dignified obedience, that subordination of the heart, which kept alive, even in servitude itself, the spirit of an exalted freedom. (Burke 1988: 170)

In response to Burke, Tom Paine's riposte in his *Rights of Man* made short shrift of Burke's claims for heredity and tradition, and this secured for Paine an indictment from the British Parliament (Keane 1995: 309–10). With a rhetoric which was less flamboyant yet more savage than Burke's, Paine nevertheless rose to similar heights of eloquence when he attacked his erstwhile friend and the latter's partiality for the French queen:

Not one glance of compassion, not one commiserating reflection, that I can find throughout his book, has he bestowed on those who lingered out the most wretched of lives, a life without hope, in the most miserable of prisons . . . His hero or his heroine must be a tragedy-victim expiring in show, and not the real prisoner of misery, sliding into death in the silence of a dungeon.   (Paine 1984: 51)

More philosophically, Paine turned the tables on Burke's appeal to nature by his counter-assertion that "it is by distortedly exalting some men, that others are distortedly debased, till the whole is out of nature" (p. 59). What is more, to argue from historical precedent, as Burke mainly did, was inconsistently to stop short of going back the whole way

till we come to the divine origin of the rights of man at the creation . . . [E]very child born into the world must be considered as deriving its existence from God. The world is as new to him as it was to the first man that existed, and his natural right in it is of the same kind . . . [But] it is not among the least of the evils of the present existing governments in all parts of Europe, that man considered as man, is thrown back to a vast distance from his Maker, and the artificial chasm filled up by a succession of barriers, or sort of turnpike gates, through which he has to pass.   (Paine 1984: 66–7)

Natural rights, Paine concludes in true Lockean style, belong to man "in right of his existence," whereas civil rights belong to man "in right of his being a member of society. Every civil right has for its foundation some natural right pre-existing in the individual, but to the enjoyment of which his individual power is not, in all cases, sufficiently competent." In short, society and social structures have a purpose, to be sure, Paine concedes; but "Man did not enter into society to become *worse* than he was before, nor to have fewer rights than he had before, but to have those rights better secured" (p. 68).

Tom Paine was not alone in England in reacting vigorously to Burke's *Reflections* on the French Revolution. Now acknowledged as an early pioneer of the rights of women, the Enlightenment thinker and writer Mary Wollstonecraft (1759–97) rushed to defend her friend, Richard Price, whose revolutionary sermon had been the target for Burke's alarmed pamphlet. In a detailed scathing attack on Burke for what she considered his emotionalism, his insincerity, his inconsistency, and "a mortal antipathy to reason," Wollstonecraft (1995: 12–13; see pp. 6–8) rejected his self-interested appeal to history and partisan tradition, and proclaimed "it is necessary emphatically to repeat, that there are rights which men inherit at their birth, as rational creatures, who were raised above the brute creation by their improvable faculties; and that, in receiving these, not from their forefathers but from God, prescription can never undermine natural rights." For good measure she followed this up two years later, in 1792, with what has become her best-known and equally spirited work, *A Vindication of the Rights of Women: with Strictures on Political and Moral Subjects*, dedicated to the French statesman and ex-bishop, Talleyrand, who had been a member of the committee which passed the Declaration of the Rights of Man. Picking up his recent observation that it was an inexplicable political phenomenon to see one-half of the human race excluded from participation in government by the other, Wollstonecraft put to him the uncomfortable question whether

> when men contend for their freedom, and to be allowed to judge for themselves respecting their own happiness, it be not inconsistent and unjust to subjugate women, even though you firmly believe that you are acting in the manner best calculated to promote their happiness? Who made man the exclusive judge, if women partake with him the gift of reason? . . . If women are to be excluded, without having a voice, from a participation of the natural rights of mankind, prove first, to ward off the charge of injustice and inconsistency that they want reason – else this flaw in your new Constitution will ever shew that man must, in some shape, act like a tyrant. (Wollstonecraft 1995: 69)

And she concluded, "I wish, Sir, to set some investigations of this kind afloat in France; and should they lead to a confirmation of my principles, when your constitution is revised the Rights of Woman may be respected, if it be fully proved that reason calls for this respect, and loudly demands justice for one half of the human race" (p. 70).

What purported to be a more rational English onslaught on the very idea of human rights was mounted by the contemporary of Burke and Paine, Jeremy Bentham (1748–1832), legal and social reformer, whose eagerly offered drafts for both an American and a French Constitution were rejected, to his intense frustration (Hart 1982: 76–8). Bentham's chief claim to fame is the assiduity with which he propounded and applied what one commentator has described as his "great vision: a complete science of morals and legislation" based on the all-sufficient Principle of Utility which he was pleased to take over from the French philosopher Helvétius (Mack 1962: 106–9). As Bentham saw it, the supreme principle in life was to aim to secure the greatest happiness of the greatest number, regarding happiness as synonymous with pleasure and thus dividing "the whole range of conscious human experience into pleasures and pains" (p. 219).

Bentham's systematic reductionism extended to what he termed the abolition of "fictitious entities," of which he had a horror, and of which he wished to rid legal language; and prominent among these chimeras were for him the ideas of natural law and of natural rights. "Implacable, and often intemperate, opposition to natural rights was one of the constants of Bentham's long career" (Sumner 1987: 111–12). The ponderous sarcasm, or what Hart terms the "panic-stricken rhetoric . . . inspired by the Terror" (Hart 1982: 79), of Bentham's analysis of the French Declaration of Rights charges it with being "dangerous nonsense" and "terrorist language" in its "perpetual abuse of words" (Waldron 1987: 46–69). In what was to become a famous aphorism on the subject, he protested, "*Natural rights* is simple nonsense: natural and imprescriptible rights, rhetorical nonsense – nonsense upon stilts," presumably meaning the height of nonsense. "*Right*, the substantive *right*, is the child of law: from *real* laws come *real* rights; but from *imaginary* laws, from laws of nature, fancied and invented by poets, rhetoricians, and dealers in moral and intellectual poisons, come *imaginary* rights, a bastard brood of monsters" (p. 69). The final reference to the illegitimate parentage of rights is not just vulgar invective, but was to be explained in a later work in which Bentham wrote, "To me a right and a legal right are the same thing, for I know no other. Right and law are correlative terms: as much so as father and son. Right is with me the child of law: from different operations of the law result different sorts of rights. A natural right is a son that never had a father" (p. 73).

Nor was Bentham's ire over natural rights confined to the terminology of the French Declaration (Burke 1988: 93). It had also earlier extended to the American Declaration of Independence, whose "inalienable" rights he considered "nonsense" (Mack 1962: 186), even although he came to have some approval for the actual success of that Revolution. "But the attack he abandoned against the American Revolution he levelled again at the French" (p. 187). In sum, Bentham opined, whatever claim is made for them, "the recognition of the nothingness of the laws of nature and the rights of man that have been grounded on them is a branch of knowledge of as much importance to an Englishman, though a negative one, as the most perfect acquaintance that can be formed with the existing laws of England" (Waldron 1987: 69).

In any case, it could well be argued, once Bentham had established the universal application of his Principle of Utility to all social and ethical issues, in seeking at all times what will bring about the greatest net happiness of the greatest number of people, then what need, or what further need, was there for any other social or ethical theory, least of all for those figments of the imagination, natural law and natural rights?

(See Mack 1962: 188–9.) Thus, as Hart (1982: 67–8) notes, in 1790 "for the first time Bentham identified the precise form of the utilitarian principle which, instead of a doctrine of natural rights, was to serve as his leading argument for democracy." This explains why Bentham could opine, "I know of no natural rights except those which are created by general utility, but even in that sense it were much better that the words were never heard of" (p. 89).

Equally wedded to the all-sufficiency of the theory of utilitarianism, which he refined in several significant ways, Bentham's disciple and successor, John Stuart Mill (1806–73), did not, however, regard natural rights with the same dismissive disdain as his predecessor. Indeed, Mill not only accepted the idea of such human rights; he even developed a justification for them on precisely utilitarian grounds. In his major work *Utilitarianism* Mill felt it necessary to devote a chapter to the consideration that "one of the strongest obstacles to the reception of the doctrine that Utility or Happiness is the criterion of right and wrong, has been drawn from the idea of Justice" (Mill 1973b: 296); and as part of his attempt to explain justice in utilitarian terms, or in terms of "expediency," he found it necessary to devote some attention to the idea of "moral" rights, as contrasted with legal rights, or rights conferred by law (p. 299).

For Mill, the notion of justice necessarily "implies something which is not only right to do, and wrong not to do, but which some individual person can claim from us as his moral right" (Mill 1973b: 305). He explains that "when we call anything a person's right, we mean that he has a valid claim on society to protect him in the possession of it, either by the force of law, or by that of education and opinion. If he has what we consider a sufficient claim, on whatever account, to have something guaranteed to him by society, we say that he has a right to it" (p. 309).

Mill, then, has no difficulty in acknowledging the idea and existence of moral rights. When it comes, however, to explaining to anyone what is the basis for such a right, or precisely why society ought to defend him in the possession of such a right, Mill comments, "I can give him no other reason than general utility" (1973b: 309); in other words in their resulting in the greatest happiness of the greatest number of people. He goes on to face the objection that this explanation does not appear to account for the strength of the moral obligation felt by people in responding to a right, and he explains that such a strength of feeling arises from "the extraordinarily important and impressive kind of utility which is concerned," that of personal security. This he considered aroused such intense feelings by comparison with "the more common cases of utility" that the difference in degree between them becomes "a real difference in kind" (p. 310). "Justice," then, Mill concludes, "is a name for certain classes of moral rules, which concern the essentials of human well-being more nearly, and are therefore of more absolute obligation, than any other rules for the guidance of life; and the notion which we have found to be the essence of the idea of justice, that of a right residing in an individual, implies and testifies to this more binding obligation" (pp. 315–16).

Commenting on the various qualifications which Mill felt constrained to introduce into Bentham's original all-purpose ethical principle of utilitarianism, Copleston (1966: 29) remarks that Mill's own ideas "strained the original Benthamite framework to such an extent that it ought to have been radically refashioned or even abandoned." And one might think this applies not least to the way in which Mill attempts to explain in terms of the greatest pleasure principle the idea of moral rights which Bentham excoriated. Thus, in his most famous work, his essay *On Liberty*, Mill draws attention to the fact that he will not develop his argument for liberty "from the idea of abstract right, as a thing independent of utility." For, he goes on in true Benthamite fashion, "I regard utility as the ultimate appeal on all ethical questions." Yet he immediately and carefully adds a qualification, "but it must be utility in the largest sense, grounded on the permanent interests of a man as a progressive being" (Mill 1973a: 136).

John Rawls describes the utilitarian view of rights by explaining how "under the conditions of civilized society there is great social utility in following them for the most part and in permitting violations only under exceptional circumstances ... utilitarianism seeks to account for them as a socially useful illusion" (Rawls 1971: 28). So far as concerned Mill himself, Copleston may be closer to the truth in his comment that once again "we receive the impression that Mill is working away from Benthamism to an ethics based on a more adequate view of the human person" (1966: 34). In other words, it may be considered at least questionable whether Mill's solely utilitarian explanation of rights, even in attempting to identify a net advantage to society which is unique or different "in kind" from other advantages, will explain what Hart (1982: 86), in commenting on Bentham, terms "the peremptory character evident in the invocation of rights as justifying demands made on others." Perhaps more logically fatal to Mill's position is the conclusion to which Hart (p. 94) further draws attention, that on the simple utilitarian view to which Mill appeals "there could never be a conflict between rights and utility"; even although, as we shall have occasion to see later (below, pp. 80, 113), one of the strongest arguments in favor of human rights lies precisely in their function as a counter and corrective to utilitarian considerations.

German Developments: Kant and Marx

In Europe not only France and Britain were exercised on the subject of human rights in theory as well as in practice. In Germany a notable intellectual contribution to the subject was made by Immanuel Kant (1724–1804), the meticulous German professor of pious Protestant parentage and possibly Scottish ancestry, who was decidedly sympathetic to the French Revolution (Reiss 1991: 262). Yet Kant also appears as a paradoxical figure in the history of the development of natural human rights. On the one hand, he rejected human nature as a basis from which to draw moral conclusions, and yet on the other hand he is rightly considered one of the most influential advocates of respect for the dignity of human beings. Seeking to establish a solid foundation on which to build a universal theory of ethics, or what he called "the supreme principle of morality" (Kant 1964: 60), Kant was quite clear that "the ground of obligation must be looked for, not in the nature of man nor in the circumstances of the world in which he is placed, but solely *a priori* in the concepts of pure reason" (p. 57).

In his approach to our experience of reality Kant introduced what he himself described as a "Copernican revolution" in human knowledge by suggesting that, rather than all our knowledge replicating or conforming to the objects which exist all around us, we should accept that we do not know objects as "things in themselves" but only through the way in which they are "known to us," that is, as they are presented to us through our mental categories of space, causal connection, and the like (Copleston 1960: 224–32). The consequence of this revolutionary approach to our knowledge of reality for the subject of human rights has been well noted by Shell (1990: 263): "For Kant, the contingent status of empirical knowledge seriously undermined the foundations of the older liberal natural rights teaching . . . To provide rights with a rational and certain foundation, Kant was forced on another track, permitting him to ground them not in nature with all its vagaries but in the absolute dictates of morality and the dignity it confers upon the moral subject." What in fact Kant was looking for was a universal and absolute moral law which would bind the wills of all rational beings and indicate to them where their duty lies. Obedience to such laws was for him the essence of morality. As he explained, "conformity with juridical laws is the *legality* of an action and conformity with ethical laws is its *morality*" (Kant 1991: 42). And he claimed to discover the fundamental ethical law, or "categorical [that is, unconditioned] imperative," by means of certain principles which could be established, he maintained, just by exercising one's reason.

The Kantian principle which most concerns us here is his claim to respect for human beings, expressed in his famous injunction: "Act in such a way that you always treat humanity, whether in your own person or in the person of any other, never simply as a means, but always at the same time as an end" (Kant 1964: 96). All commentators are careful to point out that Kant did not say that we should never use people at all as means to achieving our own ends. We do that all the time, using each other to get things done, whether to run the buses as drivers or to run the country as Members of Parliament or to run a business as directors. In fact, society could not function if it were never permissible to treat people as means. Kant carefully phrased his rule, however, to indicate that we should never treat others "merely as a means." In other words, in our dealings with others we should never reduce human beings to the status of means and nothing else. We should never forget that whatever defined function they may serve in society, or no matter how subordinate their role may be in an organization or in a process they are also human beings and as such more than simply means. For Kant they are ends in themselves, entitled to invariable ethical respect. Our behavior towards them should always bear that in mind, and never have the effect of equivalently depersonalizing or dehumanizing any person with whom we may have dealings.

When it comes to seeking the basis for such a claim to universal unqualified respect for human beings, Kant's reasoning is rather involved. At first reading, for instance, he seems to ground this claim in the simple fact of being a human person, and as such possessed of an inherent dignity. Thus, he writes that "man regarded as a *person*, that is, as the subject of a morally practical reason, . . . possesses a *dignity* (an absolute inner worth) by which he exacts respect for himself from all other rational beings in the world" (Kant 1991: 230). It is clear, however, from this statement that what makes a person so important and so entitled to respect is that it is, in Kant's words, "the subject of a morally practical reason." In other words, it is the human capacity to be moral and to exercise one's reason in discovering those moral laws to which all humans are subject which really gives human beings their unique dignity. "Morality, and humanity so far as it is capable of morality, is the only thing which has dignity" (Kant 1964: 102).

However, as Kant maintains, this human capacity for morality, or for reaching moral decisions, depends on our being interiorly free, or autonomous. As he saw it, we cannot adopt the moral laws to which we may reason from time to time unless our wills are independent from outside constraint, and, more positively, unless our wills are also able to legislate to themselves on where their moral duty lies. It is this need for freedom as a necessary condition for reasoning morally which leads Kant to conclude that "*autonomy* is therefore the ground of the dignity of human nature" (1964: 103). It is this which makes him describe "inner freedom [as] the innate dignity of man" (Kant 1991: 216–17). It is also this conclusion on the significance of freedom as essential for moral reflection and therefore as the basis of all human dignity which forms Kant's major argument for insisting that humanity in all its individual instances be treated as an end and never merely be subordinate to others as a means. And it is this centrality of the freedom to engage in morality which provides his basic argument for the existence of human rights. As Norman comments:

> respect for persons involves respect for their *liberty and autonomy*. An ethic which was confined to the *promotion* of ends would incline to paternalism . . . For the Kantian ethic, on the other hand, the basic requirement is a respect for the other person's own pursuit of his or her own ends through his or her own free action, and I am to help in the promotion of those ends only in ways which are compatible with that basic respect. (1983: 121–2)

Accordingly, Kant lays great emphasis on the notion of human rights, in so far as these identify basic freedoms which have to be respected. This is why, Norman continues, Kant commended human rights in such ringing terms: "There is nothing more sacred in the wide world than the rights of others. They are inviolable. Woe unto him who trespasses upon the right of another and tramples it underfoot! His right should be his security; it should be stronger than any shield or fortress. We have a holy ruler and the most sacred of his gifts to us is the rights of man" (1983: 193–4).

Kant views rights in general as "moral capacities for putting others under obligations," as he exemplifies by descending to details. One division of rights contrasts an innate right, or "that which belongs to everyone by nature," with an acquired right, which is brought into being by some particular act (Kant 1991: 63). So far as concerns innate rights, he is clear that there is only one right which belongs to everyone by virtue of their humanity: that of "freedom (independence of being constrained by another's choice), insofar as it can coexist with the freedom of every other." Involved in this right, or flowing from it, are others, including innate equality with others, independence of action and good reputation and behaving towards others in ways which do not diminish them (p. 63). For it is only by possessing such detailed human rights, that is, the capacity to lay others under obligation, that I can require them to respect my absolute dignity as flowing from my freedom. Only in this way, Kant concludes, can I be assured of exercising my moral autonomy to identify and discharge my own moral duties and be a rational moral being (p. 63). As Shestack (2000: 43) concludes, "Kant's great imperative is that the central focus of morality is 'personhood,' namely the capacity to take responsibility as a free and rational agent for one's system of ends."

A much more negative approach to human rights, leading to their suffering a serious eclipse, was to be taken by another great German thinker Karl Marx (1818–83), the social revolutionary who analyzed society and prescribed cures for its ills in terms of economic forces and realities, and who considered human rights to be totally self-centered. Among his early philosophical writings, Marx devoted some thought to the subject of human rights, in which he claimed to find an inherent contradiction (Marx 1992: 211–41). According to Marx, in the ideal "*political community*," which by its nature is "the *species-life* of man," "man regards himself as a *communal being*"; and this contrasts strongly with his living in "civil society," "where he is active as a *private indi-vidual*, regards other men as means, debases himself to a means and becomes the plaything of alien powers" (p. 220).

Thus, Marx (1992: 230) considered the French *droits de l'homme* as "quite simply the rights of the *member of civil society*, i.e., of egoistic man, of man separated from other men and from the community." This enabled him to conclude that "not one of the so-called rights of man goes beyond egoistic man, man as a member of civil society, namely an individual withdrawn into himself, his private interest and his private desires and separated from the community." Of course, such French "rights of man" would not satisfy the later Marx of *The Communist Manifesto*, who wanted nothing less than "proletarian uprising" throughout Europe. "[T]hough he celebrated the fall of the *ancien régime*, he never characterised it as anything other than a bourgeois revolution" (Waldron 1987: 123). It is in this context that one can appreciate the observation of Newell (1990: 342), that for Marx "behind the idealistic camouflage of the rights of man, the liberal state serves the interests of the bourgeoisie." As Peffer (1990: 324) summed up Marx's rejection of human rights, "a criticism Marx has of *both justice and rights* is that they will be otiose with the evolution of socialism into communism . . . A criticism he has of *rights* is that they embody or pre-suppose the model of man as the egoistic individual of civil society." The ideological objection of Marx to any idea of human rights is brought out by Allen Buchanan in his suggestion that Marx considered the basic civil and political rights enjoyed in capitalism to have value only in coping with the problems which were actually raised by capitalism, that is, "only when there are class-divisions and the egoism to which class-divisions give rise, under conditions of scarcity." However, Buchanan continues, "since he also believed that communism will end class-divisions and greatly reduce egoism and scarcity, he believed that conceptions of rights will not play a significant role in communism, the form of social organization which he believed would replace capitalism" (Buchanan 1985: 48).

As the influence of Marxism as a new political creed expanded in the early twentieth century and spread throughout Europe, Eastern and Western, partly as a result of the two world wars, his ideological strictures on human rights led to a severe eclipse in their intellectual and political appeal. It was only in the Catholic Church, with its strong anti-Marxist philosophy (equating Marxism with atheism), that the doctrine of human rights survived from its original application in the Industrial Revolution as a moral bulwark to defend the working class from laissez-faire exploitation (Curran 2003) as well as from Marxist totalitarianism. As Francesca Klug comments, "From a classical Marxist point of view, rights were a device for legitimising the self-interested behaviour of the propertied classes." Hence it was not surprising that, with the spread of Communist sympathies in Britain and elsewhere, "the Left became massively influenced by Karl Marx's attack on the idea of rights as hopelessly individualistic and therefore inimical to the collectivist goals of Communism. Although Marx was not entirely hostile to the French Revolutionaries' identification of the rights of citizens, he was so dismissive of the philosophy of fundamental rights as a progressive idea that this legacy was to last well into the twentieth century" (Klug 2000: 84–5). It was to take a second world war caused by the massive systematic abuse of the human rights of millions of people worldwide for the idea of human rights to re-emerge and seize public consciousness, and to assume a totally new expanding role in human history.

References

Aristotle, see Grant (1885).
Bellof, M. (1948), *Thomas Jefferson and American Democracy*, London: Hodder & Stoughton.
Bentham, J., see Hart (1982), Waldron (1987).
Bloom, A. (1990) (ed.), *Confronting the Constitution*, Washington, DC: AEI Press.

Browning, A. (1953) (ed.), *English Historical Documents VIII: 1660–1714*, London: Eyre & Spottiswoode.

Buchanan, A. (1985), *Ethics, Efficiency, and the Market*, Totowa, NJ: Rowman & Allenheld.

Buckland, W. W. (1966), *A Text-Book of Roman Law from Augustus to Justinian*, 3rd edn. Cambridge: Cambridge University Press.

Burke, E. (1988), *Reflections on the Revolution in France*, ed. Conor Cruise O'Brien, London: Penguin.

Burns, R. I. (2001) (ed.), *Las Siete Partidas*, Philadelphia: University of Pennsylvania Press.

Cicero (1928) *De re publica*, ed. T. E. Page, Loeb Classical Library, London: Heinemann.

Cicero (1960) *De inventione*, trans. H. M. Hubbell, Loeb Classical Library, London: Heinemann.

Cohler, A. M., et al. (1995) (trans.), Montesquieu, *The Spirit of the Laws*, Cambridge: Cambridge University Press.

Copleston, F. C. (1944), *A History of Philosophy*, vol. 1, London: Burns, Oates & Washbourne.

Copleston, F. C. (1960), *A History of Philosophy*, vol. 6, London: Burns & Oates.

Copleston, F. C. (1966), *A History of Philosophy*, vol. 8, London: Burns & Oates.

Cranston, M. (1958), *John Locke*, Oxford: Oxford University Press.

Cranston, M. (1973), *What are Human Rights?* New York: Taplinger.

Cranston, M. (1987), *Jean-Jacques: The Early Life and Work of Jean-Jacques Rousseau*, London: Penguin.

Cranston, M. (1991), *The Noble Savage: Jean-Jacques Rousseau*, London: Penguin.

Crocker, L. G. (1963), *Nature and Culture: Ethical Thought in the French Enlightenment*, Baltimore, MD: Johns Hopkins University Press.

Curran, C. E. (2003), *Catholic Social Teaching, 1891–Present: A Historical, Theological, and Ethical Analysis*, Washington, DC: Georgetown University.

Finnis, J. (1980), *Natural Law and Natural Rights*, Oxford: Clarendon Press.

Foner, L., and Genovese, E. D. (1969) (eds.), *Slavery in the New World*, Englewood Cliffs, NJ: Prentice Hall.

Grant, A. (1885), *The Ethics of Aristotle*, London: Longman's, Green.

Grant, M. (1971), *Cicero: On the Good Life*, London: Penguin.

Grotius, H. (1853), *De Jure Belli et Pacis*, ed. W. Whewell, London: University Press.

Habgood, J. (1993), Human Nature and Human Rights, in Habgood, *Making Sense*, London: SPCK.

Hampson, N. (1984), *The Enlightenment*, London: Penguin.

Hart, H. L. A. (1982), *Essays on Bentham: Jurisprudence and Political Theory*, Oxford: Clarendon Press.

Hawke, D. F. (1974), *Paine*, New York: W. W. Norton.

Hayden, P. (2005), *Cosmopolitan Global Politics*, Aldershot: Ashgate.

Herbert, G. B. (2002), *A Philosophical History of Rights*, Brunswick, NJ: Transaction Publishers.

Hill, C. (1965), *The Century of Revolution 1603–1714*, London: Abacus, Sphere Books.

Hobbes, T. (1974), *Leviathan*, ed. C. B. Macpherson, London: Penguin.

Holt, J. C. (1982) (ed.), *Magna Carta and the Idea of Liberty*, Malabar, Fl.: R. E. Krieger.

Jones, P. (1994), *Rights*, London: Macmillan.

Jover Zamora, J. M. (1998) (ed.), *Historia de España Menéndez Fidal*, Madrid: Espasa Calpe.

Kant, I. (1964), *Groundwork of the Metaphysics of Morals*, trans. H. J. Paton, New York: Harper.

Kant, I. (1991), *The Metaphysics of Morals*, trans. M. Gregor, Cambridge: Cambridge University Press.

Keane, J. (1995), *Tom Paine: A Political Life*, London: Bloomsbury.

Klein, H. S. (1969), Anglicanism, Catholicism, and the Negro Slave, in Foner and Genovese (1969).

Klug, F. (2000), *Values for a Godless Age: The Story of the UK's New Bill of Rights*, London: Penguin.

Kohler, O. (1981), in H. Jedin and J. Dolan (eds.), *Handbook of Church History*, vol. 6, London: Burns & Oates.

Laslett, P. (1963) (ed.), *John Locke: Two Treatises of Government*, Cambridge: Cambridge University Press.

Locke, J. (1963), *Two Treatises of Government*, ed. Peter Laslett, Cambridge: Cambridge University Press.

Lowe, E. J. (2005), *Locke*, London: Routledge.

Luther, M. (1964), Lecture on Galatians, in *Luther's Works*, ed. Jaroslav Pelikan, vol. 27, St. Louis, MI: Concordia Publishing House.

MacDonald, M. (1970), Natural Rights, in Melden (1970).

Mack, M. P. (1962), *Jeremy Bentham: An Odyssey of Ideas 1748–1792*, London: Heinemann.

Macpherson, C. B. (1974) (ed.), Thomas Hobbes, *Leviathan*, London: Penguin.

Mahoney, J. (1987), *The Making of Moral Theology: A Study of the Roman Catholic Tradition*, Oxford: Clarendon Press.

Marcus Aurelius (1961), *Meditations*, Everyman's Library, London: Dent.

Marx, K. (1992), On the Jewish Question, in Marx, *Early Writings*, ed. L. Colletti, London: Penguin.

Melden, A. I. (1970) (ed.), *Human Rights*, Belmont, CA: Wadsworth.

Mill, J. S. (1973a), *On Liberty*, in Mill, *Utilitarianism*, ed. Mary Warnock, London: Collins Fontana.

Mill, J. S. (1973b), *Utilitarianism*, ed. Mary Warnock, London: Collins Fontana.

Miller, F. D., Jr. (1995), *Nature, Justice, and Rights in Aristotle's Politics*, Oxford: Clarendon Press.

Montesquieu, Baron de (1995), *The Spirit of the Laws*, trans. A. M. Cohler et al., Cambridge: Cambridge University Press.

Newell, W. R. (1990), Reflections on Marxism and America, in Bloom (1990).

Norman, R. (1983), *The Moral Philosophers*, Oxford: Clarendon Press.

O'Brien, C. C. (1988), Introduction, in Burke (1988).

Padover, S. K. (1942), *Jefferson*, London: Jonathan Cape.

Pagels, E. (1979), The Roots and Origins of Human Rights, in A. H. Henkin (ed.), *Human Dignity: The Internationalisation of Human Rights*, New York: Aspen Institute for Humanistic Studies.

Paine, T. (1984), *Rights of Man*, intro. by Eric Foner, London: Penguin.

Paine, T. (1989), *Common Sense*, in Paine, *Political Writings*, ed. Bruce Kuklick, Cambridge: Cambridge University Press.

Paton, H. J. (1964) (trans.), Immanuel Kant, *Groundwork of the Metaphysics of Morals*, New York: Harper & Harper.

Peffer, R. G. (1990), *Marxism, Morality and Social Justice*, Princeton, NJ: Princeton University Press.

Raphael, D. D. (1967), Human Rights, Old and New, in Raphael (ed.), *Political Theory and the Rights of Man*, Bloomington: Indiana University Press.

Rawls, J. (1971), *A Theory of Justice*, Cambridge, MA: Harvard University Press.

Reiss, H. (1991) (ed.), *Kant: Political Writings*, 2nd enlarged edn., Cambridge: Cambridge University Press.

Rousseau, J.-J. (1984), *A Discourse on Equality*, trans. M. Cranston, London: Penguin.

Rousseau, J.-J. (1994), *The Social Contract*, in *"Discourse on Political Economy" and "The Social Contract,"* trans. C. Betts, World's Classics, Oxford: Oxford University Press.

Ruston, R. (2004), *Human Rights and the Image of God*, London: SCM.

Scruton, R. (1991), *A Short History of Modern Philosophy*, London: Routledge.

Shell, S. (1990), Idealism, in Bloom (1990).

Shestack, J. J. (2000), The Philosophical Foundations of Human Rights, in Symonides (2000), pp. 31–66.

Sophocles (1998), *Antigone*, ed. H. Lloyd-Jones, Loeb Classical Library, Cambridge, MA: Harvard University Press.

Sugden, C. (1996), *The Right to be Human: Biblical Studies in Human Rights*, Cambridge: Grove Books.

Sumner, L. W. (1987), *The Moral Foundation of Rights*, Oxford: Clarendon Press.

Symonides, J. (2000) (ed.), *Human Rights: Concept and Standards*, Aldershot: Ashgate.

Tierney, B. (1997), *The Idea of Natural Rights: Studies on Natural Rights, Natural Law and Church Law 1150–1625*, Atlanta, GA: Emory University.

Tuck, R. (1993), *Natural Rights Theories: Their Origin and Development*, Cambridge: Cambridge University Press.

Villey, M. (1962), *Leçons d'histoire de la philosophie du droit*, Paris: Dalloz.

Waldron, J. (1987) (ed.), *Nonsense upon Stilts*, London: Methuen.

Warnock, M. (1998), *An Intelligent Person's Guide to Ethics*, London: Duckworth.

Weinreb, L. L. (1987), *Natural Law and Justice*, Cambridge, MA: Harvard University Press.

Weinreb, L. L. (1992), Natural Law and Rights, in Robert P. George (ed.), *Natural Law Theory: Contemporary Essays*, Oxford: Clarendon Press.

Wollstonecraft, M. (1995), *"A Vindication of the Rights of Men"*, with *"A Vindication of the Rights of Women"* and *"Hints,"* ed. Sylvana Tomaselli, Cambridge: Cambridge University Press.

Chapter ②

The Modern Human Rights Movement

The subject of human rights entered a new era in the aftermath of the Second World War (1939–45). In the words of one individual closely involved in this postwar development, "one of the causes of the Second World War was the cynical, studied and wholesale violation of human rights by Nazi Germany. This, unlike any previous war, was a war to vindicate human rights" (Humphrey 1984: 12). It is against this background that we can appreciate the full force of the opening sentence of the founding Charter of the United Nations Organization when it was promulgated in June 1945:

> We the peoples of the United Nations determined to save succeeding generations from the scourge of war, which twice in our lifetime has brought untold sorrows to mankind, and *to reaffirm faith in fundamental human rights, in the dignity and worth of the human person, in the equal rights of men and women and of nations large and small* . . . have resolved to combine our efforts to accomplish these aims. (*UN Charter* 1995: preamble; emphasis added)

Of this aim on the part of the United Nations to endorse a program of universal human rights a later Secretary-General, Boutros Boutros-Ghali, commented, "The United Nations Charter . . . expressly places the Organization under an obligation to encourage 'respect for human rights and for fundamental freedoms for all without distinction as to race, sex, language, or religion' and makes that respect the very foundation for the achievement of its goals" (*The UN and Human Rights* 1995: p. 6). The purpose of this chapter is to explore the role of the United Nations Organization in promoting the modern human rights movement, and to consider the growing expansion of that movement in modern times.

The Charter of the United Nations Organization

The influence of the United States of America on the modern human rights movement is nowhere more evident than in its central contribution to setting up and giving direction to the United Nations Organization, including what emerged as its prominent concern for universal human rights. The history of the United States of America, which from the first founded its national and international political identity on the rights-based Declaration of Independence, as we have seen (pp. 22–4), made it entirely natural and almost instinctive for that country to appeal to the notion of human rights as the appropriate instrument for reconstructing world society after the horrors of the Second World War. And one can trace the more immediate origin of such US concern to the famous "Four Freedoms" State of the Union speech which President Franklin D. Roosevelt delivered to the American Congress in January 1941. When Britain stood alone in Europe against Nazi Germany, and Roosevelt, even before the USA entered the war, was concerned to ensure that Britain received the supply of armaments essential to pursuing its struggle, he famously declared his vision for the postwar world (Roosevelt 1941: 672):

> In the future days, which we seek to make secure, we look forward to a world founded upon four essential human freedoms.
> The first is freedom of speech and expression – everywhere in the world.
> The second is freedom of every person to worship God in his own way – everywhere in the world.
> The third is freedom from want – which, translated into world terms, means economic understandings which will secure to every nation a healthy peacetime life for its inhabitants – everywhere in the world.
> The fourth is freedom from fear – which, translated into world terms, means a world-wide reduction of armaments to such a point and in such a thorough fashion that no nation will be in a position to commit an act of physical aggression against any neighbour – anywhere in the world.

The underlying legitimation of all these freedoms was the idea of human rights. As Roosevelt concluded, "Freedom means the supremacy of human rights everywhere. Our support goes to those who struggle to gain those rights or keep them."

It was this early presidential reference to "human" rights which helped to canonize the term and to launch it on its historical development through America's major contribution to the deliberations of the United

Nations Organization. It was not surprising, then, that the following year, after the USA had entered the war, a "Declaration by United Nations" (the first use of the phrase "united nations," coined by Roosevelt), committed its twenty-six signatories to an all-out united war effort, and included in its preamble the conviction held by all parties "that complete victory over their enemies is essential to defend life, liberty, independence, and religious freedom, and to preserve human rights and justice in their own lands as well as in other lands" (Russell 1958: 51–3).

The proposal to organize these united nations as "a permanent arrangement for collectively maintaining the future peace" was considered by the "Big Four" allies, the United States of America, the Soviet Union, Great Britain, and China, at the Dumbarton Oaks Conversations which were held outside Washington in August–December 1944 (Russell 1958: 1–2). Among the various points of contention which inevitably arose was the proposal which was contained in the draft document submitted by the United States that the future General Assembly of the United Nations should be able to make recommendations "for the promotion of the observance of basic human rights" (Luard 1982: 1. 31–2). None of the other participating states had referred to this subject in their respective papers, and in fact initially Britain and the USSR were opposed to any mention of human rights, at least partly on the ground that it would constitute interference in the domestic affairs of sovereign member-states. Nevertheless, the US State Department had determined that human rights issues were "too important to be ignored in planning for an international organization that set its objectives in terms of world peace" (Russell 1958: 423).

The meeting to inaugurate the United Nations Organization duly assembled at San Francisco on April 25, 1945, President Roosevelt having died and been succeeded as President of the USA by his vice-president, Harry S. Truman. The atmosphere at the United Nations Conference on International Organization was one of "great expectations by many delegations of achieving higher living standards and expanded rights for mankind through the new world Organization" (Russell 1958: 776). Prior to this San Francisco meeting various countries had submitted observations and amendments relating to the references to human rights contained in the draft document which had been agreed at Dumbarton Oaks as a basis for deliberation; and in the course of the Conference's early sessions sundry other proposals were made with respect to the subject of human rights and its place in the UN's initial Charter.

The preamble to the Charter naturally set the tone of the spirit and agenda of the United Nations Organization, as shown in the strong opening statement referring to human rights quoted at the beginning of this chapter. However, the composing of a UN Declaration of detailed human rights was postponed for the time being, although the determination of many of the participating countries to make human rights a UN priority was clear, as also was the continuing reservation of some parties about appearing, or presuming, to intervene in the internal affairs of sovereign states (see Russell 1958: 780–1).

The document produced by that inaugural meeting of the UN, the Charter of the United Nations, of course contained vastly more than what was agreed as UN policy on human rights. Nevertheless, that the subject of human rights came after much debate to be explicitly identified in the preamble to the UN Charter is an indication of how significant and crucial future respect for human rights was considered to be by the fifty nations represented at San Francisco. In addition, the subject also figured at several other critical points in the whole document (*UN Charter* 1995). Thus, article 2 of the Charter envisages one of the purposes of the UN as "to achieve international cooperation . . . in promoting and encouraging respect for human rights and for fundamental freedoms for all without distinction as to race, sex, language, or religion." Article 55 provides that "with a view to the creation of conditions of stability and well-being which are necessary for peaceful and friendly relations among nations . . . the United Nations shall promote: . . . universal respect for, and observance of, human rights and fundamental freedoms for all without distinction as to race, sex, language, or religion." In pursuance of these aims article 13, par. 1, empowers the General Assembly to initiate studies and make recommendations for the purpose of ". . . assisting in the realization of human rights and fundamental freedoms for all without distinction as to race, sex, language, or religion." The Economic and Social Council, which was set up under the General Assembly, is likewise empowered in article 62, as the most appropriate agent for this activity, "to make recommendations for the purpose of promoting respect for, and observance of, human rights and fundamental freedoms for all." Article 68 further empowers the Council to set up "commissions . . . for the promotion of human rights." Finally, with respect to dependent territories and the Trusteeship System envisaged for them, article 73 of the Charter identifies a basic objective of this system as being "to encourage respect for human rights and for fundamental freedoms for all without distinction as to race, sex, language, or religion, and to encourage recognition of the interdependence of the peoples of the world."

The Charter was signed in June 1945, to enter into force on the following October 24. In the Closing Plenary Session President Truman, addressing the representatives of the fifty participating countries, declared with reference to their Charter's undertakings on human rights:

> I shall send this Charter to the United States Senate at once . . . Under this document we have good reason to expect an international bill of rights, acceptable to all the nations involved. That bill of rights will be as much a part of international life as our own Bill of Rights is a part of our Constitution. The Charter is dedicated to the achievement and observance of human rights and fundamental freedoms. Unless we can attain those objectives for all men and women everywhere – without regard to race, language, or religion – we cannot have permanent peace and security in the world. (*Documents of UN Conference* 1945: vol. 1, pp. 26, 683).

The Universal Declaration of Human Rights

Among the internal bodies which the UN Charter created in order to pursue its various ends, the Economic and Social Council was instituted as an intergovernmental body under the authority of the General Assembly charged with making studies and recommendations on a number of issues including "respect for, and observance of, human rights . . . for all" (*UN Charter* 1995: art. 62.2). The Economic and Social Council was to pursue its aims by setting up various commissions, including a commission for "the promotion of human rights" (art. 68). Thus, in June 1946 the Economic and Social Council set the terms of reference and composition of the Commission on Human Rights and also presented its secretariat with the formidable tasks of compiling a yearbook on "law and usage referring to human rights" as well as studying the evolution of human rights, including the preparation and publication of a survey of the development of human rights (*UN Yearbook on Human Rights* 1949: 457–8). The secretariat, dismayed by the resources and expertise implied by this grandiose request, asked for guidance on various factors of their remit, which they considered more suited to a scientific institute than to an international political organization (UN Econ. Soc. Council Records 1947: 4 (2): 1–3).

A usefully documented account of some of the work of the Human Rights Commission was produced by Simpson (2001: 411–56) in a study which is more concerned with the later European Convention on Human Rights, and which tends to be concerned with legal considerations, primarily with British concern to safeguard its sovereignty against intervention in national affairs by other parties (for example, pp. 245–8). In general, he adopts a belittling tone towards the work and production of the Commission, as well as towards the final Universal Declaration, of which he asserts that "on its own it represented little more than an exhalation of pious hot air" (p. 11). Being more interested in international law and the inner concerns of the British Foreign Office, he had no interest in what interests us, the background to human rights, and he mentioned the philosophical debates only as one of the "controversies which left no obvious traces on the final form of the Declaration" (p. 453), while, on the significant religious discussions he noted only that at one stage in the Third Committee "there was considerable controversy, which had first arisen in the Commission, as to whether the declaration should contain some reference to the Deity, the Creator, or to Nature, by way of providing a philosophical basis for the document" (p. 454). So far as concerns the final successfully approved Declaration he concentrated on the criticisms it received and the defensive responses, limiting his comment on the positive side to the observation (p. 459, n. 284) that "the adulatory literature is vast."

In the circumstances it is not surprising that Simpson makes no mention of the help forthcoming to the secretariat and the Commission on Human Rights from another UN body, the United Nations Educational, Scientific and Cultural Organization (UNESCO), which set up its own Committee on the theoretical and philosophical bases of human rights and instituted an inquiry among leading thinkers and writers around the world on their views on the subject. In the preface to its detailed questionnaire the Committee (UNESCO 1949: 255) noted: "the world of man is at a critical stage in its political, social and economic evolution. If it is to proceed further on the path towards unity, it must develop a common set of ideas and principles. One of these is a common formulation of the rights of man." Of the sixty replies received, some were published at the time in the United Nations weekly *Bulletin* (*UN Bulletin* 1947: 3) while a collection of replies selected for the variety of their views was subsequently published in a UNESCO Symposium, which also included the Committee's final report to the Commission on Human Rights (UNESCO 1949: 258–72). The material on human rights thus produced was included in the 408-page documented draft outline prepared for the Drafting Committee by the secretariat and constituted "perhaps the most exhaustive documentation on the subject of human rights ever assembled" (*UN Bulletin* 1947: 3. 639).

Other interest in the work of the UN Human Rights Commission came from a much wider public, including religious bodies and legal and non-governmental organizations (NGOs) throughout the free world who had contributed to the strong wave of interest in human rights which had been building up since 1943, and on whose behalf many representative groups now encouraged and monitored the deliberations of the new Commission (Morsink 1999: 1–2, 9–10).

At its first session, in January–February 1947, the Commission on Human Rights elected the widely respected widow of President Roosevelt, Mrs Eleanor Roosevelt, as its chair. The Chinese scholar Dr Peng-chu Chan was elected as vice-chair and Dr Charles H. Malik, the Lebanese ambassador and Harvard philosopher, was appointed the Commission's rapporteur, while Professor John P. Humphrey of the secretariat acted as its secretary. These formed the basis of a Drafting Committee to produce a draft bill of rights using the material prepared by the secretariat (*UN Yearbook on Human Rights* 1949: 462–3).

Commenting on the working of this Human Rights Commission, Mrs Roosevelt recalled later in her autobiography that "early in the meetings of the commission we discovered that while it would be possible to reach some kind of agreement on the Declaration, we were going to be in for a great deal of controversy with the Russian representatives, particularly Dr Pavlov, who attempted at every opportunity to write a bit of Communist philosophy into the document . . . This naturally became a bit monotonous but the Russians never gave up trying" (Roosevelt 1992: 317). A more detailed description of the basic ideological polarization on human rights which emerged within the Commission is provided by Tony Evans, in an analysis inspired by the Italian Marxist thinker, Antonio Gramski, of the Soviet resistance to what Evans terms the US bid for hegemony and moral leadership in the postwar world. When the Commission on Human Rights was convened, Evans records:

> it was the socialist states that mounted the early resistance to a liberal conception of rights. These states shared a view of history that understood the post-war world as an era of transposition from a capitalist to a socialist order. From this it followed that any durable international agreement on human rights should reflect the values of a future social order, not those of the past. These values included economic and social rights like the right to work and social security. As discussion of the Declaration and Covenants continued, the socialist states repeatedly highlighted their own "progressive" approach and denigrated that of the USA, which they claimed clung conservatively to outmoded values.   (Evans 1998: 8; see p. 4)

Such socialist stress on economic, social, and cultural rights, which was supported by some of the less developed countries, explains, Evans continues (1998: 9–10), why "the US found it increasingly difficult to sustain domestic support for full engagement in the human rights debate," on account of the conservative and isolationist fears within the USA that a full human rights program including economic, social, and cultural rights would eradicate "the traditional social and political freedoms for which America stood" and erode the constitutional and law-making rights of the individual states.

A slightly more nuanced account of the early debates about the place to be accorded to economic and social rights is provided by Glendon, who observes (2001: 185) that, "contrary to later belief, the countries within the Soviet sphere of influence were neither alone nor the most vigorous in pushing for the inclusion of social and economic rights. Though the details of these provisions were a continuing source of controversy within the Commission, no nation opposed them in principle." As she points out, the presence of Eleanor Roosevelt assured that her late President husband's stress on "freedom from want" must act as a touchstone for the Commission and, indeed, its parent body in their deliberations. It was really and regularly a matter of what emphasis such rights should receive in comparison with the more traditional political and civil rights. However, Glendon (2001: 42–3) does recognize that "nowhere was Eleanor Roosevelt's ability to influence U.S. policy more evident than in her success in persuading a reluctant State Department to accept the inclusion of social and economic rights in the Declaration."

It was, then, a tribute to the diplomatic skills of Eleanor Roosevelt, internally as well as nationally, that on the occasion of the Report of the Human Rights Commission to the Economic and Social Council in March 1947, the rapporteur, Dr Malik, could speak for the Commission in explaining that the bill of human rights would be the United Nations' answer to the question: "What is man?" and would give meaning to the phrase "dignity and worth of the human person," which was to be found in the Preamble to the Charter.

> The elaboration of the bill of rights [Malik continued] was fraught with three grave dangers. The first was that of legalism or getting lost in legalistic distinctions and niceties. The second danger was that of instrumentalism, allowing the instrumental things of life to obscure the essence of man. The last and most important was that of totalitarianism. It was not to be feared that the rights of the State would not be properly represented. But the danger existed that the individual human person might be forgotten. Unless the bill of rights embodied man as he really was, the declaration would merely express the dominant forces of the age, which did not respect man sufficiently. (UN Econ. Soc. Council Records 1947: 4 (1). 108–9)

The reception given to the Commission's working report by the Economic and Social Council was favorable, and included commendation by Dr Peng-chu Chan, head of the Chinese UN Delegation, a respected and erudite literary figure, described by Glendon as "a Chinese Renaissance man" (2001: 33; see p. 133). He observed that "the bill envisaged should be based on the aspiration for a new humanism. The fact that rights of men were included in thirty-five or forty of the world's constitutions indicated that a large measure of agreement was possible in spite of differences of philosophy or ideology" (UN Econ. Soc. Council Records 1947: 4 (1). 110–11). Many suggestions of rights to be included or recognized were also made by Council members (pp. 111–12), and drafts were also submitted to the Commission by governments and non-governmental organizations (*The UN and Human Rights* 1995: p. 24).

Eventually the Commission submitted its final version to the Economic and Social Council, and notwithstanding general differences in ideology, and in spite of specific rights and details calling for many compromises, the general mood of satisfaction was expressed by the representative from Turkey when he noted that "it was encouraging to reflect that after two world wars men of all creeds and climes had been able to devise a common standard of rights for all mankind" (UN Econ. Soc. Council Records 1947: 4 (1). 656).

Thus approved, the draft UN Declaration on Human Rights reached the General Assembly in August 1948 (*The UN and Human Rights* 1995: p. 24), and this eventually referred it for examination and comment to its Third Committee. Reflecting on the behind-the-scenes labor which had been involved in securing consensus for the entire document, Eleanor Roosevelt wrote, "We worked for two months, often until late at night, debating every single word of that draft Declaration over and over again before Committee Three would approve its transmission to the General Assembly" (Roosevelt 1992: 320). Finally, at its third session the General Assembly of the United Nations proclaimed the Declaration as a whole on December 10, 1948 by 48 votes to none, with 8 abstentions (*The UN and Human Rights* 1995: pp. 153–5). Commenting on the final vote, Mrs Roosevelt wrote:

> in the end there was no vote cast against the Declaration in the General Assembly, but there were some disappointing abstentions. The Soviet Union and its satellite countries abstained, since the Russian delegate contended that the Declaration put emphasis mainly on "eighteenth-century rights" and not enough on economic, social and cultural rights. The delegate from Saudi Arabia abstained, saying he was quite sure King Ibn Saud would not agree to the interpretation of the Koran. South Africa also abstained, I was sad to note; its delegate said that they hoped to give

their people basic human rights, but that the Declaration went too far. Two small countries were absent. (Roosevelt 1992: 320)

One of the most influential contributors to the document's composition, Dr Charles Malik, had earlier observed that "The present Declaration . . . is the definitive explication of the pregnant phrase of the preamble [of the Charter], 'the dignity and worth of the human person' " (Malik 1948: 519). Commenting now on the successful completion of the Declaration, Dr Malik explained:

> the resulting formulation reflects the fundamental convictions of the present age in regard to what constitutes the inherent dignity and worth of man. The remarkable thing about this achievement is that it is not the product of one brain or one school of thought alone. For two years all the United Nations participated in this work, or had a full chance to participate, and every point of view was expressed and thoroughly debated, so that the document is a genuine international product.
>
> (1949: 4)

He concluded, "Whoever values man and his individual freedom above everything else cannot fail to find in the present Declaration a potent ideological weapon. If wielded in complete goodwill, sincerity, and truth, this weapon can prove most significant in the history of the spirit. It can never be said, from now on, that the conscience of organized, responsible humanity has left ambiguous what inherently belongs to man's own humanity." In less rhetorical terms an unsigned article in the same issue of the *United Nations Bulletin* (1949: 6. 9) concluded: "What resulted was necessarily a composite of many political, economic and sociological ideas, differing systems of law, and cultural traditions. This is precisely what gives the first international declaration of the human rights of man its value and its place in history."

The Universal Declaration of Human Rights (*The UN and Human Rights* 1995: pp. 152–5) which resulted from these years of debate and patient compromise is a carefully constructed document possessing a strong internal coherence and comprising three major sections: civil and political rights; economic, social, and cultural rights; and the importance of rights for international order. The preamble, recalling the United Nations original Charter's reaffirmation of faith in fundamental human rights, and declaring that "Human rights are based on the 'inherent dignity . . . of all members of the human family'," provides the basis of article 1, which proclaims, with conscious echoes of the triad of values contained in the French Declaration of the Rights of Man, that "All human beings are born free and equal in dignity and rights. They are endowed with reason and conscience and should act towards one another in a spirit of brotherhood." Article 2 then defines the rights which are enumerated in the Declaration as applying to everyone "without distinction of any kind."

Article 3 introduces the first group of rights (civil and political) as "the first pillar of the declaration": "Everyone has the right to life, liberty and security of person." These rights are then developed in articles 4–21, enlarging on the following topics: no slavery or servitude (art. 4); no torture or cruel, inhuman, or degrading treatment (art. 5); recognition before the law (art. 6); equality before the law (art. 7); legal right to remedy (art. 8); no arbitrary arrest, detention, or exile (art. 9); fair and public hearing (art. 10); presumption of innocence (art. 11); protection of privacy (art. 12); freedom of movement (art. 13); right to asylum from persecution (art. 14); right to a nationality (art. 15); right to marry and found a family (art. 16); right to own property (art. 17); right to freedom of thought, conscience, and religion (art. 18); right to freedom of opinion, expression, and information (art. 19); right to peaceful assembly and association and non-association (art. 20); and right to participate in government and election (art. 21).

The second basic element of the Declaration is then articulated, as an introduction to the group of economic, social, and cultural rights: "Everyone, as a member of society, has the right to social security and is entitled to realization, through national effort and international cooperation and in accordance with the organization and resources of each State, of the economic, social and cultural rights indispensable for his dignity and the free development of his personality" (art. 22). These rights are then specified and expanded on in relation to the subjects of: work and working conditions (art. 23); rest and leisure (art. 24); standard of living adequate for one's self and one's family (art. 25); education directed to the full development of the human personality (art. 26); and free participation in the cultural life of the community (art. 27).

Finally, the concluding section of the Universal Declaration identifies the right to a peaceful international order favorable to the realization of rights and freedoms (art. 28), and then points out the need to have regard for the sort of community in which human rights and freedoms can be enjoyed. Not only is it the case, as many of the participating nations stressed, that "Everyone has duties to the community in which alone the free and full development of his personality is possible" (art. 29.1). In addition, everyone shall be subject to laws "securing due recognition and respect for the rights and freedoms of others" (art 29.2).

As one begins then to track the fortunes of this historic document it is worth bearing in mind its originally limited purpose and its inherent limitations. As Falk expressed these (2000: 6), the Universal Declaration of Human Rights "was set forth as a comprehensive image of human dignity toward which states would individually move, but at their own pace and in a manner respectful of their own sovereignty."

Continental Developments

The 1948 Universal Declaration of Human Rights can be subjected to various criticisms, yet there is much to be said for the conclusion expressed by Glendon (2001: 240) that "the framers took encouragement from the fact that human beings are capable not only of violating human rights, but also of imagining that there are rights to violate, of articulating those rights in declarations and constitutions, of orienting their conduct toward the norms they have recognized, and of feeling the need to make excuses when their conduct falls short." Moreover, the Declaration "addressed the great majority of the current or foreseeable issues of its time" (*The UN and Human Rights* 1995: p. 27), and in so doing exercised dramatic influence on the spread of interest in human rights in the various continents of the world. Thus, two years later in 1950 the members of the Council of Europe signed a *European Convention on Human Rights* (1995: 13–36) in which they noted the UN Declaration and affirmed that one of the methods to pursue their aim of greater unity between their European members was "the maintenance and further realisation of Human Rights and Fundamental Freedoms" (see Donnelly 2003: 138–41).

Another subsequent regional agreement which was influenced by the UN Declaration was the *American Convention on Human Rights*. Already in 1948 the Ninth International Conference of American States, meeting in Bogota, had produced an American Declaration of the Rights and Duties of Man, which opened with the affirmation, "All men are born free and equal, in dignity and in rights, and, being endowed by nature with reason and conscience, they should conduct themselves as brothers one to another" (Brownlie 1997: 489). Now, "the culmination of Latin American interest in human rights" (p. 495) saw the participating states belonging to the Organization of American States claim to be "reaffirming their intention to consolidate in this hemisphere, within the framework of democratic institutions, a system of personal liberty and social justice based on respect for the essential rights of man" (*The UN and Human Rights* 1995: p. 248). In so doing, the American Convention noted that "the essential rights of man . . . are based upon attributes of the human personality" (ibid.), and it reiterated with a

Rooseveltian echo "that, in accordance with the Universal Declaration of Human Rights, the ideal of free men enjoying freedom from fear and want can be achieved only if conditions are created whereby everyone may enjoy his economic, social, and cultural rights, as well as civil and political rights" (*The UN and Human Rights* 1995: p. 249).

A third major continental agreement which followed from the UN Declaration was the 1981 *African Charter on Human and Peoples' Rights* (*The UN and Human Rights* 1995: pp. 284–91), issued by members of the Organization of African Unity (OAU), in which there is evidence of African preconceptions and aspirations. The signatories bow to the American Convention in recognizing "on the one hand, that fundamental human rights stem from the attributes of human beings, which justifies their international protection," but they qualify this individual note with the community-regarding affirmation "on the other hand, that the reality and respect of peoples' rights should necessarily guarantee human rights." This concern for peoples rather than individuals is also clear in the reaffirmation of the pledge made in the OAU's Charter "to eradicate all forms of colonialism from Africa, to coordinate and intensify their cooperation and efforts to achieve a better life for the peoples of Africa and to promote international cooperation having due regard to the Charter of the United Nations and the Universal Declaration of Human Rights." The African and postcolonial agenda is also evident in the stated conviction "that it is henceforth essential to pay particular attention to the right to development and that civil and political rights cannot be dissociated from economic, social and cultural rights in their conception as well as universality and that the satisfaction of economic, social and cultural rights is a guarantee for the enjoyment of civil and political rights" (*The United Nations and Human Rights* 1995: p. 284).

Further international acknowledgment of the importance of human rights was to be found among Arab nations, which had been invited by the UN Economic and Social Council to take part in the discussions led by the Commission on Human Rights, and which were further invited to attend the UN 1968 Teheran Conference. At that Conference (*The United Nations and Human Rights* 1995: pp. 247–8) the Arab states were successful in having the agenda include reference to the question of Israeli-occupied territories resulting from the 1967 war, and as a consequence the League of Arab States set up a Permanent Arab Commission on Human Rights whose competence includes all matters in the Arab world which relate to human rights and is set out in an Arab Charter on Human Rights which was eventually approved in 1994 (Robertson and Merrills 1996: 238–42).

Within the United Nations itself in the immediate aftermath of its Universal Declaration work was pursued within the Economic and Social Council on identifying, promoting, and protecting particular groups of rights, such as those applying to women, prisoners, children, and refugees; and various recommendations and statements were issued in the next few years (*The UN and Human Rights* 1995: pp. 29–36). The Human Rights Commission itself was more concerned in its early years in exploring its proposal that "in addition to a Declaration, there should be a binding multilateral treaty on human rights" (*The UN and Human Rights* 1995: p. 39). After considerable debate and widespread consultation the Commission was authorized to bring forward not one, but two, International Covenants on Human Rights, one on Economic, Social and Cultural Rights (*The UN and Human Rights* 1995: pp. 229–34), and the other on Civil and Political Rights (pp. 235–44), which entered into force in 1976 and to which over 120 States worldwide are now parties, with the undertaking to report periodically to the Economic and Social Council (Brownlie 1997: 114–43). The thinking behind producing binding international covenants in the field of human rights was that "as the legal expression of the moral principles underlying the Universal Declaration of Human Rights, these two Covenants were seen as instruments that would encourage States to give greater impetus to their human rights commitments" (*The UN and Human Rights* 1995: p. 48). Much of the other UN work on human rights in these years is chronicled and documented in its publication, *United Nations Action in the Field of Human Rights* (*UN Action* 1994).

To celebrate the twentieth anniversary of the Declaration of Human Rights the year 1968 was designated as International Year for Human Rights, and the International Conference on Human Rights held that year in Teheran was attended by delegations from eighty-four states with the specific objective "to reaffirm the will of the international community to put a stop to gross denials of human rights and step up both national and international efforts and initiatives in the human rights field" (*The UN and Human Rights* 1995: p. 69). In its Proclamation (pp. 247–8), the Teheran Conference was forthright in identifying what it considered serious human rights abuses in various parts of the globe, and it affirmed, *inter alia*, that "since human rights and fundamental freedoms are indivisible, the full realization of civil and political rights without the enjoyment of economic, social and cultural rights is impossible" (*The UN and Human Rights* 1995: p. 248).

An important new expansion of human rights was formalized in 1986 with the adoption by the UN General Assembly of a *Declaration on the Right to Development* (*The UN and Human Rights* 1995:

pp. 74–80, 322–4), which clearly echoed the 1981 African Charter on Human and Peoples' Rights, noted above. As described in the opening article of the Declaration, "the right to development is an inalienable human right by virtue of which every human person and all peoples are entitled to participate in, contribute to, and enjoy economic, social, cultural and political development, in which all human rights and fundamental freedoms can be fully realized." In expressing development in these terms the Declaration was questioning the idea held hitherto with regard to the so-called developing countries, on the whole unsuccessfully, that the main objective of economic activity was to improve economic and financial indicators. "Instead it placed human beings, individually and collectively, at the centre of all economic activity, making them both the central subject and principal beneficiary of development" (*The UN and Human Rights* 1995: p. 75). The Declaration was the culmination of ten years of drafting and deliberation in the United Nations, reflected in a 1981 report in which the then Secretary-General drew the conclusion that "any development strategy which directly involves the denial of fundamental human rights, in whatever name or cause it may be undertaken, must be deemed to be a systematic violation of the right to development." In such situations often conditions of underdevelopment involved for millions of people the denial of access to basic essentials of human survival and the imposition of living conditions which were totally incompatible with human dignity (*The UN and Human Rights* 1995: p. 76).

The 1993 Vienna World Conference on Human Rights

The modern human rights movement saw a significant further step taken at the first major international conference on human rights after the dramatic internal collapse of the Eastern European Soviet bloc, convened in Vienna in 1993. Preparations for the Vienna Conference were worldwide, with thousands of non-governmental organizations involved as well as the States Members of the UN (*The UN and Human Rights* 1995: p. 93), all aiming, in the words of Boutros Boutros-Ghali in his Opening Address, to inquire into the progress made in the field of human rights since the Declaration of 1948, to identify the obstacles encountered, and to find ways to overcome them. "What I mean to say, with all solemnity, is that the human rights we are about to discuss here at Vienna are not the lowest common denominator among all nations, but rather what I should like to describe as the 'irreducible human element,' in other words, the quintessential values through which we affirm together that we are a single human community" (*The UN and Human Rights* 1995: p. 442).

Drinan brings out well the historic significance of this United Nations Conference on Human Rights in Vienna (Drinan 2001). Shortly after the founding of the United Nations, the descent of the Iron Curtain midway across Europe had kept East and West polarized politically and economically for more than forty years; and human rights had to some extent been a cold war political weapon which the United States in particular aimed regularly at the Soviet bloc. As Evans (1998: 10–11) explained, "the conflict over differing conceptions of human rights offered a focus for cold war rhetoric that dominated international politics for over four decades." Now, Drinan observes (2001: 16), with the fall of the Berlin Wall and the collapse of Communism, "participants in the Vienna conference wanted to feel that the first fifty years of the intellectual human rights movement had been superseded by an entirely new era in the development of democracy and human equality." The result was an updating and modernizing of the Universal Declaration of Human Rights, comprising "an astonishing proclamation of the rights of humanity" which was subscribed to by 171 nations, including "delegates from the newly liberated countries in central and eastern Europe" (Drinan 2001: pp. x, 16), and whose "panoramic view" of human rights was strongly influenced by "the thousands of nongovernmental organizations (NGOs) who were present in Vienna and who had carefully worked to make sure that the major issues related to world law and human rights were taken up in the final document" (Drinan 2001: p. xii).

Despite the less enthusiastic comments by Evans (1998: 18; see p. 202) on the claimed unanimity of the deliberations and work of the Vienna Conference even after the end of the cold war, the final results, for all their occasional signs of ambiguity and compromise, do constitute a remarkable human achievement. The Vienna Declaration and Programme of Action (*The UN and Human Rights* 1995: pp. 448–64) recalled the origin and history of the human rights movement since the end of the Second World War in "recognizing and affirming that all human rights derive from the dignity and worth inherent in the human person, and that the human person is the central subject of human rights and fundamental freedoms, and consequently should be the principal beneficiary and should participate actively in the realization of these rights and freedoms" (p. 448).

It also singled out "several key areas on which the Organization should focus its efforts in the years to come," including "the interdependence of the right to development, democracy and other fundamental human rights" (p. 94), and it created the post of United Nations High Commissioner for Human Rights (pp. 109–10). In addition, the Vienna Conference gave new emphasis to the idea that "all human rights are universal, indivisible and interdependent and interrelated" (p. 450), and this recognition gave the Conference the opportunity to stress particularly, in addition to the right to development, the rights of children and migrant workers and the need to eliminate all forms of discrimination and torture (p. 98). In addition, the United Nations set itself numerous human rights projects to be pursued at international level as the world moved into a new century, as the then Secretary-General subsequently observed in the closing chapter of his study, *The United Nations and Human Rights 1945–1995*. As he concluded, "The United Nations must continue to mobilize its efforts, so that human rights may one day emerge at last as the common language of humanity" (*The UN and Human Rights* 1995: p. 125).

Fresh, if controversial, impetus was given to the drive towards recognizing human rights worldwide by the appointment as the first United Nations High Commissioner for Human Rights of the distinguished lawyer and former President of Ireland, Mary Robinson (Horgan 1997). Charged with integrating human rights concerns into all the activities of the United Nations, she traveled widely in order to work at first hand with the governments of various countries in which there were reports of problems or alleged violations of human rights, including China, East Timor, and various African countries. It was widely believed that her activities as no respecter of persons – nor of governments – brought disapproval from both the United States and Israel which led to her term of office not being extended. As Ian Williams wrote, in publishing an interview with Dr Robinson, "It's common knowledge that her defense of the Durban Conference against Racism, which U.S. and Israeli representatives walked out of, her views on the Israel–Palestine conflict and her condemnation of the U.S. treatment of Iraqi prisoners at Cuba's Guantanamo Bay provoked the Bush administration to oppose the extension of her term" (Williams 2002).

On the occasion of the fiftieth anniversary of the Universal Declaration of Human Rights Mary Robinson highlighted the significance of their impact in claiming:

> We must learn that human rights, in their essence, are empowering. By protecting human rights, we can create an environment for living in which each individual is able to develop his or her own gifts to the fullest extent. Providing this assurance of protection, in turn, will contribute to preventing so many of the conflicts based on poverty, discrimination and

political oppression which continue to plague humanity. The vicious cycle: violations of human rights – conflicts – which in turn lead to more violations – must be broken. I believe we can break it only by ensuring respect for all human rights. The reaction to conflict always comes too late from the perspective of those whose rights have been violated. Now is the time for us to assume collective responsibility and develop the institutions and processes to anticipate, deter and prevent gross human rights violations. (Robinson 1998: 257)

It has to be recognized, of course, that the history of the UN Human Rights Commission was more than somewhat checkered in the agreements reached and implemented, not least because its participating members were not all notable for their own human rights records and some cynically found their rotating membership a useful way of stifling criticism of themselves and their allies. After serious complaints offered by the Secretary-General (Annan 2005), the Commission was replaced in May 2006 by an elected Human Rights Council, whose members, the Secretary-General and the President made a point of noting, would conduct a regular review of the human rights records of all countries, beginning with themselves. The United States of America voted against the reform on the ground that it did not go far enough (UN News Service, 9 May 2006).

Wider Human Rights Developments

In the closing decades of the twentieth century the considerable impetus given to the human rights movement worldwide by the UN also continued to influence groupings and events outside that organization. So far as Europe was concerned, David Hoffman and John Rowe (2003: 25) note that, after the Second World War,

> there was a movement within Europe in favour of a federal European state, to promote greater peace and security, and prevent a resurgence of a militarily strong Germany. Part of this movement was for the protection of human rights, especially from those with the experience of being oppressed by their own governments . . . The British Foreign Office, under Foreign Secretary Ernest Bevin, was a prime mover in the development of regional protection of human rights within Europe, although it was not in favour of a federal Europe.

Accordingly, in 1949 the Council of Europe was set up "to achieve a greater unity between its members," with aims which included "the maintenance and further realisation of human rights and fundamental freedoms."

In 1950 the Council produced the *European Convention on Human Rights and Fundamental Freedoms (The UN and Human Rights* 1995: pp. 156–63; *European Convention* 1995: 13–36), followed by various Protocols specifying implications and applications of the Convention (Jacobs and White 1996). This came into force in 1953, and the European Court came into being in 1959 (Hoffman and Rowe 2003: 26). The High Contracting Parties to the European Convention significantly linked the future of Europe with human rights in their opening affirmation "that the aim of the Council of Europe is the achievement of greater unity between its Members and that one of the methods by which that aim is to be pursued is the maintenance and further realisation of Human Rights and Fundamental Freedoms." Further, it was no doubt considered appropriate that in the continent which saw the origin of the Second World War and which was its major battlefield they should reaffirm not just "the belief" in human rights which the United Nations had identified, but now their own "profound belief in those Fundamental Freedoms which are the foundation of justice and peace in the world and are best maintained on the one hand by an effective political democracy and on the other by a common understanding and observance of the Human Rights upon which they depend." Moreover, the European governments were aiming now not simply to record collective aspirations and utter high-flown sentiments about human rights. They were "resolved, as the Governments of European countries which are like-minded and have a common heritage of political traditions, ideals, freedoms and the rule of law, to take the first steps for a collective enforcement of certain of the Rights stated in the Universal Declaration" (Jacobs and White 1996: preamble). Consequently, in order to secure effective observance of the Convention by the countries signatory to it they set up a European Commission on Human Rights which would receive complaints from individuals or groups alleging violation of rights by participating countries "after all domestic remedies have been exhausted" (Jacobs and White 1996: arts. 19–37), and a European Court of Human Rights to adjudicate on cases referred to it by the Commission or by a participating government (Jacobs and White 1996: arts. 19, 38–56).

In 1961, the Council of Europe further introduced the European Social Charter which was aimed at recognizing and protecting rights entailed by the dignity of workers (Brownlie 1997: 363–82). In 1975, in the final act of the Helsinki Conference on Security and Co-operation in Europe, thirty-five states, including the USA and the USSR, agreed to a principle of "Respect for human rights and fundamental freedoms" in which they undertook to "promote and encourage the effective exercise of civil, political, economic, social, cultural and other rights and freedoms all of which derive from the inherent dignity of the human person and are essential for his free and full development" (Brownlie 1997: 395). Within Europe as a whole the most significant recent development in human rights began to take shape with the proposal at Nice in 2000 of a *Charter of Fundamental Rights and European Citizenship*, which was agreed upon as a central plank in the move to create a Constitution for the enlarged European Union. Forming Part II of the draft EU Constitution, the fortune of this charter of fundamental rights of the EU is inevitably linked to the much contested question of the future of European federalism (EU Charter 2005). Pending that eventuality, in 2005 the European Commission set up an independent Agency for Fundamental Rights, with the role of providing the EU institutions and member states with appropriate assistance and expertise in the field with effect from 2007 (*Europe Infos* 74: Sept. 2005).

Another area of society which has seen considerable development this century in concern for human rights has been the Christian churches. Examining human rights in a theological perspective, the Church of England bishop, Richard Harries, notes that "all talk about human rights presupposes a recognition of the dignity and worth of the human person," and adds, "the worth and dignity of the human person is basic to the Judaeo-Christian-Islamic tradition" (Harries 1993: 1–2). Against this background Harries observes that the modern movement of Christian concern for human rights is strikingly exemplified by Liberation Theology, which engages Christians today in "a new commitment to the poor." As expounded by José Bonino, one of the foremost exponents of Latin American liberation theology, Harries observes (pp. 9–10) that "for the vast majority of the world today the basic 'human right' is 'the right to a human life' . . . [T]he drive towards universality in the quests of the American and French Revolutions, the aspirations in the *UN Declaration*, finds its historical focus today for us in the struggle for the poor, the economically and socially oppressed, for their liberation." At the more institutional and international level Harries points to the human rights pronouncements of the World Council of Churches and of the Roman Catholic Church.

The latter body in particular has developed a cumulative and impressive body of social teaching which began from the papal defense of the European working class against laissez-faire capitalism during the Industrial Revolution and which has since developed to a stage in which the subject of human rights has emerged to take a central place (Curran

2003, Hollenbach 1979). So much so, that the greatest religious gathering of the twentieth century, the Second Vatican Council of the bishops of the entire Catholic Church, meeting in Rome (1962–5), gave considerable attention to the subject of human rights. The Council noted how "from a clearer awareness of human dignity there is a movement in various parts of the world to renew the politico-juridical order for the better protection of the rights of the person in public life." It expressed the view that "the safeguarding of the rights of the person is a necessary condition for citizens, individually and together, to be able to take an active part in the life and conduct of the state" (Tanner 1990: vol. 2, p. *1121). And it further claimed its own God-given mandate in asserting that "the church is empowered by the gospel entrusted to it to proclaim the rights of humanity and to recognize and value the modern movement to promote these rights everywhere" (Tanner 1990: 2. *1095). It was to discharge his perceived duty to proclaim human rights that Pope Paul VI visited the United Nations in 1965, and warmly recognized that what they were proclaiming were "the fundamental rights and duties of man, his dignity and his freedom" (Pope Paul VI 1965: 883). In like manner his successor, the Polish Pope John Paul II, became widely recognized for his impassioned championing of human rights in the course of his many evangelizing journeys around the world. As the London Catholic weekly *The Tablet* (October 11, 2003) commented, in recognizing the twenty-fifth year of his pontificate, "Above all, [John Paul II] has been the Pope of peace and human rights, crying out as the voice of the voiceless in country after country, and whenever the world's powers have resorted to force to settle their differences." So, thirty years after Paul VI had applauded the UN, his successor John Paul II addressed the General Assembly in 1995 on the fiftieth anniversary of its founding. He recalled that on his own previous visit to the UN in 1979 he had noted that "the quest for freedom in our time has its basis in those universal rights which human beings enjoy by the very fact of their humanity"; and he now described the Universal Declaration of Human Rights as "one of the highest expressions of the human conscience of our time" (Pope John Paul II 1995: 295).

In addition to UN, Christian, and other intergovernmental and governmental activities, a multitude of other groups have sprung up worldwide and are increasingly active in the interests of human rights. One of the most prolific in its publications and campaigns is Human Rights Watch (HRW), which publishes an annual World Report and maintains a full and continually updated website on the Internet entitled "Defending Human Rights Worldwide" (HRW 2005). Another internationally prestigious group is Amnesty International, whose initial concern for the fate of political prisoners has mushroomed, as its website shows (AI 2005), to include many other issues involving disregard for human rights. Indeed, the most striking modern evidence of the growing interest in, and concern for, human rights worldwide is the number and quality of the websites on the Internet which the web-engine Google records as devoted to the subject, including the United Nations itself (<http://www.un.org/rights>) and the Human Rights Web (<http://www.hrweb.org>), the latter providing a comprehensive approach to the whole subject, and more than 38 million other sites, including those concentrating on the application of human rights in various countries throughout the world.

British Developments

We have already noted the momentum generated in various continents by the 1948 UN Universal Declaration and the subsequent cumulative development of interest in human rights in Europe, Latin America, Africa, and the League of Arab States. It is of interest finally to return to the 1950 European Convention for the Protection of Human Rights and Fundamental Freedoms and to note the way in which it came to influence the attitude to human rights in Britain. The UK was the first country in Europe to ratify the European Convention on Human Rights in 1951. Subsequently the British Government accepted from 1966 the right of individuals to petition against it under the Convention as well as recognizing the compulsory jurisdiction of the European Court. "The UK committed itself – in fact, if not in legal form – to acquiescing in the judgements of the European Court and, if necessary, to amending the UK law to bring it into conformity with the Court's rulings" (King 2001: 71). Meetings of the British Commonwealth regularly focused on the conduct of various member states which were considered delinquent in their respect for basic human rights, notably in their 1991 Harare Declaration on democracy and human rights (Harare 1991), and were addressed on the subject by successive British prime ministers, on one occasion drawing from *The Times* (October 21, 1993) the editorial observation that "without human rights, the Commonwealth stands for nothing." A new British Labour Government in 1997 announced its intention of using human rights as a more effective yardstick in its foreign policy, including the export of arms, a policy which showed little subsequent evidence of being implemented. Into the late 1990s, partly as a consequence of various expressions of social unrest, a widespread and heated debate took place in Britain on the creation of a British Bill of Rights which could be connected in some way with the European Convention of Human Rights and Fundamental Freedoms (Gordon and Wilmot-Smith 1996; especially Dworkin 1996). In 1997 a Human Rights Bill was proposed, which the Prime Minister, Tony Blair, explained "will give people in the UK opportunities to enforce their rights under the European Convention in British courts rather than having to incur the cost and delay of taking a case to the European Human Rights Commission and Court in Strasbourg." In addition, he commented, "it will enhance the awareness of human rights in our society" (Grosz, Beatson, and Duffy 2000: 415–16).

In 1998, then, the Human Rights Act (HRA) was passed by the British Parliament, to take effect from 2000, basically incorporating the European Convention on Human Rights into British law (Klug 2000). At that time the British government did not see a need to create a human rights commission for the United Kingdom, in spite of the view expressed by the influential British Institute of Human Rights (2002: 3) that the Act's "potential for creating a human rights culture in the United Kingdom is undermined by the lack of a Human Rights Commission." However, in June 2003 a new Department for Constitutional Affairs was set up to incorporate much of the Lord Chancellor's Department, including the Human Rights Unit; and in 2004 the British government brought together the work of various equality commissions by setting up a new body, the Commission for Equality and Human Rights (CEHR), whose purpose is to challenge discrimination across society and to take responsibility for new laws on age, religion or belief, and sexual orientation, thus for the first time providing institutional support for human rights. This was paralleled by the independent charity, the British Institute of Human Rights, based in London, which aims at working for "some of the most disadvantaged and vulnerable communities in the UK" (British Institute of Human Rights). In addition to all this increased planning and activity connected with domestic rights in Britain, the Foreign and Commonwealth Office Commission (2005) showed an increasing interest in international human rights and their role in British foreign policy, and from 1998 it introduced an *Annual Report on Human Rights* aimed at illustrating how the Government is working to advance the cause of human rights around the world.

Conclusion

In drawing this chronicle of human rights to a close we may fairly observe that the modern human rights movement has been, and continues to be, an astonishing moral phenomenon. Continuing the unfolding of rights from their first stirrings in the Middle Ages to modern times, the whole trajectory of human rights has proved a remarkable development in human moral consciousness, to such an extent that it might be difficult to argue that its advent on the moral scene can be an entirely novel event; it must have had some preparatory intimations, or at least preparations, within the human mind. We have argued in our first chapter that neither the classical world nor the culture of the Jewish and Christian Bibles had an explicit awareness of the idea of subjective rights, which emerged only in medieval canon law, to be applied through the late Scholastic articulation of natural law and natural rights to arrive at the full-blown political concept of natural rights as deployed in the revolutionary eighteenth century. Nor, it appears, is the explicit language of natural rights, far less human rights, to be found in the sacred documents of any other of the world's great religions or in any other culture. Nevertheless, it does appear that what has become the sophisticated terminology of natural and human rights can claim a congenial commonality with many, if not most, of the great ethical traditions in history, religious and secular, or can find a similar seed in them. As we noted in chapter 1, in the classical culture the ideas of justice and of nature possessed of a normative role provided the base of what were to become human rights. Likewise, in the biblical culture the idea of humans being created in the *imago dei*, the divine image, provides a powerful basis of unique human distinctiveness and dignity which can readily generate for each individual so constituted moral claims on his or her fellows. In considering evidence adduced from Islamic, African, Confucian, and Hindu cultures and thinking, Donnelly (2003: 71–84) rightly rejects all attempts to claim that human rights had a foothold in such non-Western cultures before the modern era; but he is happy to grant that there have existed "substantive similarities at the level of basic values" which recognize human good and human dignity and are expressed in terms of duties (p. 75). As such, just as in Western pre-medieval thought, a cultural and ethical patrimony is ready to hand for development to articulate the moral leverage of human rights. Shestack describes this challenging development as follows: "religious philosophers of all faiths are engaged in the process of interpreting religious doctrines towards the end of effecting a reconciliation with basic human rights prescriptions. This process is largely through hermeneutical exercise, namely reinterpretation of a religion's sacred texts through both historical explication and a type of prophetic application to modern conditions" (2000: 36).

Likewise, the UNESCO report composed in support of the task given to the Human Rights Commission to survey human rights in history produced a series of remarkable statements to do with cultural similarities and parallels (Maritain 1949). Glendon comments that responses to the UNESCO study "indicated that the principles underlying the draft Declaration were present in many cultural and religious traditions, though not always expressed in terms of rights. Somewhat to the UNESCO group's surprise, the lists of basic rights and values submitted by their far-flung correspondents were broadly similar" (Glendon 2001: 76; see pp. 73, 186, 191–5). And, as we shall see later, various non-Western representatives taking part in the sectional and plenary UN discussions on the draft Declaration made it quite clear that basically the idea of human rights was not entirely foreign to their culture and way of thinking, as much modern intercultural and interreligious research is in the process of confirming (see Bloom, Martin, and Proudfoot 1996). What Glendon describes as the dawning awareness of natural rights which occurred in the West as the ideas of natural right and equality "spoke to as yet unnamed longings . . . awakened sleeping hopes, fired imaginations, and changed the world" (1991: 10–11) need not be an experience confined to that society.

Drawing, then, on the moral inheritance of late Scholasticism and seventeenth- to nineteenth-century political reflection and events, finding articulation in the cultures of the world's major modern democracies, stimulated to new growth and global expansion in reaction to totalitarian savagery and with the aim of preventing its recurrence, and developing new expressions commensurate with the end of colonialism and with economic and technological advances, this cumulative and worldwide drive to give formal voice to humanity's moral claims in terms of basic human rights appears well-nigh unstoppable. At the end of the twentieth century, looking back over fifty years of the modern human rights movement, Richard Falk presented an upside and a downside. The upside was that human rights had contributed "an extraordinary cumulative impact . . . in international political life in the course of the last half-century." This impact had shown itself in a variety of ways, including changing the language of international relations and of diplomacy by introducing "an objective, shared set of standards" and "a common normative language" for governments, international institutions, and civil society. It had inspired the creation of normative documents, including the two historic and binding Covenants of 1966, additional treaties on refugees, women, racial discrimination, torture, and children, and many Declarations on other topics. It had enhanced concern for human rights within the UN system itself, especially through the 1993 Conference on Human Rights and Development, and the establishment of the post of High Commissioner for Human Rights, "ensuring both budgetary support and agenda salience for human rights within the UN, despite downsizing pressures." It had focused and forwarded internal popular struggles for freedom from oppression and had legitimized international support. It had provided aims and strong legal and moral support for national and transnational human rights associations. And it had created a role for tribunals to prosecute extreme violations of human rights as crimes against humanity (Falk 2000: 53–6).

In contrast, the downside which Falk summarized lay in the enormous challenges which he foresaw still remained for the next fifty years, among which "the prime challenges are improving the process of implementation, separating geopolitical practice from the domain of human rights, and enhancing the impression that leading states are as subject to comparable criteria of evaluation as are weak and vulnerable states" (Falk 2000: 9), all of this in an increasingly global context in which it will be necessary to cope with "the main drift of change in the direction of a highly marketized, non-sustainable, and grossly unequal set of relations among the peoples of the world, with weak structures of legal authority and even weaker sentiments of human solidarity" (p. 34). Falk's measured conclusion, with which it is difficult to disagree, was that "the achievements in human rights over the course of the last fifty years are extraordinary, but the obstacles to full realization seem as insurmountable as ever" (p. 56).

Nor is the modern human rights movement without its critics and its opponents. For all its strengths, impetus, and potential, the theory of human rights contains numerous challenging difficulties which must be addressed to justify its claim to impose serious moral obligations on all human beings in the interests of their fellows. The following two chapters are devoted to analyzing and meeting those difficulties.

References

Amnesty International (2005), available from <http://www.amnesty.org> accessed Feb. 2006.

Annan, K. (2005), *In Larger Freedom*, United Nations General Assembly, available from <http://www.un.org/largerfreedom/contents.htm> accessed Feb. 2006.

Bloom, I., Martin, P. J., and Proudfoot, W. L. (1996) (eds.), *Religious Diversity and Human Rights*, New York: Columbia University Press.

British Institute of Human Rights, available from <http://www.bihr.org/> accessed Feb. 2006.

British Institute of Human Rights (2002), *Annual Review for 2002*, London: King's College.

Brownlie, I. (1997) (ed.), *Basic Documents on Human Rights*, 3rd edn., Oxford: Clarendon Press.

Curran, C. E. (2003), *Catholic Social Teaching, 1891–Present: A Historical, Theological, and Ethical Analysis*, Washington, DC: Georgetown University.

Documents of the United Nations Conference on International Organization (1945), vol. 1: Closing Plenary Session, June 26, 1945, Doc. 1209 P/16 June 27, 1945, San Francisco: United Nations.

Donnelly, J. (2003), *Universal Human Rights in Theory and Practice*, 2nd rev. edn., Ithaca and London: Cornell University Press.

Drinan, R. F. (2001), *The Mobilization of Shame: A World View of Human Rights*, New Haven, CT: Yale University Press.

Dworkin, R. (1996), Does Britain Need a Bill of Rights?, in Gordon and Wilmot-Smith (1996).

European Convention on Human Rights: Collected Texts (1995), Brussels: Council of Europe Press.

European Union Charter (2005), available from <http://www.federalunion.org.uk/europe/charter.shtml> accessed Feb. 2006.

Europe Infos, Commission of the Bishops' Conferences of the European Community, Brussels.

Evans, T. (1998), Power, Hegemony and Human Rights, in Evans (ed.), *Human Rights Fifty Years On: A Reappraisal*, Manchester: Manchester University Press.

Falk, R. A. (2000), *Human Rights Horizons: The Pursuit of Justice in a Globalizing World*, London: Routledge.

Foreign and Commonwealth Office (2005), *Annual Report on Human Rights*, London: Foreign and Commonwealth Office.

Glendon, M. A. (1991), *Rights Talk: The Impoverishment of Political Discourse*, New York: Free Press.

Glendon, M. A. (2001), *A World Made New: Eleanor Roosevelt and the Universal Declaration of Human Rights*, New York: Random House.

Gordon, R., and Wilmot-Smith, R. (1996) (eds.), *Human Rights in the United Kingdom*, Oxford: Oxford University Press.

Grosz, S., Beatson, J., and Duffy, P. (2000), *Human Rights: The 1998 Act and the European Convention*, London: Sweet & Maxwell.

Harare Commonwealth Declaration on Democracy and Human Rights (1991), London: Commonwealth Secretariat.

Harries, R. (1993), Human Rights in Theological Perspective, in R. Blackburn and J. Taylor (eds.), *Human Rights for the 1990s*, London: Mansell.

Hoffman, D., and Rowe, J. (2003), *Human Rights in the UK: An Introduction to the Human Rights Act 1998*, Harlow: Pearson Longman.

Hollenbach, D. (1979), *Claims in Conflict: Retrieving and Renewing the Catholic Human Rights Tradition*, New York: Paulist Press.

Horgan, J. (1997), *Mary Robinson: A Woman of Ireland and the World*, Dublin: O'Brien Press.

Human Rights Watch (2005), available from <http://www.hrw.org/> accessed Feb. 2006.

Humphrey, J. P. (1984), *Human Rights and the United Nations: A Great Adventure*, Dobbs Ferry, NY: Transnational Publishers.

Jacobs, F. G., and White, R. A. C. (1996), *The European Convention on Human Rights*, Oxford: Clarendon Press.

King, A. (2001), *Does the UK Still Have a Constitution?* London: Sweet & Maxwell.

Klug, F. (2000), *Values for a Godless Age: The Story of the UK's New Bill of Rights*, London: Penguin.

Luard, E. (1982), *A History of the United Nations*, New York: St. Martin's Press.

Malik, C. (1948), International Bill of Human Rights, *United Nations Bulletin*, 5 (July 1).

Malik, C. (1949) An International Achievement, *United Nations Bulletin*, 6 (Jan. 1).

Maritain, J. (1949), *Human Rights: Comments and Interpretations*, London: Wingate.

Morsink, J. (1999), *The Universal Declaration of Human Rights: Origins, Drafting and Intent*, Philadelphia: University of Pennsylvania Press.

Pope John Paul II (1995), Address to the Fiftieth General Assembly of the United Nations Organization, *Origins*, Washington, DC: CNS Documentary Service, vol. 25.

Pope Paul VI (1965), Discours aux Nations Unies, *Acta apostolicae sedis*, vol. 57, Vatican City: Vatican Press, pp. 877–85.

Robertson, A. H., and Merrills, J. G. (1996), *Human Rights in the World*, Manchester: Manchester University Press.

Robinson, M. (1998), The Universal Declaration of Human Rights: The International Keystone of Human Dignity, in Barend van der Heijden and Bahiaq Tahzib-Lie (eds.), *Reflections on the Universal Declaration of Human Rights: A Fiftieth Anniversary Anthology*, The Hague: Martin Nijhoff.

Roosevelt, E. (1992), *The Autobiography of Eleanor Roosevelt*, New York: Da Capo Press.

Roosevelt, F. D. (1941), *The Public Papers and Addresses of Franklin D. Roosevelt*, vol. 4: *1940 volume*, London: Macmillan.

Russell, R. B., assisted by Muther, J. E. (1958), *A History of the United Nations Charter: The Role of the United States, 1940–45*, Washington, DC: Brookings Institute.

Shestack, J. J. (2000), The Philosophical Foundations of Human Rights, in Symonides (2000).

Simpson, A. W. B. (2001), *Human Rights and the End of Empire: Britain and the Genesis of the European Convention*, Oxford: Oxford University Press.

Symonides, J. (2000) (ed.), *Human Rights: Concept and Standards*, Aldershot: Ashgate.

Tanner, N. P. (1990) (ed.), *Decrees of the Ecumenical Councils*, London: Sheed & Ward; Washington, DC: Georgetown University Press.

UN News Service, <http://www.un.org/apps/news/printnews.asp?nid=18411>.

United Nations Action in the Field of Human Rights (1994), New York and Geneva: United Nations.

The United Nations and Human Rights 1945–1995 (1995), intro. by Boutros Boutros-Ghali, Secretary-General of the United Nations, New York: Department of Public Information, United Nations.

United Nations Bulletin, Lake Success, NY: United Nations Department of Public Information (ceased publication in June 1954).

United Nations, Charter of the (1995), New York: Department of Public Information, United Nations.

United Nations Economic and Social Council Official Records, New York: United Nations.

United Nations Educational, Scientific and Cultural Organisation (UNESCO) (1949), *Human Rights: Comments and Interpretations*, London and New York: Allan Wingate.

United Nations Yearbook on Human Rights, New York: United Nations.

Williams, I. (2002), The Salon Interview: Mary Robinson, in the internet newsletter *Salon Premium* <http://www.salon.com/people/interview/> accessed Feb. 2006.

Chapter ③

Clarifying Human Rights

The worldwide growth of the human rights movement and the multiplication of human rights declarations and manifestos have been remarkable following the end of the Second World War, and the attraction as well as the impetus of the idea of human rights in the modern world are difficult to gainsay. In the words of one commentator, human rights today "provide an accepted international currency for moral and political debate" (Almond 1993: 259). Yet, in spite of its considerable popular, political, and intellectual attractions, the idea of human rights also meets with strong objections and opposition, perhaps more concerted today than in the past. As we noted in the first chapter, the anti-rights polemic was led in the eighteenth century by Jeremy Bentham who branded talk of human rights as social terrorism and as the height of philosophical nonsense – nonsense upon stilts, as he expressed it (see pp. 29–31). Today that opposition to the very idea of human rights is represented by MacIntyre, who has roundly rejected human rights as fictions which are as incapable of proof as are witches and unicorns (MacIntyre 1981: 67).

Nor are other difficulties with the theory or the appeal to human rights far to seek. There is complaint at the tendency to multiply human rights by bringing ever more, and more trivial, moral claims under their banner, in a process which leads not just to the unwarranted proliferation of human rights but also to a rhetorical debasement of the currency of rights. Again, concern for human rights is accused of cultivating and encouraging a polemical and adversarial atmosphere in society and of disrupting the established social order. Many critics condemn the idea as radically individualistic and as expressive of a concern for self which disregards one's duties to others and the interests of the wider community. A further major line of objection to the whole idea of fundamental and universal human rights takes the form of identifying them as a peculiar expression of a particular culture, that of Western liberal individualism, which is alien to the history, culture, and values of many other peoples, yet attempts to impose its own morality on other cultures around the world in a form of ethical imperialism. Finally, some opponents of the ethical theory of human rights justify their opposition by maintaining that rights theory and language are actually unnecessary from an ethical point of view, since the moral claims which they purport to make can be expressed in other moral terms and can be established at least as validly in other ways.

The charge sheet as thus set out against human rights is an impressive and formidable one, which calls for careful consideration and reflection if rights are to retain credibility and moral authority. The purpose of this chapter, then, is to analyze and comment on these charges brought against human rights theory before exploring the more positive considerations which justify and commend it as a powerful ethical tool, as a prelude to concentrating in the following chapter on what considerations might be adduced to establish the existence of human rights.

Some Useful Distinctions

By way of introduction, some basic distinctions can help to clarify the debate about human rights. One of the earliest modern writers on the subject, Maurice Cranston, makes an important preliminary distinction between *legal* rights and *moral* rights. Legal rights are understood as those which are "conceded and enforced by the law of the realm" (Cranston 1973: 4). Such rights vary from country to country, and in particular countries might cover actions such as a right to receive social welfare, a right to be protected from sexual or racial discrimination, a right to trial by jury, or a right to be informed of the ingredients of a particular food on sale. By contrast, moral rights are not rights which are conferred or enforced by the government or in a particular state. They exist independently of legislation; in fact, in a view which goes back as far as Locke, they can be said logically, if not historically, to pre-exist legislation and, indeed, may often be the basis or reason for a new law and a new legal right being introduced in a particular society. The distinction is simply stated by Amartya Sen: "It is best to see human rights as a set of ethical claims, which must not be identified with legislated legal rights" (Sen 1999: 229). Further, the connection between the two types of rights is well expressed by Brian Orend (2002: 26–7) in his observation that "the contemporary human rights movement has, as probably its main goal, the effective translation of the moral values inherent in human rights theory into meaningful and concrete legal rights."

The outstanding modern illustration of the difference between legal and moral rights must be the apartheid regime which existed into the twentieth century in South Africa. Black South Africans were prevented by law from moving freely around the country, from engaging in collective labor negotiations, and from behaving in other ways like white South Africans; they had no legal rights to engage in such activities. Yet the strong international disapproval of the South African system of government was due precisely to the fact that by such legal disqualifications the moral rights of black people were being systematically ignored or violated. The Sullivan Code of conduct subscribed to by many multinational businesses as a condition of their continuing to operate in South Africa was aimed precisely at respecting those moral rights of black South Africans by actually breaking the apartheid laws and thus undermining the legal, yet immoral, apparatus of apartheid from the inside (Sullivan 1998).

Cranston (1973: 4) makes another useful distinction applying to human rights when he points to a difference between *universal* moral rights and *special* moral rights. The latter can arise from one's special status in society, such as that of being a child or a consumer, or from a special relationship, such as having been promised something or having been given permission to do something. By contrast, universal moral rights are not circumscribed in any such way, but apply to everyone everywhere and under all circumstances.

Another important clarification which can shed considerable light on discussions about human rights distinguishes between a *liberty* and a *claim*, and has become attached to the name of Wesley N. Hohfeld (1919). The major contribution of the Hohfeldian analysis of rights, directed by him at legal rights but adopted by many others for moral rights also, is his distinguishing between some rights as what he calls "privileges," sometimes referred to as a "bare liberty," and other rights which he identifies as "claims." Exploring Hohfeld's distinction, we can note that where privileges, or mere liberties, are concerned attention is focused on the individual possessor of the right, who is simply at liberty to act or not to act as he or she wishes, and who does not have a duty to refrain from acting. Sumner (2000: 292) expresses this aspect well when he writes that such "rights define protected spaces in which individuals are able to pursue their own personal projects." For instance, I have a right to buy and own a dog, that is, I am at liberty to do so, or to walk down the street, in the sense that there is nothing to prevent me or morally restrain me from acting in this way. It would be quite different if I wished to buy or own a dangerous dog, or if I wanted to walk down the middle of a busy road, for then my "privileges" or liberty rights would have to be importantly qualified by considerations relating to other people. By contrast with liberty rights, in the case of claim rights attention is focused not so much on my freedom to act, but more on other people, and on what I can morally require them to do in order to help me.

Liberty rights include a claim on others not to prevent me from exercising those rights, and they are sometimes (rather confusingly) referred to as *"negative"* rights, imposing, as Orend (2002: 31) expresses it, "a correlative duty which calls only for *inaction* on the part of the duty-bearer." By contrast, claim rights are viewed more as *"positive"* rights, in that they require that people take active steps to help me exercise my right. This difference between negative and positive rights is explained by Cooney's comment (1998: 878–9) that "negative rights theory holds that the overriding moral principle is non-interference . . . And the theory of politics it typically supports is that of laissez-faire. This hands-off style of government follows the motto, 'that government which governs least, governs best,' and provides, it is argued, less danger of governmental infringement on rights." By contrast, Cooney notes, positive rights are understood as "requiring some positive response, i.e., some act of commission, and not simply the acts of omission supplied by the principle of non-interference."

Other writers, however, such as Henry Shue (1996), are dissatisfied with making too sharp a disjunction between liberty rights and claim rights, and with identifying the former as negative, calling only for non-intervention, and the latter as positive rights, involving social provision. There is an obvious need, for example, for a society to ensure that liberties are universally respected, by setting up various resources and institutions at public cost precisely for that purpose. It is this awareness of the need at times, for example, to take steps to defend someone's right to exercise their freedom which led Sen (1988: 56 n. 25) to refer to "a positive concept of negative freedom"!

In fact, the use of the terms "negative" and "positive" to apply to different types of rights appears strained and not at all self-evident. Indeed, they more readily suggest that I have some rights (negative ones) which allow me *not to do* certain things, such as not to take an active part in a war declared by my government or not to pay a particular tax, if I judge these actions unethical, as contrasted with other rights I possess (positive ones) which allow me *to do* certain things, such as to marry or to emigrate. The distinction being looked for appears to be captured better by the difference to which White (1985:

13) draws attention, between *"active"* rights, or rights to do something, and *"passive"* rights, or rights to have something done to one. Even here, however, the idea of a "passive" right seems strangely contradictory, since of its nature a right appears to be an active power which I possess. Perhaps the simplest expression of the distinction between Hohfeldian liberty rights and claim rights could be to understand it as the difference between *a right to act* as contrasted with *a right to receive* (see White 1985: 17–19). However we describe it, this distinction between two quite different kinds of moral claims which we have upon others, the claim not to be hindered and the claim to be helped or supported, is frequently of the utmost significance, nowhere more so than in the contrasting meanings which can be given to "the right to die."

Thus, on the one hand, the claim to have a right to die can be understood as a right to be allowed to die, uttered in a libertarian sense as meaning a right when in a deteriorating state of health not be kept alive and not to be prevented from dying. Understanding the claim of a right to die in this way can be used to justify drawing up a "living will," or an advance medical directive, in which the individual identifies types of burdensome treatment to which they do not wish to be subjected in the terminal stage of their life. In sharp medical, as well as moral and legal, contrast to this liberty to be allowed to die one's death is the alternative interpretation of a right to die when it is appealed to as the basis of a claim to require other people to help bring about one's death, either by a form of assisted suicide or by active euthanasia, or "mercy killing."

A wider explanation of the basic Hohfeldian difference between rights not to be hindered and rights to be helped takes the form of distinguishing between terming some (active) rights as *"libertarian"* in the sense of expressing the freedom, or liberty, to engage in some activity without let or hindrance from others; while other (passive) rights can be called *"welfare"* rights, pointing to rights which require the provision of aid or help from others. This expression of active rights as libertarian rights and of passive rights as welfare rights gives a political slant to the distinction which we have already noted between, on the one hand, the early political and civil active rights which formed the basis of eighteenth- and nineteenth-century claims and campaigns and, on the other hand, the more recent passive, that is, social, economic, and cultural, rights which achieved such prominence in the twentieth century and which focus attention on claims for the provision of certain welfare services by society. The development of the latter is well noted by Henkin (1990: 18):

Individual human rights as a political idea derives both conceptually and historically from Euro-American ideas, rooted in individual autonomy and supported by conceptions of popular sovereignty and social contract. The rights implied in those ideas were rights of autonomy and freedom, limitations on government, immunities from undue, unreasonable exercise of authority. But in the nineteenth century there began to grow another sense of right, rooted not in individual autonomy but in community, adding to liberty and equality the implications of fraternity.

Almond (1993: 260) expands the contrast between the two kinds of rights: "while the eighteenth-century notion of rights was protective and negative, setting limits to the treatment which governments might mete out to their subjects, the modern conception adds to these a positive element, by including rights to various kinds of welfare goods." She makes the useful additional political point that the latter social and economic rights, to such items as education or health, actually justify greater government involvement through taxation, whereas the former political and civil rights argue for the restraint of government. Habermas (1993: 68) refers to the same distinction in terms of "negative rights of freedom" and "positive rights of participation," and makes the political point regarding the latter that "in complex societies, of course, claims to a fair share of scarce social resources – positive rights to basic goods such as food and housing, health care, education, and opportunities for work – can be satisfied only through organisations. In this context individual rights and duties are transformed into institutional rights and duties; the organised society as a whole is the subject of obligations – claims to positive rights are raised against it." Only such a line of reasoning to societal obligations arising from individual rights can make sense, for instance, of the right to work claimed in article 23 of the Universal Declaration (*The UN and Human Rights* 1995: pp. 152–5), which implies that society is required in one way or another to make provision for employment.

Further helpful clarification in considering human rights comes from attempting to introduce some sort of priority among various moral rights, or "to provide a hierarchical arrangement to address the intuition that some rights seem more basic, primary, or fundamental than others" (Cooney 1998: 877). Opponents of human rights, for instance, regularly make derisive play of the UN Declaration's claim in article 24 to a universal human right to "periodic holidays with pay," since it is evident that such a right presupposes the existence of certain social and labor structures and conventions in society which are manifestly not universally obtainable. However, although, viewed in isolation, such a claimed right may appear to trivialize the subject of human rights, nevertheless it can be justified when it is viewed in context, as specifying a means in some cultures to give expression to the more fundamental "right to rest and leisure" which is the controlling right in that particular article of the Declaration. Henkin (1990: 32, 33 n.) observes that many rights are human in that they are universal, while others, such as the right "to form a trade union, or to enjoy vacation with pay," apply to workers in industrialized societies. Yet he notes, "these too are universal in that they apply to all to whom they are relevant." Another interesting illustration of how various rights can interrelate as ends and means is provided by Orend in distinguishing between first-level and second-level specifications of human rights objects, the first level comprising security, subsistence, liberty, equality, and recognition, and the second level more or less consisting of those further more specific rights identified in the Universal Declaration of Human Rights (Orend 2002: 117–26). He makes the interesting additional comment that "the burden of proof is always on the claimant proposing a brand new second-level specification for human rights" (p. 124).

In other words, some rights can be seen as foundational, basic, or primary, "including those such as life, liberty, privacy, and few others," while others can be classed as implied, derivative, or secondary rights, "those which can be implied by, or derive their existence from, foundational rights" (Cooney 1998: 877–8). As Cooney explains, "an implied right like the right to health care, for example, can be derived from the right to life. Implied rights are not only founded upon foundational rights, but can often provide some instrumental value and additional meaning to them" (Cooney 1998: 878). Possibly the most informative terms for describing this priority of some rights over others is to distinguish between *basic* human rights which can be considered those which are general and universal, on the one hand, and, on the other, *instrumental* human rights, which can be considered as means to achieving or expressing or specifying basic rights, and which may vary according to circumstances of culture, time, and place.

The idea of basic human rights is explained by Onora O'Neill in terms of such basic human needs as food, shelter, and clothing, clean water and sanitation, and some parental and health care, from which she concludes (2000: 118) that "these *basic needs* may provide a basis for arguing for *basic rights*." Detailed treatment of such basic rights is developed significantly by Henry Shue (1996) in his study on *Basic Rights: Subsistence, Affluence, and U.S. Foreign Policy*. He characterizes "basic rights" as "a shield for the defenceless against at least some of the more devastating and more common of life's threats . . . everyone's minimal reasonable demands upon the rest of humanity." He identifies basic rights as those whose enjoyment is essential to the enjoyment of all other rights, and he instances what he considered three basic human rights of physical security, subsistence, and liberty (1996: 18–19), subsistence including minimal economic security (p. 23) and liberty including freedom of physical movement (pp. 78–82). In fact, Shue points out in the afterword to his second edition that he had never intended to limit basic rights to these three (p. 157); but his work had, in fact, as its subtitle indicates, a political agenda of attempting to influence United States foreign policy, or "to rescue from systematic neglect within wealthy North Atlantic nations . . . the priority of subsistence rights" (p. 65), which in the circumstances he considered not only basic, but also "strategically critical rights" (p. 157).

Rawls is aware in his study of *The Law of Peoples* of Shue's identification of some human rights as basic, and he agrees with Shue's giving primacy among these to subsistence (1999: 65 n.1). However, he himself prefers to concentrate on "a special class of *urgent* rights," among which he includes freedom from slavery, liberty of conscience, and security of ethnic groups (p. 79). Rawls had not said much about human rights in his earlier work, *A Theory of Justice*, in which he focused on constructing just relationships among individuals within a state (1971: 8). However, in expanding his theory in *The Law of Peoples* (1999) to encompass the relations between states themselves at an international level, by analogy with individuals within one state – not entirely successfully, according to some critics (see Singer 2004: 176–80) – he then sees a particular role for human rights as constituting one of the two criteria which he requires for "decent hierarchical societies," a criterion externally regulating recourse to war and internally limiting a state's power over its members (1999: 79). In so doing, Rawls does not express any particular interest in the provenance or nature of human rights, referring to them only as "what have come to be called human rights" (1999: 65) and later declining to base them on any particular "theological, philosophical, or moral conception of the nature of the human person" (1999: 81). He is content to view them as "universal rights" in the sense that "their political (moral) force extends to all societies, and they are binding on all peoples and societies, including outlaw states" (1999: 80–1).

One approach to identifying priorities among rights which has achieved recent notice and popularity is the "capability" thesis introduced by Sen which concentrates on the lived context of individuals and groups (Sen 1993). This moves away from considering the broad aim of impersonal economic growth and general welfare on the scene of international justice to adopt the criterion of identifying and fulfilling the real capabilities and functionings which individuals require in different situations within an overall goal of maximum individual freedom and human flourishing. One commentator defines Senian capabilities as "a combination of capacities and opportunities" (Raes 2002: 45); and another sums up Sen's approach as "we have a right to what we ought to have the capability to do" (Dowling 2005: 32).

Sen's development of the idea of "capabilities" can be seen as aiming to add precision to the content of basic rights in differing situations by gearing it to "a person's ability to do valuable acts or reach valuable states of being," which Sen also calls the various "functionings" the person is able to achieve (Sen 1993: 30). "The approach is based on a view of living as a combination of various 'doings and beings,' with quality of life to be assessed in terms of the capability to achieve valuable functionings" (p. 31) and the aim being to help people realize their capabilities. The crucial point is that different individuals may vary considerably in the weights which they attach to different functionings and in allocating value to different objects, particularly, so far as Sen is concerned, regarding the freedom to choose among different types of life, "which can *inter alia* include goals other than the advancement of his or her own well-being" (p. 35). Thus, as Cohen comments:

> Sen called for attention to something like opportunity (under the title "capability"), but it was not welfare, or not, at any rate, welfare alone, which Sen thought people should have the opportunity to achieve. Instead, he drew attention to the condition of a person (e.g. his level of nutrition) in a central sense captured neither by his stock of goods (e.g. his food supply) nor by his welfare level (e.g. the pleasure or satisfaction he obtains from consuming food). (Cohen 1993: 10)

So far as concerns basic rights, Sen also adds the useful clarification, which also confirms his position, that "there is a tendency to define basic needs in the form of needs for *commodities* (e.g., for food, shelter, clothing, health care), and this may distract attention from the fact that these commodities are no more than the *means* to real ends (inputs for valuable functionings and capabilities)." This enables him to stress that the relationships between commodities and "capabilities" can vary enormously among individuals, and to conclude that "the capability approach can accommodate the real issues underlying the concern for basic needs, avoiding the pitfall of 'commodity fetishism'" (Sen 1993: 40 n. 30).

A question which this classifying of rights inevitably raises is whether it is possible to separate what might be considered *absolute* rights which, it is claimed, cannot morally under any circumstances be overridden, from other *relative* rights which at times may be overridden and can be required to cede to some stronger moral claim. Dworkin (1984) is rightly famous for his striking phrase that "rights are trumps," in the sense that the playing of the rights card cuts across utilitarian calculations which may be leading to a conclusion harmful to an individual or to a comparative minority. As Isaiah Berlin sardonically commented (1969: 192) of the utilitarian maximizing of human happiness, " If happiness is the sole criterion, then human sacrifice, or the burning of witches, at times when such practices had strong public feeling behind them, did doubtless, in their day, contribute to the happiness of the majority." It is only the steady, unremitting appeal to individual rights which can stem and turn such popular tides. However, as every bridge player knows, it is almost always possible to overtrump. In other words, not all moral rights are equally compelling, and situations can arise when one right must give way to another. Indeed, if there are any truly absolute human rights there can be only one, since in theory all human rights can at some time find themselves in conflict with other rights, unless, as Donnelly comments (2003: 95 n. 6; see Freeden 1991: 35), "we implausibly assume that rights never conflict with one another."

It remains possible, then, in various situations to prioritize between rights, and to work out how one can take precedence over another, difficult though this must be at times to decide. De George noted: "although it is possible to argue persuasively that some rights are more basic than others, it is not always possible to rank rights or to see clearly which rights take precedence in specific cases" (1999: 100). Even if one can abstract basic rights from the whole gamut of human rights, however, as Freeden observes, "in principle, with the exception of the abstract right to exist, the ranking of basic rights is difficult to uphold; but in practice there may be greater urgency in upholding some rights rather than others; the right not to suffer torture in an unsavoury dictatorship, the right to nutrition in a drought-ridden country, the right to types of welfare and social assistance in a number of capitalist systems. If at all, this reinforces a culturally relative rather than universal and intrinsic basis for ranking rights" (1991: 103).

A final distinction which it is helpful to be aware of is how people consider the traditional *natural* rights and the more common *human* rights to be related. The intellectual descent of the idea of "natural" rights is twofold, one chronologically viewing them as pre-social and the other metaphysically understanding them as arising from human nature. As Tierney notes, "natural" can mean either "a primeval state of affairs or an intrinsic permanent characteristic of any being" (1997: 49). Thus, the sixteenth- to seventeenth-century appeal to "natural" rights underlying social contract theories envisaged the rights as belonging to the human state of existence which was postulated or conjectured as chronologically "preceding," logically if not historically, all forms of society and all social rules and conventions. Such (primitive) natural rights were considered as continuing to hold sway in society, providing a basis for, as well as taking precedence over, society's own laws. However, natural rights were also more metaphysically considered as being grounded in human nature, as distinct from social convention, and as being expressions of the natural law, or "law of (human) nature." In this sense the development of the idea of rights in the Middle Ages, "was symptomatic not of a change in the content of natural law but of a change in the form in which it was conceived. People began to think of God's natural laws as investing them with titles so that transgression of those laws wronged not only God but also the human beings who were harmed by the transgressors. In that way natural law came to be seen as a source of natural rights" (Jones 1994: 37–8). Once human beings began to be seen as all equally the possessors of fundamental, even God-given, natural rights then the political question inevitably arose why some individuals should be justified in lording it over others, and the way was opened to developing various theories of social contract or agreement among, at least theoretically, political equals (see Jones 1994: 78).

In modern times, however, the ideas of natural law and even of human nature have become generally discredited, or at least seriously questioned, and the modern preference is to refer to "human" rights rather than to "natural" rights, on the grounds that such rights apply equally and inalienably to all human beings precisely because of their being human, without there being any need to enter into metaphysical explorations of the meaning of a "shared human nature." As Stirk and Weigall explain (1995: 108), with human rights "arguments usually rest on some conception of a human or (perhaps more precisely) a person as a being with needs and interests that must be met if he or she is to live a fully human life." One could, of course, argue that all human beings are such precisely in so far as they each equally possess a shared human nature; but if that were generally accepted today it would be in a weak sense of the term "nature" as simply equivalent to "human being," and not ascribing particular significance or moral purchase to the notion of nature in any stronger more metaphysical sense. It is this thin approach to nature which Tierney appears to have in mind when he comments (1997: 2 n. 4): "I use the terms natural rights and human rights interchangeably. The term 'human rights' is often used nowadays to indicate a lack of any necessary commitment to the philosophical and theological systems formerly associated with the older term, 'natural rights.' But the two concepts are essentially the same. Human rights or natural rights are the rights people have, not by virtue of any particular role or status in society, but by virtue of their very humanity."

In a similar approach, Jones (1994: 72) observed that the idea of human rights descended from that of natural rights, a view to which Herbert (2002: 293) took strong exception, asserting that the "greatest philosophical ambiguity" concerning human rights is that they are the contemporary version of natural rights. Herbert argued, or, rather, asserted, against Jones, that "the difference between natural rights and human rights is the result of more than merely removing the metaphysical underpinnings of the original idea of natural right." The classical natural right of Hobbes and Locke, Herbert explained, "never imposed obligations on anyone." It was just the pre-society liberty to seek one's personal safety and well-being. As such, "natural right had none of the obligatory moral character of the contemporary idea of human rights. It produced no pure concern for the suffering of others, nor any obligation to assist them. It neither required nor recognized human dignity as its foundation" (p. 293). Herbert's main concern here seemed to be to distinguish sharply between first-generation civil and political rights, Hohfeld's "mere liberties," and second-generation social, economic, and cultural rights, and to ascribe the former, and only the former, to seventeenth-century thinkers; and few people will be found in general to disagree with that. It does not follow, however, that, as Herbert asserted, the moral liberty to protect oneself, at least so far as Locke was concerned, implied no moral obligation on others to respect that liberty, whether in a pre-social existence, or a fortiori within society, whose role includes the task of protecting that liberty; in which case it is strange to claim that this liberty "never imposed obligations on anyone," as Herbert maintained. Moreover, once one has established that even mere liberties, or what is called "negative rights" often require interventions by society and others to enable them to be respected and observed, it is no large step to conclude that the extent of such interventions, or indeed the contents of rights, can expand to cover a wider social context, including social, economic, and cultural considerations. From which it seems to follow that there is a much closer logical and historical connection between modern human rights and earlier natural rights than Herbert was disposed to permit.

At first sight, Freeden also appears to want to distinguish between human rights and natural rights, since he comments (1991: 61–2) that "to talk about human rather than natural rights is to link rights with human nature in a non-traditional manner." However, he goes on to argue that human nature "is, in all of its aspects, the product of human interpretation as much as of biological, chemical and environmental processes." In other words, "nature" is partly a cultural construct, a feature which may be more clearly indicated as such by substituting the term "human." The result appears to be, then, that "natural" rights are as malleable as human rights, and there is no basic difference between them.

Another writer who does wish to maintain a clear distinction between natural rights and human rights, Pogge, notes what he considers certain advantages involved in the historical transition from the language of natural rights to that of human rights. The move away from the tradition of (divinely created) nature as metaphysically and morally significant makes the language of rights accessible to those who do not accept moral realism (as, for instance, Mackie (see chapter 4, p. 134)); and it emphasizes that all humans equally, and only humans, have such rights (Pogge 2002: 57). In addition, however, Pogge proposes an argument to retain natural rights as well as human rights, so that, as he explains, "through the language of natural rights, one can demand protection of persons against any threats to their well-being and agency; through the language of human rights, one demands protection only against certain 'official' threats" (p. 58). Behind this distinction which he wishes to sustain between natural and human rights lies a wish on his part to restrain the scope of human rights to an "institutional" context of legal claims against offending governments and their agents, while acknowledging that this institution-directed understanding of human rights which he is proposing "diverges from a familiar one that conceives a human right to X as a kind of meta-right: a moral right to an effective legal right to X" (p. 45).

This latter appears a strange, rather than a "familiar," understanding of human rights, implying that my human right, for instance, to life or to property is a moral right that there should exist a legal right to protect life or to possess property. It appears, in fact, that Pogge is to be understood as seeing "human" rights primarily only as legal claims against offending official bodies ("coercive social institutions") or their officials, as distinct from claims against parties which do not fall under this description, that is, private individuals or groups; and these last are the parties he identifies against whom one might however, he proposes, claim "natural" moral rights (Pogge 2002: 44–5). There may be no objection to narrowing the normal understanding of the general term "human rights" in this way, as Pogge does, or for keeping and reserving natural rights to claims against individuals or private bodies or groups; but there appears little justification for so doing, particularly when it is recognized as at variance with the usage of the United Nations, as we shall see later (p. 98). In a sustained critique of Pogge's "institutional" reading of human rights claims, in which Pogge defines human rights as exclusively to be claimed against offending institutions and their agents, Orend (2002: 130–6) finds this approach implausible. As he explains, "a prime moral reason for thinking that we have human rights is concern that we not be grievously harmed in connection with our vital human needs. Since both individuals and institutions can deal us such unjustified grievous harm, it is only reasonable to conclude that they must both bear duties of a kind correlative to human rights" (p. 134). Orend does not draw attention to Pogge's consequently retaining the term "natural" right to apply to claims which can be made against non-institutional offenders, but, of course, once the reason for requiring a restricted use of "human" rights has been refuted, there is no need for maintaining this peculiar distinction.

Orend's own approach is to maintain a clear distinction between natural rights and human rights because he rejects natural rights as what he considers a discredited theory and opts for "a more compelling and contemporary theory of human rights" (2002: 18–19): a theory which regards human rights as simply reasons for acting in certain ways. Orend eschews "the metaphysical option" of regarding human rights as somehow properties of persons, on the grounds that they cannot be displayed for all to see: "a human right, like any other right, is *not* a property of persons; rather, it is *a reason to treat persons in certain ways.*" For him, in fact, rights are literally no more than reasons for acting. "We find at the very heart of human rights, a set of especially powerful reasons informing us how we should treat each other and how we should shape our shared social institutions. *In the final analysis, rights are reasons*" (p. 19). In other words, rather than base human rights on reasons, as most people who favor them attempt to do, Orend actually identifies rights with reasons.

Later, however, he appears to concede a little more independent reality to rights when he explains that "a right is an entitlement that endures even when the right-holder is not actually making a verbal claim and yet, most crucially, a right remains a justified claim, or demand, on the behaviours of others and the shape of local institutions" (Orend 2002: 24). Describing a right in this way as an "entitlement" appears to go beyond considering rights as simply reasons, and to be approaching the idea not that a right is a personal property (which Orend rejects), but that a right is a personal prerogative, or *power*, whether a legal power conferred by positive law, or a moral power possessed by virtue of being human. In fact, there is very good reason, rooted in history, ethical analysis, and experience, for accepting the view which developed through such influential thinkers as Gerson, Grotius, and Suarez, as we have seen in chapter 1, that human rights are more than reasons; they are powers possessed by individual human beings which entitle them to make on their fellows serious moral claims corresponding to their own needs.

Vardy and Grosch also want to distinguish between natural and human rights, although they concede they are in a minority in so doing. They argue for rejecting the idea of "natural" rights on the somewhat strange ground of "their not being self-evident," perhaps confusing "natural" with its popular meaning of being "obvious." As for human rights, these appear to them to be human artefacts, "the actual products of moral, social and political agreements made between human beings. Such agreements try to establish those conditions thought necessary for a decent existence" (Vardy and Grosch 1994: 193). The weakness of this position, however, is that it does not seem to feel a need to identify any criteria for identifying what it is that makes for such a "decent existence" for human beings. In other words, it does not take account of the consideration that human rights should be seen not merely as created by such agreements, or conventions, among human beings, but that there is at a deeper level a basis for such agreement, something about being human which gives antecedent rise to moral claims on other humans and to their general recognition, which is not unlike what the idea and theory of natural rights have traditionally aimed to do.

Rights and Duties

The connection between rights and duties is one which can at times give rise to bewilderment; and consideration of the links between them can throw further light on how we are to understand human rights. The distinctions introduced by Hohfeld were directed at legal rights rather than at moral rights, and in this context of legal rights he distinguished between claim rights, liberty rights, powers, and immunities. When these four types of rights are transferred from the legal to the moral world it is the claim rights which are generally considered the strongest, in the sense that having such a right entitles me to make certain appropriate claims on other people (Jones 1994: 12–13; see also pp. 47–8). As Jones explains, "To have a claim-right is to be owed a duty by another or others" (p. 14). Yet it is worth recalling the point made above, that liberty rights also can enable me to claim not to be hindered by others as I go about exercising my freedom, so that they have a duty not to impede me.

It can be illuminating to start at the other end, beginning with the idea of duties and proceeding to consider to what extent they imply, or create, rights. The notion of duty, of course, can sometimes be understood in a restricted sense of the behavior appropriate to one's distinct role or status in society, as when one speaks of the duties of one's state or profession, or of the duties attached to, or peculiar to, a particular appointment or position. White (1985: 23) makes the point that "A policeman can be on point duty and a nurse on night duty. I may even be able to stand duty for someone else. My duties commence and finish with my work." What is interesting is that such duties which are attached to one's role or which are undertaken as implied with certain relationships, such as being a parent or making a promise, appear to generate moral rights in others, entitling the latter to require certain ways of behaving on the part of those who have undertaken the duty. This corresponds to the distinction we have noted introduced by Cranston (1973: 7) between universal moral rights on the one hand and on the other, special moral rights generated by a particular relationship. White, however, does not accept any automatic correlation between duties in one party giving rise to rights in others, arguing that "a doctor has certain duties to his patients, a teacher to his pupils and a sovereign to his subjects which do not give them any rights . . . as when the doctor dutifully does not indulge the patient's desire for drugs, the teacher keeps his pupil's nose to the grindstone, and the sovereign sees that his subjects are always militarily prepared" (White 1985: 62). Yet it seems to be more the case that these instances would be examples of those to whom a duty is owed attempting to abuse the correlative right which this does confer on them, and seeking to influence the duty-holder to act unethically. By contrast it seems obvious that patients do have a right that their doctor seek their best medical interests, pupils do have a right to be taught competently by their teachers, and the citizenry do have a right to be governed properly.

It does not follow from this, however, that every right is the logical consequence of a duty, or follows from a duty. It is possible to argue in the legal sphere, as Bentham appears to have done, that laws which create offenses impose legal duties on everyone and consequently the beneficiaries of those duties possess corresponding legal rights (see Jones 1994: 27–8), in a line of argument which proceeds from the existence of a law enjoining legal duties to infer the existence of legal rights. However, even in the moral sphere O'Neill attempts to establish a systematic priority of duties or obligations over rights, arguing that to begin from rights incurs the risks of neglecting serious duties or obligations which are not correlative to rights, as well as underestimating moral virtues (O'Neill 1996: 140). Returning to the subject in 2000 she maintained that "the most questionable effect of putting rights first is that those rights for which no allocation of obligations has been institutionalized may not be taken seriously" (O'Neill 2000: 126). Given what she considered the ineffectiveness of claiming rights, especially economic rights to food, protection, etc., which cannot be allocated to corresponding identifiable obligation bearers, she preferred to proceed in a Kantian manner by establishing some basic principles of obligation as the starting point for justice, a move which she considered is less ambitious than many comprehensive attempts to construct human rights and one which can proceed in more realistic stages (pp. 136–7).

Finally, in her 2002 BBC Reith Lectures (O'Neill 2002), in the course of a wide-ranging series of reflections on the subject of trust within society, O'Neill mounts a surprisingly sharp attack on human rights, or rather, on the human rights movement, "one of our most sacred cows." "We fantasise irresponsibly that we can promulgate rights without thinking carefully about the counterpart obligations, and without checking whether the rights we favour are consistent, let alone set feasible demands on those who have to secure them for others . . . We need *genuine* rights . . . We are pursuing distorted versions of [them]" (O'Neill 2002: 18–19). Later she moves from criticizing the human rights movement to address her objections to human rights themselves. She claims that human rights are gestured at more often than seriously argued for, that the list proclaimed in the 1948 Universal Declaration is "untidy and unargued" (p. 27) and, like others, she homes in on the proclaimed "supposed" "right to holidays with pay" (p. 28) as irrelevant to the billions of people who are not paid employees. Drawing closer to her customary main charge that duties are prior to rights, O'Neill complains that the Declaration has almost nothing to say about duties, while it and other subsequent UN and European documents are silent on "*who* is required to do *what* for *whom*, or *why* they are required to do it" (p. 28) And yet, she comments, "duties are the business end of justice: they formulate the requirements towards which declarations of rights gesture" (p. 29). The priority of attention given to rights, she further suggests, may be because this helps to conceal the cost of respecting them, a cost which would be clear if we started from obligations (p. 29). And unless and until we can identify who is obliged, and to what extent they (especially "weak or failing states" (p. 30)) are capable of meeting their obligations, it makes little practical sense to speak of rights. "Without competent and committed persons and institutions, duties are not met; where they are not met, rights are not respected; and where rights are not respected, democracy is unachievable . . . [Yet] democracy *presupposes* rights, and rights presuppose duties" (p. 31); and Kant again is appealed to as the advocate for thus centering morality on duties (pp. 33–4), leading O'Neill to conclude once again "that we have duties that provide a basis for rights" (p. 35).

As a prelude to responding to these claims of the priority of moral duties over moral rights, it is worth noting that preferring to give the priority to rights does not have to involve a claim to provide a complete account of morality, nor to adopt exclusively a rights-based theory of ethics. If the human rights theory carries with it risks of monopolizing all moral consideration, as O'Neill and others claim – and what theory does not? – the solution must be to ensure that when rights occupy center stage precautions are regularly taken to avoid their driving all other moral considerations off the scene.

That having been said, the most powerful reason for according priority to moral rights over their corresponding duties lies in the answer to the simple questions, What is the origin of such moral duties as contrasted with legal duties which originate in the law? And what is the purpose of such moral duties? To concentrate on duties in order to establish them piecemeal in Kantian fashion, or to work out from them which moral rights they give rise to, is to disregard what it is precisely which gives rise to those moral, as distinct from legal, duties or obligations in the first place, thus approaching situations as experienced, or a posteriori, rather than by way of Kantian a priori intellectualism. It then appears much more reasonable to argue in the opposite direction to Bentham and O'Neill, recognizing first the possession of certain moral rights, such as rights to life and liberty, and concluding that the possession of such rights entitles their owner to make appropriate claims on others.

Moreover, so far as concerns O'Neill's contention that rights which cannot be allocated are ineffective and should yield to identified obligations, Feinberg (1980: 153) has interesting comments to make. In some situations where a right is conceived of as a need, or entitlement to some good, it need not involve a duty on any identifiable individual. This Feinberg terms the "manifesto sense" of rights, that is, a sense "in which a right need not be correlated with another's duty" (p. 153), a scenario which O'Neill invokes against the effective force of rights, as we have seen. However, Feinberg accepts "the moral principle that to have an unfulfilled need is to have a kind of claim against the world, even if against no one in particular." And he continues by describing such claims, which are based simply on need, as "permanent possibilities of rights, the natural seed from which rights grow." As a consequence, he concludes, "when manifesto writers speak of them as if already actual rights, they are easily forgiven, for this is but a powerful way of expressing the conviction that they ought to be recognized by states here and now as potential rights and consequently as determinants of *present* aspirations and guides to present policies. That usage, I think, is a valid exercise of rhetorical licence" (p. 153).

Feinberg's recognition that such claims "ought to be recognized" as potential rights is readily understandable in the light of appreciating that part of the dynamic of rights when no duty-owner is evident is to require that a search for such a one be instituted as a matter of urgent justice. Typical here may be the sad and all too common instances dramatized on TV of countless children dying of hunger through a national government's disregard, incompetence, corruption, or sheer inability to meet famine. It is the victims' needs which seize the center of the moral stage, and it is a succeeding, but imperative, question to demand, who, then, is obliged to respond to this? Perhaps, in fact, in default of an obvious duty-holder, such as a national government, or when they cannot or will not meet their obligation, the prima facie reply to this question must always be, anyone who is aware and able – any other nation, any organization, any individual. It is not an insight exclusive to Christianity to note that one's neighbor is whoever one encounters who is in need (see Luke 10: 29–37). We are, after all, talking here of *human* rights, rights possessed by a member of the one human family, which lay a claim on all other humans, in so far as the resulting obligation is commensurate or compatible with any other duties to which they may already be subject. Sen (1999: 230) expresses it simply: "while it is not the specific duty of any given individual to make sure that the person has her rights fulfilled, the claims can be generally addressed to all those who are in a position to help."

By way of a final ad hominem comment on O'Neill's position on the priority of moral obligations over rights, it is relevant to note that the other main target of her criticism in her Reith Lectures was the printed media, much of which she finds gravely deficient in not living up to its public ethical responsibilities (O'Neill 2002: 88–100). She offers several practical suggestions to improve the performance of the British press in this regard, short of legal regulation (pp. 97–8), and concludes, "only if we build a public culture – and above all a media culture – in which we can rely on others not to deceive us will we be able to judge whom and what we can reasonably trust" (p. 98). But if we go on to ask, just why should the press take the trouble to accept its moral responsibilities to improve its performance and to give up deceiving us, as O'Neill maintains it does? Surely the best reason for the press having such responsibilities can only be because we have a right to be told the truth and not to be deceived.

Even in the legal sphere it appears that a major purpose in introducing a new law is to provide protection of the public; that is, to recognize that individuals have a prior moral claim to be protected, which the law now attempts to meet by introducing legal duties to protect them. It may be true, then, that, as Jones (1994: 14) comments, in the absence of a duty there can be no claim right; but this is not because duties always give rise to rights. It is because moral rights give rise to moral duties. In the moral sphere the very point of recognizing rights is to create the possibility of making claims on others, who when identified have corresponding moral duties to respect those claims. "Duties presuppose rights," as Harries observes (1993: 7): "my duty not to murder presupposes the rights of other human beings to life." On the other hand, Harrison does take a realistic approach when he writes, "the central point is that if you really want to see what you have got when you are told that you have a right, see what duties are laid on other people" (Harrison 1983: 94). Yet presumably the main point remains that it is not enough to identify what duties are laid on others, but to appreciate precisely why this should be the case. As we have written elsewhere, "Starting from duty may clarify, but only starting from right or, more fundamentally, from the right-bearer can justify" (Mahoney 1990: 329). Whatever may be said in the legal sphere, then, it does appear within the area of morality that, apart from special duties or responsibilities undertaken or accepted in some situations, rights come first: "duties as correlatives of rights – your duty not to invade my privacy may be justified by my right to privacy – is one of the hallmarks of fundamental rights" (Klug 1996: 42).

Of course, who is subject to such duties arising from various rights depends on the rights in question as well as on particular circumstances. Thus, to take the example of one possessing a right to life, and a claim not to have it violated or endangered, there is a corresponding moral duty on all comers to respect that right. There is also a corresponding duty on the public authorities to provide a context of safety and of public order precisely to ensure that the right to life really is recognized and respected. In a welfare state there could also be a further duty incumbent on government to provide at least the basic necessities of housing, health, and employment to enable that right to life to be enjoyed. In instances of disastrous famine or of calamitous natural disasters the almost instinctive or spontaneous reactions of the international community and of the public in general leave one in no doubt that they feel impelled to respond to calls on their help.

The Proliferation of Rights

In the light of these basic distinctions and comments aimed at clarifying the central issues surrounding human rights, it is now appropriate to consider the major objections which have been, and are, mounted against them. Of these possibly the most common is the allegation that human rights are proliferating uncontrollably, involving an increase of what is frequently referred to as the rhetoric of human rights as well as a debasement of their currency. For example, while Mary Ann Glendon, the Learned Hand Professor of Law at Harvard Law School, provided a highly positive and sympathetic account of the composition of the Universal Declaration of Human Rights (Glendon 2001), and is clearly in favor of human rights, she earlier deplored the degree to which she considered political discourse in the United States had recently become impoverished through the "strident language of rights" pervading every area of life and in its litigiousness dislodging other more possibly accommodating considerations (Glendon 1991: p. x). As she summed up her argument, "the new rhetoric of rights is less about human dignity and freedom than about insistent, unending desires" (p. 171). There was therefore, Glendon concluded, a need, not for the abandonment but for the "renewal of our strong rights tradition" (p. xii) through scaling down the rhetoric of rights and the interminable recourse to legal resolutions of social issues. In agreement with this need, Dworkin comments simply that "the language of rights now dominates political debate" (Dworkin 1978: 184).

Few people would be found to disagree with Glendon in confirming her plea to American culture (and commending it to other cultures, where necessary)

> for refining our deliberations concerning such matters as whether a particular issue is best conceptualized as involving a right; the relation a given right should have to other rights and interests; the responsibilities, if any, that should be correlative with a given right; the social cost of rights; and what effects a given right can be expected to have on the setting of conditions for the durable protection of freedom and human dignity. (Glendon 1991: 177)

However, it is relevant to note that in a sustained response to the allegations by Glendon, and others of a similar mind, that human rights are proliferating unhealthily, Samuel Walker (1998) identifies her as a leading figure in the current of American thought which has been given the name of communitarianism. In the reaction of some academics in the 1970s to John Rawls's theory of justice (Rawls 1971) which stresses the individual and their rights (Walker 1998: 145), and to the political activities of the American Civil Liberties Union (ACLU) which has encouraged a rapid growth of individual rights claims in American life (Walker 1998: 26), numerous critics, according to Walker, have claimed that "the rights revolution has destroyed community in America, cultivating an unhealthy set of values and undermining the fabric of daily life" (p. xi). As a consequence, Glendon, along with the other leader of the intellectual and political communitarian wave of thinking, Amitai Etzioni, argued, in Walker's words, "that we have given far too much attention to individual rights and have neglected both the needs of the larger community and the importance of individual responsibility" (Walker 1998: 25), appealing instead to "a noble sentiment: that we should think more about the general wellbeing of society and less about our own selfish interests" (p. xiii).

To the contrary, Walker argues that "the growth of rights has enlarged and enriched the dimensions of community in America, fulfilling the core values of American democracy" (Walker 1998: p. xi), while critics of rights propose "an imagined or invented view of the past. It is ideology masquerading as history, and becomes a blunt instrument for advancing a specific political agenda" (p. xv). Walker provides a detailed examination of the criticisms proffered against the current "rights-dominated" American ethos and of the contents of the communitarian program, with numerous cautionary case studies illustrating the unjust conditions which existed prior to what he calls "the rights revolution" in America. In the process he provides evidence to show that, so far as the United States is concerned, "the rhetoric about an endless 'minting' of new rights is wildly hyperbolic," nor are they as dangerously radical as they are charged to be (p. 44). As he explains, "the American preference for rights emerged in large part out of a recognition of the undesirable consequences of limitations imposed in the name of the general welfare" (p. 57).

As he adds, "most of the writing on the issue of rights and community quietly slides over the difficult questions related to the community side of the equation. There is a vast literature on the problems related to the rights side of the equation: the scope of free speech, the relationship between church and state, the meaning of due process, and so on. There has been far less written on the community side of the equation. In particular, the communitarian critics of rights have tended to take 'community' as a given – and a problem-free given at that" (Walker 1998: 63–4). In short, Walker concludes, unlike the communitarians, "the rights revolution, in my view, has in fact offered a definition of community, one that is grounded in the principles of inclusion and tolerance. These are the values advanced by a strong commitment to freedom of speech, privacy, and other civil libertarian values . . . The issue, in short, is not 'rights' versus 'community' at all. It is rather a question of what vision of community we seek to establish, and how the development of various rights contributes to that end" (p. xviii).

So important is the popular concern about an undue multiplication of rights and about excessive appeals to them, often exploited in some quarters of the press, that it is worth pursuing this particular line of objection in a little more detail. In his influential 1993 study, *The Spirit of Community: Rights, Responsibilities and the Communitarian Agenda*, Etzioni aimed to replace concern for individual rights and entitlements with commitment to responsibilities and duties in society, as part of which he notoriously proposed a moratorium on the manufacture of new rights (Etzioni 1993). The warm response to this anti-rights move in many quarters found such support that Avineri and de-Shalit (1996: 1) were able to observe that the debate between individualists and communitarians became "one of the most important and fascinating issues of political philosophy in the 1980s."

Francesca Klug had interesting details and comments to add on this sociopolitical movement, which she considers has affinities with the Moral Majority in the United States of America and also had a deep influence in some philosophical and political circles in Britain. As she explained, "the assertion that we have too many rights and not enough duties in the United Kingdom has been given intellectual backing by a group of (mainly) American philosophers cum political activists known as communitarians." As she carefully points out, Etzioni is not an opponent of rights, although his agenda, composed for an American rights-overfriendly context, included the aim of declaring "a moratorium on the minting of most, if not all, new rights" (Klug 1996: 39; see p. 55). In her later work, *Values for a Godless Age: The Story of the UK's New Bill of Rights*, Klug provides an interesting description of the growing popularity and influence of this communitarianism in the British political establishment in the 1990s, and of its influence on the Labour Party's search for a "third way" in politics which would stress the central role of the community (Klug 2000: 55–66). She comments: "at the heart of Etzioni's thinking lies the idea that the notion of duty needs to be restored to its former hegemonic position" (p. 57). It seems to have been what Klug identifies as the transatlantic influence of these communitarian ideas which provided the background to the resounding claim uttered at the British Labour Party conference of 1997 by Prime Minister Blair that "A decent society is not based on rights. It is based on duty. Our duty to each other." To which *The Economist* (October 25, 1997) tartly riposted, "Those are fine sounding words, but one of those duties is to respect each other's rights." Someone had evidently been reading Tom Paine:

> While the Declaration of Rights was before the [French] National Assembly, some of its members remarked, that if a Declaration of Rights was published, it should be accompanied by a Declaration of Duties. The observation discovered a mind that reflected, and it only erred by not reflecting far enough. A Declaration of Rights is, by reciprocity, a Declaration of Duties also. Whatever is my right as a man, is also the right of another; and it becomes my duty to guarantee, as well as to possess.   (Paine 1987: 114)

It is difficult to avoid a feeling when reading Etzioni and similar communitarian writers, in the United States as in Britain, that nostalgia and golden-age reminiscences of a simpler, more settled life are at work, if not overtly, then at least beneath the surface (see Bellah et al. 1985, Selbourne 1997). Mulgan (1995) refers perceptively to communitarianism's "socially conservative guise, where community is used as a code-word for shoring up older institutions that can no longer either win legitimacy or deliver." Keeley (1996: 549–60) likewise made an important point, in a favorable review of Derek L. Phillips's *Looking Backward: A Critical Appraisal of Communitarian Thought* (Phillips 1993), in concluding that "most of his book is devoted to showing that communitarians have decent hearts but faulty memories . . . the 'good old days' were not as rosy as depicted in communitarian accounts." And similar illustrations from British history can confirm that those who are afflicted by chronic nostalgia are ever prone to be selective and partial in their reminiscences, as we have seen in Edmund Burke's far from impartial reading of English history (see pp. 26–8). It is also to be feared that neo-communitarian sentiments contain tendencies to elitism and to authoritarianism and more or less subtle social coercion when appeals to a change of heart prove predictably unsuccessful.

In spite, then, of the eloquent deploring of the proliferation of rights, especially to the detriment of responsibilities, which is to be heard regularly in British, as well as American, society, it does not seem self-evident that rights have had their own for far too long. David Fergusson (1998: 169), for instance, is in no doubt that "the language of rights has an important function in articulating a moral consensus against some of the most flagrant abuses in our time." He does justice (pp. 140–1) to communitarian concerns about "the corrosive effects of individualism," the loss of a sense of belonging together and of sharing common values, concerns and interests. Yet he also (p. 144) recognizes and illustrates "the oppressive conditions under which families and communities existed in the past," as well as acknowledging the "latent oppressiveness" of communitarianism, including xenophobia and "the imposition of the standards of one community upon all others." And he reports Seyla Benhabib to the effect that the communitarians are correct to recognize the ways in which traditions, communities and practices shape our identities, adding her qualification that "this should not preclude an ability to criticize, challenge, and question the content of these identities and the practices they prescribe" (Fergusson 1998: 148).

Interestingly, another movement of thought which accords central significance to the idea of community and which has recently been growing in political interest and appeal takes an entirely different approach to the subject of human rights by locating them at the very center of an international community. Claiming its initial inspiration in the possibly testy remark of the Greek Cynic, Diogenes of Sinope (d. *c.*324 BCE), who responded to a query about his nationality that he was a "citizen of the world" (*kosmopolites*) – he had been banished from his native city (Copleston 1944: 120) – cosmopolitanism envisages the entire human race as constituting a single world community in which concern for global equality and justice is ideally expressed in the paramount idea of universal human rights. As modern exponents of the cosmopolitan movement have concluded, and as we shall have occasion to examine in the final chapter (see pp. 183–5), "A central concern and goal of cosmopolitan democracy is the worldwide protection of human rights" (Archibugi and Koenig-Archibugi 2003: 285).

At heart, much of this talk of the danger of human rights proliferating and swamping other considerations is aimed at establishing, or redressing, a basic balance between one's personal needs and the needs of others, to put the choice very simply, and few moderate people would be found to disagree with this. At few points in history, of course, will such a balance be found in absolute equilibrium. For one thing, as Habgood (1993: 108) observed, "if assertions of rights represent the leading edge of moral insight, then proliferation is inevitable." Moreover, it is possible for philosophical and political pendulums to swing too far in the other direction. Even some who may feel some sympathy for (neo-) communitarianism and for the warm glow of the traditional values whose passing it regrets, may nevertheless experience certain apprehensions about it, especially as it becomes popularized in a swell of public opinion and is hijacked by various political and other pressure groups.

Moreover, the apparently inexorable increase in human rights is not as arbitrary nor as random or eclectic as some critics complain. There is a historical development and an evolution to be observed in the emergence of fundamental moral rights since they first began to appear on the twelfth-century scene, as well as a trajectory which points to the emergence and identification of further such rights in the future. The Italian political philosopher, Norberto Bobbio, has captured this well in explaining that

> human rights however fundamental are historical rights and therefore arise from specific conditions characterized by the embattled defence of new freedoms against old powers . . . Religious freedom resulted from the religious wars, civil liberties from the parliamentarian struggles against absolutism, and political and social freedoms from the birth, growth and experience of movements representing workers, landless peasants and small holders. The poor demand from the authorities not only recognition of personal freedom and negative freedoms, but also protection against unemployment, basic education to overcome illiteracy, and gradually further forms of welfare for sickness and old age – all needs which the wealthy can provide for themselves.   (Bobbio 1996: pp. x–xi)

Bobbio here is distinguishing between what have become described as the first generation of human rights, the classic liberties of Locke, of the nascent America, and of revolutionary France, and the second generation which comprises the social, political, and cultural rights more redolent of socialism which began to secure recognition after the havoc created by the Second World War. He continues, however, that there is now emerging a third generation of rights which

> arise from the danger posed to life, liberty and security by the growth in technological progress. Three examples at the heart of current debate will be sufficient: the right to live in an unpolluted environment, which has been the basis for the ecological movements that have shaken both individual countries and the international system; the right to privacy, which has been seriously endangered by the ability of public bodies to store information concerning a person's life, and hence control behaviour without the person knowing; and finally the right to the integrity of one's genetic inheritance, which is already stirring up debate in international organizations; this goes far beyond the right to physical integrity proclaimed in Articles 2 and 3 of the European Convention on Human Rights.   (Bobbio 1996: 69; see p. xi)

It therefore provides little consolation to those who complain of the constant proliferation of human rights to appreciate, so far as Bobbio foresaw the future, that

It does not take much imagination to realize that development of technology, the transformation of social and economic conditions, widening knowledge and the intensification of the means of communication will produce such changes in the organization of human life and social relations as to engender favourable conditions for the creation of new needs and therefore new demands for freedoms and powers. (Bobbio 1996: 19; see Klug 2000: 9–10, 135–9)

In a manner similar to Bobbio's, the comprehensive study, *Human Rights in the Twenty-First Century: A Global Challenge*, by Kathleen E. Mahoney and Paul Mahoney (1993), identifies a future increase in human rights reflecting new aspects of various conditions of life relating to food, health, environment, minorities, and disabled persons, and also resulting from technological advances in mass communications, information technology, and reproductive techniques.

Nor is the expansion of human rights due exclusively to new technological developments or to political events: in some cases it is more the manifestation of a deepened awareness of the intrinsic dignity of some classes of human beings who had been previously undervalued, thus overthrowing what previous generations had considered "natural." As Freeden explains:

Many rights are, of course, still being discovered or invented. The rights of women – both as human beings and women-specific – are still being spelled out in rights-compendia. Indeed, historically changing views of human nature have already applied to non-trivial attributes of women, or of homosexuals. Conceptions of women have evolved beyond the view that ascribed to them intellectual inferiority side by side with moral superiority. Homosexuals are currently engaged in the process of removing the label of moral perversity from their sexual proclivities. Yet in the past those descriptions seemed to many to be self-evident just as their obverse may now claim the status of self-evidence. (1991: 41)

Of course, in spite of all this justification for foreseeing an inevitable increase of instrumental human rights, or new expressions or applications of fundamental rights dependent on changing circumstances, it remains obviously true that there are, and can be, many real and potential abuses of human rights claims; and there is a continual need for a moderating critical approach to irresponsible demands made on society, on governments, or on other people, whether by individuals or groups, in the name of human rights. Sumner makes the useful cautionary point that "a fixation on rights may lead us to exaggerate conflict and competition and to overlook possibilities for cooperation and reconciliation"

(Sumner 2000: 297). Nevertheless it is worth recalling that historians of the human rights movement regularly point out that all the major historical documents throughout history which advocate rights invariably balance this program by including an acknowledgment of the needs also for responsibilities, at the very least that of respecting the human rights of others (see UN Commission 1985).

Looking to the more general claim that individuals today are much more prone to appeal to their rights than to listen to the stern voice of duty, the simple fact, of course, is that, as Habgood comments (1993: 97), "there need be no conflict between rights and duties"; and he quotes Tom Paine's statement made as early as *The Rights of Man* that "a declaration of rights is, by reciprocity, a declaration of duties also. Whatever is my right as a man is also the right of another; and it becomes my duty to guarantee as well as to possess." In point of fact, it was a regular theme in the discussions leading to the UN Universal Declaration of Human Rights that rights and duties go together. Not only did the preamble in its final form require that all men "should act towards one another in a spirit of brotherhood," which clearly implies having a sense of responsibility towards the "brotherhood of man," or in more inclusive language "human solidarity," or, in less rhetorical terms, the common good. More explicitly, the final article points out that "Everyone has duties to the community in which alone the free and full development of his personality is possible" (art. 29.1); and everyone shall be subject to laws "securing due recognition and respect for the rights and freedoms of others" (art 29.2). "These last clauses, which were drafted after long debate, express the idea embodied in the Declaration of relations among human beings, society and the State, namely, that each should yield to the requirements of the general welfare as defined by the organised community, whose *raison d'être* remains, in any case, the promotion of human rights through democracy" (*The UN and Human Rights* 1995: p. 25).

Individuals-in-Society

Underlying the misgivings expressed about the apparent proliferation of human rights to the detriment of duties appears often to be a perceived tension between the individual and the community, and the apprehension that the idea of increasing moral rights vested in individuals is leading, or will lead automatically, to social divisions or to the fragmentation of society. In point of fact, however, the very idea of rights attaching to the individual as such in the community entails moral respect for the rights of every individual on the part of every other individual, as we have just seen Tom Paine explain. The point is well developed by Gewirth (1993: 43–6) in his writing of "the community of rights" as involving "a certain communitarian conception of human relationships, one that is focused on mutuality of consideration and social solidarity." For few human rights, if any, are held in isolation or in a social vacuum. As Bernard Levin once expressed it with his customary elegance, my right to stick out my fist ends where someone else's nose begins. Harries gets to the root of it: "Freebooting individualism is a denial of the essential nature of human personhood. We are persons only in relation to other persons. The other person's welfare is my welfare" (Harries 1993: 11).

Underlying this observation by Harries lies a whole current of philosophical reflection found in the work of three twentieth-century thinkers, Jacques Maritain, John Macmurray, and William Temple, each of whom distinguishes importantly between the human person and the human individual, and views the person as precisely an individual-in-society. Temple, for instance, presumes and highlights the difference simply in calling for "a democracy of persons, not only of individuals" (Temple 1987: 72; see p. 15). Earlier, Maritain (1940: p. vii) set out to examine the relationship between the human person and society by analyzing the notion of person and developing the difference between individuality and personality, "two notions which are usually confused and whose distinction I consider to be highly important." For Maritain (pp. 60–2), coming from an Aristotelian and Thomist metaphysical tradition, individuality is that which makes any particular being unique and separates it off from all others, even from similar beings, as an individualized member of a class. By contrast, personality in humans is what makes for being a person or a self, that is, an intelligent, reflecting, willing, and loving subject, a center of characteristically human reception, action, and, above all, interaction. "The subjectivity of the person . . . demands the communications of intelligence and love. Because of the very fact that I am a person and that I express myself to myself, I seek to communicate with *that which is other* and with *others*, in the order of knowledge and love" (p. 64).

Spelling out the social implications of this distinction between individuals and persons, Maritain then observes, "it is essential for personality to tend towards communion. We must insist on this point which is often forgotten: the person, by virtue of his dignity, as well as of his needs, requires to be a member of society . . . Society, properly speaking – human society – is a society of persons" (1940: 67). This then in turn enables Maritain (pp. 69–70) to define the aim of society as the common good of all its members, provided this is recognized as "a common good of human persons," not as a simple collection of private goods, nor a good belonging to a whole which absorbs its parts for its own ends. "Under pain of being itself denatured, such a good implies and demands the recognition of the fundamental rights of the person . . . It involves, as its chief value, the highest possible accession (an accession compatible with the good of the whole) of persons to their life as persons, and to their freedom of expansion."

Maritain thus distinguishes between individuality as that in us which divides and separates us from each other, and personality as that in us which impels us to interrelate with others in society. (It is the human person who for him constitutes Aristotle's "political animal.") The practical influence of Maritain's thinking on the workings of the UN Human Rights Commission is brought out by the recognition by Novak of the early solution found to the dilemma on how "to bridge the gap between the Anglo-American zeal for the term *individual* and the Soviet insistence on the *State*." As Novak observed, in directing the work of the Commission Charles Malik preferred to use the "more capacious notion" of "person" to stress its social overtones rather than the term "individual." And he concludes, "From the very first words of the Preamble, then, the Universal Declaration avoids the term *individual* and takes care to surround the term *person* with references to the expanding circle of communities and associations in which" it always exists (Novak 1999: 39–42).

Some fifteen years after Maritain's reflections, the philosopher John Macmurray in Scotland was at pains to develop what one commentator has described as "the full mutuality of persons in relation" (Macmurray 1995: p. xvi). In the second volume of his 1953–4 Gifford Lectures he remarked that "any human society is a moral entity. Its basis is the universal and necessary intention to maintain the personal relation which makes the human individual a person, and his life a common life" (1995: 128; see Costello 2002: 326–9). And this reflection on the essentially communal nature of personal identity, as distinct from individuality, was equally emphasized by William Temple in 1941 when he referred to Maritain's "valuable distinction" which recognizes that a person's individuality "is what marks him off from others; it is a principle of division." By contrast, "personality is social, and only in his social relationships can a man be a person" (Temple 1987: 71; see Craig 1963: 131–2).

To sum up these considerations on the valuable distinction between individuals and persons, one can recall the observation of Julian Huxley (Teilhard de Chardin 1975: 20) that, speaking in evolutionary terms, "a person [is] an organism which has transcended individuality in personality." This being so, then the line of solution to criticisms of over-indulgence in human rights at the expense of society can lie in recognizing the real dangers of individualism, as an excessive emphasis on that which separates human beings from each other, while maintaining the need for personalism, or the recognition of the centrality of persons, and of personal rights, as something to be protected and promoted in any humane society.

Selfishness and Social Divisiveness

This consideration of the role of society as being to protect and promote the interests and human rights of all the persons who comprise it provides a line of response to the further objection sometimes raised that directing one's attention to human rights expresses or engenders irresponsible self-interest and social divisiveness. The former contention, however, is based on several presuppositions, of which the most common, particularly in some Christian quarters, is the notion that self-regard is morally wrong, and that concern for one's own interests is ethically to be discouraged. As Lynn Sharp Paine expresses it, "it is sometimes thought that morality or ethics is concerned only with what is good for others as distinct from what is good for oneself." Her reply, however, is to contend correctly, echoing the view of the eighteenth-century philosopher, Joseph Butler (Duncan-Jones 1952), that "the moral point of view requires not that individuals deny their personal needs and aspirations and consider only the interests of others, but rather that individuals see their personal interests and objectives in relation to those of others" (Paine 1996: 478).

Another misconception underlying the charge that concern for human rights is invariably egotistical and self-serving is the presupposition that the only rights one considers worth promoting are one's own or those of a closed and privileged circle of one's fellows or fellow victims. The rebuttal to this, however, was put finely by Tom Paine in his expostulation against Burke's similar attack, when he wrote: "my idea of supporting liberty of conscience and the rights of citizens, is that of supporting those rights in *other people*, for if a man supports only his *own* rights for his *own sake*, he does no moral duty" (Hawke 1974: 204). From the Christian point of view it may very well be the case that some individuals who are suffering deprivation or denial of fundamental human rights perceive the passive, even willing, acceptance of such a situation as a personal calling to a life of utter dependence on a power beyond the temporal, or as giving personal witness to higher transcendent values than those of earthly survival and flourishing. In the face of such lived faith, others can only stand in reverence and respect. Yet such an intimately personal vocation is not one to be lightly presumed as issued indiscriminately to other people, far less to everyone. Martyrdom is not something to be prescribed for others; and it has often been all too easy for the spectator of human injustice to find a religious rationalization in appeals to divine providence or to the consequences of human sin or, as Edmund Burke did, to a hoped-for compensation in the afterlife (see p. 27). The Hebrew and the Christian Bibles are at one in recognizing that "those who oppress the poor insult their Maker, but those who are kind to the needy honour him" (Proverbs 14: 31; NRSV). As we have seen in the previous chapter, the humanitarian struggle for human rights for all human beings is one which the Christian churches have come to recognize lies at the heart of the gospel of good news which they feel impelled to preach universally to the whole of society. It is one of many lessons which can be learned from the struggle for civil rights on the part of blacks and women in Western society in the twentieth century, not to mention from the whole development of liberation theology, that human degradation is not to be confused with Christian humility, and that acquiescing in the domination of some individuals and groups in society by others who just happen to have more power simply cannot be considered compatible with Christian or human moral values.

Quite unlike the other charges which we have been considering against human rights, and which we have been attempting to mitigate or to dispel, the accusation that concern and campaigning for human rights can be socially divisive and civilly disturbing may very well on occasion be completely justified. It may be, of course, that it is not appeals to rights which harm society but that it is a divided and disturbed society which increases appeals to rights. Orend, for instance, takes issue with the charge that human rights foster selfishness and social divisiveness, commenting that "it is deeply unclear whether the rise in rights talk has actually caused a collapse in public-spiritedness, or rather whether such a collapse was brought about by something else, and that an ethics of rights simply speaks more accurately and honestly to the aspirations of the new age." Indeed, he goes on, perhaps "rights, far from rupturing, actually fill in a moral gap left behind by the collapse of traditional 'community values.' Rights are actually a more appropriate and plausible candidate to dominate moral and political life in our time, because they reflect, better than any of their competitors, the salient aspects of life in the modern world" (Orend 2002: 177), whether that be the modern, globalized, intensely competitive world where erosion of human rights may be a slow, almost imperceptible, process, or those parts of the world where rights are overtly abused by brutal regimes. Certainly in the latter case, Orend (p. 183) comments, "realizing rights may, admittedly, destabilize those regimes that violate rights, but it is by no means obvious that tranquillity and stability ought to be the overriding values in such countries."

There can, in fact, be occasions when claims for human rights actually *should* be socially challenging, including situations when such rights are claimed, not for oneself, but for third parties, or for whole sectors or strata of society, such as the poor, the unemployed, and the unhoused, or even for whole subjugated peoples. What Sassen (2005: 144) describes as the situation in the United States of "the substantive exclusions suffered by lawful citizens," often partly the calculated result of racial and housing factors, has applied also to other Western countries, including Britain and France; and all have resulted in varying degrees of civil unrest and violent protest. Complaints of the divisiveness of rights talk are characteristically uttered by the secure and powerful in society, and it may well be understandable if those who are safe in the enjoyment of their own rights can feel threatened if the social equilibrium is about to be disturbed. As Preston observed (1983: 125), "to consider the institutions of society from the angle of those who experience the rough end of them is not something that their more affluent fellow citizens find easy. Only slowly are the poor being heard, only slowly are they acquiring power to affect things and not just to be pushed around."

Frequently, if not invariably, appeal to rights arises in a context of social weakness and vulnerability and from the experience of injustice or of unfairness, all of which call to be remedied as a matter of human decency. The people on the receiving end may be powerless in certain relationships in political, social, cultural, financial, and even physical terms, but to speak of them as having rights is to ascribe to them at least a *moral* power, appeal to which ought to be a defense and a genuine empowerment. On many such occasions what is being deliberately disturbed, and rightly, is not so much genuine social solidarity, as social complacency and social elitism, or even social collusion, with privilege and prejudice tenaciously holding a society in their grip under a veneer of harmony and patrician tranquillity. Then what is perceived by those in possession, and sometimes rightly, as aggressiveness arises from the justified reaction to perceived injustice on the part of rights claimants or their defenders. As O'Neill explains (1986: 105), "those who complain that their rights have not been respected do not approach the established order as humble *petitioners*, but as wronged *claimants*." For, it may be added, the appeal to human rights appears to have this similarity with appeals to one's moral conscience, that they tend to be invoked only when they appear to be under threat, or more accurately only when the person perceives he or she is at risk of being treated, or of being forced to act, in ways with which they profoundly disagree on moral grounds. As Donnelly observes (2003: 8), "we typically talk of rights only when they are at issue." To a degree, also, the appeal to human rights often takes the form of being a last resort, when other ways or levels of objecting have proved ineffective, and this can help to explain the often adversarial and morally challenging way in which appeals to human rights typically find expression.

Ethical Imperialism?

One of the most important objections raised against the very idea of human rights applying universally is that which views them as of Western origin and therefore as alien to other cultures, so much so that attempting to impose human rights on other, non-Western, countries is tantamount to exercising a form of unwarranted ethical imperialism. In the final chapter we shall explore the relevance of human rights to the modern phenomenon of globalization, and this will lead us to examine the general question of whether there can be such things as universal ethical standards of behavior which apply everywhere around the globe, or whether cultures vary and differ so much from each other that it is impossible to identify moral values which would apply equally in every one of them. The particular charge to be considered here, however, is not so much whether universal ethical standards are to be found worldwide as whether the particular expression of ethics in terms of human rights which we have been considering can be considered applicable to cultures other than the Western one in which they first came to birth.

   The major expression of considering human rights an alien imposition on non-Western cultures developed in the twentieth century in the growing identification of distinctive "Asian values," as contrasted with Western, and human right, values. In particular, the contrast was drawn between human rights and the Asian values which were prized as part of Eastern culture as well as being claimed as the engine of the economic miracles which had at the time been achieved by several Asian societies (see Donnelly 2003). Thus, in 1997, when Malaysia was hosting annual discussions between Southeast Asian nations and larger powers including the United States, China, and Japan, the

Malaysian Prime Minister proposed that the UN Declaration of Human Rights should be revised to reflect better the concerns of developing nations. In this move to redefine human rights Malaysia was supported by Indonesia and China, and also by the Philippines (*Economist*, August 2, 1997), where a columnist in the *Manila Chronicle* (August 18, 1997) supported the contention "that Asian values are different from those of the West and should be respected." Some months earlier, in a valedictory article in the *Economist* (January 4, 1997), the outgoing governor of Hong Kong, Chris Patten, had opined that "if we accept the concept of Asian values, we have to deny the universality of human rights."

However, evidence that one should treat with considerable reserve claims for peculiarly or exclusively Asian values was put forward in the same year in Japan at the first world congress of the International Society for Business, Economics and Ethics, in a paper delivered by the distinguished Indian Harvard economist and philosopher Amartya Sen. In considering the idea of "Asian values," Sen (1997: 5–15) observed that the term "Asia" covers a vast heterogeneous region, which has been subject to very uneven development and very late economic progress. This made one wonder, he commented, why it took Asian values so long to provide their present rich economic fruits; and he concluded that to speak simply of Asian values is an unhelpful stereotyping and an indulgence in over-generalization. In a later treatment of the subject Sen provided a detailed examination of sources from various Asian religions and cultures, including the Confucian, Buddhist, Hindu, and Muslim, to explode the claimed existence and authority of "Asian values" (Sen 1999: 231–9; see 244–6), and to conclude that "the modern advocates of the authoritarian view of 'Asian values' base their readings on very arbitrary interpretations and extremely narrow selections of authors and traditions" (pp. 239–40).

A previous interesting commentary from a business point of view on the significance of so-called "Asian values" was provided in a speech delivered in Singapore in 1995 and reported in *Asian Business* (January 1996: 36–8) by a Hong Kong banker on what he considered key challenges facing Asia's managers in the new millennium. These included the challenge arising from "conflict of values," or, as he put it, the tensions in conducting business between what are perceived to be traditional values, often labelled "Asian," and modern values. He was in no doubt that modernization is eroding some values which are described as "Asian," such as respect for hierarchies, Asian-style consensus, the centrality of the family, a culture of obedience and of deference to superiors and elders, and a sense of responsibility to the community. Yet he also made the point which Sen would echo, that "no one has yet demonstrated adequately that the values labelled 'Asian' are so very different from those long espoused in much of the West." In fact, as he observed amusedly, a German Canadian friend of his had recognized this cluster of so-called "Asian values" as part of what the West long ago came to call "the Protestant work ethic"!

On there being, in fact, a particular place for human rights in an Asian context, it is interesting to note the remark of the Nobel Peace Prize recipient in 1991, Aung San Suu Kyi, that "the proposition that the Burmese are not fit to enjoy as many rights and privileges as the citizens of democratic countries is insulting" (see Kearney 1994: 346 n. 90). Of this powerful popular figure Sen observed that she "has no less legitimacy – indeed clearly has rather more – in interpreting what the Burmese want than have the military rulers of Myanmar, whose candidate she had defeated in open elections before being put in jail by the defeated military junta" (Sen 1999: 247). In a wider Asian context it is particularly valuable to note the outspoken comment contained in a *Report* of a Human Rights Workshop which was held in the East Asian Pastoral Institute in Manila in 1994, to the effect that "All too often the alleged dichotomy between eastern and western values is merely a pretext (brought forward by governments, not by suffering people) to excuse repressive policies" (East Asian Pastoral Institute 1994: 3). And Patten, in his *Economist* article (January 4, 1997) about the "myths" of Asia, quoted above, had no sympathy with any suggestion of Asia possessing its own unique values when he dismissed the claims for non-Western and superior "Asian values" as being "put with bullying panache by some leaders of an authoritarian disposition to justify the curbs placed on the freedom of those they rule." Likewise, Glendon observes of the UN Universal Declaration of Human Rights that "When leaders of authoritarian governments claim that the Declaration is aimed at imposing 'foreign' values, their real concern is often domestic: the pressure for freedom building among their own citizens" (Glendon 2001: 224).

Commenting on the adopting of human rights language by the United Nations, Twiss (1998: 161) observed that "the fact that the language of rights was employed was doubtless due to the dominance of the Western legal tradition in the international area, but the mutually agreed-upon judgment about the proscription of certain acts and the protection of certain values was not simply a Western moral judgment." In fact, it is noteworthy how many politicians and statesmen of Asian origin were happy to subscribe in the United Nations debates to the agreements reached in formulating the international Declaration of Human Rights.

The British representative, Mr Davies (*Documents of UN Conference* 1945: 882–3), wondered that "never before had so many nations joined together to agree on what they considered to be the fundamental rights of the individual. More than 50 nations with differing systems of government and differing social structures, religions and philosophies had adopted by an overwhelming majority the articles of the draft declaration under discussion " Typical of individual contributions to the discussion was the statement of the leader of the Indian delegation, taking pains to point out that he was "speaking as an Asiatic," that "there is one great reality, one fundamental factor, one eternal verity which all religions teach, which must be remembered by all of us, the dignity of the common man, the fundamental human rights of all beings all over the world." In recent times a striking confirmation of this compatibility of human rights and Asian cultures, as well as a remarkable recognition of the growing international recognition of human rights, was the award in 2003 of the Nobel peace prize to the distinguished Iranian woman human rights lawyer Shirin Ebadi, who, in the report of the *Economist* (October 18, 2003), "insists on the essential compatibility of Islam and human rights."

From further East Dr Chan, the Chinese delegate at the UN, was more than happy to educate his colleagues on the way in which, far from human rights being an alien Western imposition, he considered European thinking on human rights to have been influenced by Chinese thought. "In the 18th century," Chang explained, "when progressive ideas with respect to human rights had been first put forward in Europe, translations of Chinese philosophers had been known to and had inspired such thinkers as Voltaire, Quesnay, and Diderot in their humanistic revolt against feudalistic conceptions. Chinese ideas had intermingled with European thought and sentiment on human rights at the time when that subject had been first speculated upon in modern Europe." And he concluded without any qualification that the Universal Declaration in its final form would "serve as a basis and a programme for the humanisation of man" (UN Records 1948: 48).

Finally, the issue of ethical imperialism was explicitly faced by the 1993 Vienna conference on Human Rights. Drinan noted:

> At the opening of the Conference China protested that human rights are a western construct and that cultural relativity should excuse Asian nations from some of the mandates of the human rights law built up by the United Nations and its ancillary bodies. But during the conference in Vienna this contention faded and was withdrawn. The Vienna declaration made it clear that human rights – civil, cultural, economic and political – are interrelated, interdependent, and indivisible. (2001: p. xi)

From all this it is difficult to avoid the conclusion that the confidence with which unique Asian values are claimed as distinctive and as to be preferred in the East over so-called Western human rights does not bear much close examination, especially since the waning of the Asian economic success which had earlier seemed to fuel it. Human Rights Watch (HRW World Report 1998) was totally dismissive of the idea of "a supposed 'Asian concept of human rights'," according to which Asian officials in many countries insist that "Asian people prefer order to freedom" as the best means to secure economic growth. On the contrary, HRW claimed, recent economic and environmental setbacks in various Asian countries were exacerbated by the suppression of freedoms of expression and association resulting in a lack of accountability of governments to their people. As a consequence, "the Asian threat to the universality of human rights lost credibility." For, as Donnelly also commented, perhaps the most important explanation for the prevalence of cultural arguments favoring so-called Asian values is that "they are used by vicious elites as a way to attempt to deflect attention from their repressive policies." To which he adds the well-directed admonition that "well-meaning Westerners with a well-developed sense of the legacy of Western colonialism indirectly support such arguments when they shy away from criticizing arguments advanced by non-Westerners even when they are empirically inaccurate or morally absurd" (Donnelly 2003: 100).

It may finally be suggested that generally, when discussion develops about contrasting Eastern and Western moral values, it comes down to pointing up the difference between Eastern community values and Western individual values. Yet this cannot be taken to mean that there is no concern for community in the West, nor any interest in individuals in the East. Even in the West many people are devoted to their families and dependants; and one of the most serious social issues currently preoccupying Europe and the USA is how the community can provide adequate care for the increasing numbers of its elderly members, particularly as medical technology increases life expectancy. Conversely, concern for the individual is growing in the East, whether as a result of Westernization in the wake of world business or because the weaknesses and liabilities of excessive loyalty to community or family or business company are becoming increasingly apparent in modern daily life, including in the worlds of Asian politics and business.

Perhaps, in fact, the most that should be concluded is that both sets of values, those which focus on the community and those which center on the individual, are to be found in the East as well as the West, but with varying degrees of emphasis or priority at different times or in different situations. Human rights declarations and statements regularly attempt to ensure that both clusters of values are to be respected; and keeping both in mind can serve to warn against absolutizing either the individual or the group, whether that be one's family, one's firm, or one's class or country. We have already considered the quite strong reaction even in the West today against what is considered excessive individualism, as contrasted with legitimate individuality and personalism; and history also has lessons to teach about the authoritarian abuses and deadening weight which can be exercised by groups and communities, even the best-intentioned, in the West as well as in the East.

A Challenge to All Cultures

For the human rights record even in the West is by no means unsullied in recent years, as can be seen in the case of Britain and the United States of America. So far as concerns Britain, in his 1990 pamphlet campaigning for a British Bill of Rights, Ronald Dworkin, as Professor of Jurisprudence at Oxford University, drew up a formidable indictment against the human rights behavior of both major political parties while in government in Britain, commenting that "the list of liberties compromised or ignored in Britain in recent years is a long, sad one," many of them involving suppression of freedom of expression in print or on the air in the name of official secrecy, or invading privacy in the name of national security, or limiting the rights of suspects (Dworkin 1990: 2–9). As he commented (pp. 16–17), "Britain has been a frequent defendant before the European Court . . . Since 1965 twice as many petitions have been lodged against it as against any other member, and it has lost more serious cases than any other nation." However, should it incorporate the European Convention on Human Rights into its domestic law, he concluded (p. 22), "Britain could become once again a leader in defining and protecting individual freedom, instead of a sullen defendant giving ground to liberty only when ordered to do so by a foreign court." As to whether Britain's actual respect for fundamental human rights has improved following on the passing of the 2000 British Human Rights Act eight years later, we might conclude for the present that the jury is still out, particularly so far as concerns the treatment of immigrants, asylum seekers, and those under suspicion of terrorism.

The other great champion in history of the significance of human rights, the United States of America, also possesses an ambivalent record with regard to its own behavior in this field. In his forthright essay entitled, after the Amnesty International motto, *The Mobilization of Shame*, Drinan produced at the beginning of the new millennium a sustained critique of the United States' record on human rights which found fault with many of its actions or lack of actions in this field, notably its failure to ratify the UN Covenant on Economic, Social and Cultural Rights (Drinan 2001: 128). He noted how Secretary of State, John Foster Dulles, removed Mrs Eleanor Roosevelt from her post on the UN Commission on Human Rights in protest against the proposal that the United States become a party to a UN human rights treaty approval, and he commented that "all of Dulles's successors up to Henry Kissinger regarded human rights as a hindrance to the pursuit of great power politics" (pp. 84–5). More recently, Drinan allows (p. 6), the United States has become, at least in principle, much more interested in human rights behavior around the world, although still seriously delinquent in its domestic social policy and "reluctant to guarantee economic rights, which arguably [are] to some extent inconsistent with the principles of capitalism."

Drinan's particular criticism of the routine behavior of the United States towards many of its prison populations as "appalling" was given strong contemporary confirmation in the aftermath of the terrorist attack on the New York World Trade Center on September 11, 2001, when Harold Hongju Koh, who had been Assistant Secretary of State for human rights in the Clinton administration, had occasion to draw attention to America's new attitude towards respecting human rights in the wake of that deeply traumatic experience. As he pointed out in a 2003 London lecture (*Economist*, November 1, 2003), one consequence of 9/11 was that the Bush administration "radically shifted its emphasis on human rights . . . Bush administration officials have now reprioritized 'freedom from fear' as the number-one freedom we need to preserve. Freedom from fear has become the obsessive watch-word of America's human-rights policy." In illustration of this contention Koh listed and expanded on several areas which he considered pointed to "a human rights policy fixated on fear" leading to this "transformation of human rights." One feature was "a reduced American human-rights presence through the rest of the globe," as a consequence of which, Koh suggested, "America's anti-terrorist activities have given cover to many foreign governments who want to use 'anti-terrorism' to justify their own crackdowns on human rights."

It is acknowledgments such as these by Dworkin, Drinan, and Koh on the human rights records of major Western powers which ironically help to enforce the realization that human rights confront all cultures with the basic moral requirements of how to treat human beings. In fact, all human cultures without exception are subject to constant scrutiny, evaluation, and challenge by a doctrine of human rights, and none is ethically sacrosanct or immune from such critique. It is true that the doctrine of human rights found its origin and its early development in Western society, which one writer (Gorecki 1996: p. xvi) considers a source of pride: "the idea of human rights constitutes an invaluable product of Western Civilization, its unique gift to all societies." Moreover, as Jürgen Moltmann observed, "like other universal ideas – mathematics for instance – human rights have . . . become independent of the particular European history in which they developed, and now seem plausible and convincing simply on their own account, whenever people become aware that they are not merely Americans or Russians, black or white, men or women, Christians or Jews, but that they are first and foremost human beings" (Moltmann 1990: 120).

The point seems worth stressing. Henkin (1990: p. xi) makes it clear that "human rights is not Western cultural imperialism. If the idea of human rights developed in the West, so did other political and economic ideas that underlie modern international life – 'sovereignty,' the state, democracy, market economics, socialism, development, international law and institutes." As he adds, "the West itself was slow to accept the idea of human rights: the most terrible human rights violations in modern history were committed during [the twentieth] century in the heart of Western Europe." O'Neill (2000: 117) is no less uncompromising in noting that "the European colonial expansion, which has shaped the present world economic and political order, was achieved in part by invasion, genocide, expropriation, transportation, slavery and proselytizing that Europeans would have condemned as unjust in dealings with those whose standing they acknowledged."

A final approach, then, to the charge of a Western imposition of human rights on other cultures is to accept the differences between various cultures and traditions as the product of history, and to view human rights not as an imposition but as a challenge: and not as an imposition on some cultures by others but as a challenge to every culture.

The Strengths of Human Rights

A final objection raised against the idea of human rights is that they are actually unnecessary, since the purpose which they are intended to serve can just as easily be achieved by other moral means. Before the idea of human rights emerged on the medieval scene as a moral theory, existing ways of exploring moral behavior following the classical sources of Plato, Aristotle, and the Bible were presumably quite satisfactory. If human rights create duties in others, as we have seen, then presumably it is ethically quite sufficient to explore the idea and extent of people's moral obligations in various situations without reference to rights, especially if in so doing we can avoid all the difficulties surrounding rights with which this chapter has attempted to deal. For instance, in his enormously influential work, *A Theory of Justice*, John Rawls has little formally to say about human rights. It is enough for his thesis to claim that "each person possesses an inviolability founded on justice that even the welfare of society as a whole cannot override" (Rawls 1971: 3), although he did later develop his position to envisage respect for human rights as integral to any political regime which claimed to belong to a just society of peoples (Rawls 1993, 1999; see above p. 78). Moreover, concentration on the idea of moral rights does much less than justice to areas of human behavior which are not susceptible to a rights approach, such as, notably, friendship, but also obligations which are not the correlative of rights, commonly called "imperfect duties," such as generosity or kindness. Jones (1994: 207–9) is correct to opine that "our conceptions of people's rights do not exhaust the range of our moral thinking and an attempt to think only in terms of rights would result in a severely attenuated morality."

The response to this objection is twofold. Firstly, once again it is worth stressing that rights do not by any means encompass the whole of human morality. But secondly, if the language of rights is used, its purpose is not just to replicate what other moral theories might produce. Its aim is to reflect and to express particular ethical features which might belong to some situations and which would profit from being newly highlighted in some way. This consideration leads us to move beyond examining the objections which can be, and have been, raised against the idea of rights and to explore the positive advantages which the doctrine possesses.

When Kant enjoins that we ought to treat humanity both in ourselves and in others as an end and never merely as a means, human rights can provide some intellectual and empirical ground for this major ethical intuition by pointing to the inalienable dignity and worth of individuals on which rights theory is based and which make human rights the objects of indispensable respect. Likewise, when utilitarianism in its various forms appeals to the protean idea of human happiness, or of human good or, today, of human preferences, as the sole criterion of ethical evaluation of behavior, human rights provide an identikit of what actually constitutes such human well-being. As Finnis (1980: 221) has shown, human rights theory is of value in actually identifying what are the indispensable components and conditions of such human flourishing in every individual: "Since rights must be and are referred to by name, modern rights-talk amplifies the undifferentiated reference to 'the common good' [or 'the greatest happiness'] by providing a usefully detailed listing of the various aspects of human flourishing and fundamental components of the way of life in community that tends to favour such flourishing in all." These fundamental components are likewise summarily described by Gewirth (1993: 36) in his treatment of rights as freedom and well-being: freedom as the necessary condition for truly human action; and well-being as both the condition and the purpose of the exercise of freedom, including life, physical, mental, and emotional integrity and security, access to truth and various other aspects of what combine to constitute a satisfying life in society which is claimed by, and for, so many people today.

Interestingly, however, while human rights can add useful precision to theories of the common good and to the aim of utilitarianism in its various forms, they also have a particularly powerful advantage in countering any utilitarian moves to sacrifice the individual person to the interests of the majority. For, as we have already noted (above pp. 79–80), it is one fatal weakness of utilitarianism that it is counter-intuitive in its unavoidable propensity to create victims of minorities, that is, of those unfortunates who do not happen at any particular time to belong to "the greatest number" whose greatest happiness is being studiedly pursued. O'Hear (1991: 274) expresses this well when he refers to those "who might find themselves at the bottom of the utilitarian heap, increasing the total sum of human happiness, to be sure, but not their own." By contrast, rights theory asserts that people should be treated as equals and are all entitled to equal respect and concern. In the fine phrase of Dworkin's (Waldron 1984: 153), as we have seen, "rights are trumps," and outrank calculations which, it may be claimed, will on balance make the community better off but only at the expense of some individuals.

This phrase of Dworkin's also illustrates the values of rights language by comparison with other ethical ideas and terms. This is what Hart (1982: 86) calls attention to, when he refers to "the peremptory character evident in the invocation of rights as justifying demands made on others." For reference to rights has a particular moral cutting edge, so that advocates of rights "see it as an important advantage that rights focus on an issue from the point of view of the victim or the oppressed, rather than from the perspective of those with power" (Almond 1993: 263). Talk of human rights also brings into play as a matter of course not just the idea of basic equality but also the influential idea of universality, with its implication that human rights must be immune to the demeaning behavior of petty local tyrants or bullies. As Habgood comments (1993: 100), "Rights which belong to human beings as such, whether conceived individually or socially or both together, can be pressed as overriding all other considerations, all excuses, all displays of power, and can do so in theory with the support of the whole international community." Hoffman and Rowe (2003: 10) make a salutary comment in this context when they maintain that "An interference with rights *always* needs to be justified."

Finally, human rights also offer a further major advantage in providing a powerful candidate for resolving in principle the debate between cultural diversity and transcultural ethical values. For a major characteristic of the modern human rights movement is that it is considered to apply to all human beings without exception around the globe, and regardless of many variables, including gender, ethnicity, caste, and culture, as we shall consider in more detail later (pp. 170–1). It does not follow from this that various human rights can simply be read off and applied in every culture without some adjustment and, indeed, some ethical maneuvering or casuistry in the light of local conditions and circumstances. But in principle, human rights theory claims, and with some measure of agreement and success, that there is common ethical ground to be found in the most diverse of countries and cultures. This appears to be more clearly the case when we can clarify and specify our understanding of the fullness of the human rights theory and consider the various difficulties and objections which are brought against it, as we have attempted to do in this chapter. With the intellectual ground thus cleared of such possible distractions it is now possible to focus in the following chapter on the most fundamental question which can be raised about them, how one goes about establishing human rights.

References

Almond, B. (1993), Rights, in Peter Singer (ed.), *A Companion to Ethics*, Oxford: Blackwell.

Archibugi, Daniele, and Koenig-Archibugi, Mathias (2003), Globalization, Democracy and Cosmopolis: a Bibliographical Essay, in Archibugi (ed.), *Debating Cosmopolitics*, London: Verso.

Aung San Suu Kyi (1992), In Quest of Democracy, *Journal of Democracy*, 2 (1).

Avineri, S., and de-Shalit, A. (1996) (eds.), *Communitarianism and Individualism*, Oxford: Oxford University Press.

Bellah, R. N., et al. (1985), *Habits of the Heart: Individualism and Commitment in American Life*, New York: Harper & Row.

Berlin, I. (1969), *Four Essays on Liberty*, Oxford: Oxford University Press.

Bobbio, N. (1996), *The Age of Rights*, trans. Allan Cameron, Cambridge: Polity Press.

Cohen, G. A. (1993), Equality of What? On Welfare, Goods, and Capabilities, in Nussbaum and Sen (1993).

Cooney, W. (1998), Rights Theory, in Ruth Chadwick (ed.), *Encyclopedia of Applied Ethics*, London: Academic Press.

Copleston, F. C. (1944), *A History of Philosophy*, vol. 1, London: Burns, Oates & Washbourne.

Costello, J. E. (2002), *John Macmurray: A Biography*, Edinburgh: Floris.

Craig, R. (1963), *Social Concern in the Thought of William Temple*, London: Victor Gollancz.

Cranston, M. (1973), *What are Human Rights?* New York: Taplinger.

de George, R. T. (1999), *Business Ethics*, 5th edn., Upper Saddle River, NJ: Prentice Hall.

Documents of the United Nations Conference on International Organization (1945), San Francisco: United Nations.

Donnelly, J. (2003), *Universal Human Rights in Theory and Practice*, 2nd rev. edn., Ithaca, NY: Cornell University Press.

Dowling, E. (2005), The Capability Approach and Human Rights, in Smith and van den Anker (2005).

Drinan, R. F. (2001), *The Mobilization of Shame: A World View of Human Rights*, New Haven, CT: Yale University Press.

Duncan-Jones, A. (1952), *Butler's Moral Philosophy*, Harmondsworth: Penguin.

Dworkin, R. (1978), *Taking Rights Seriously*, Cambridge, MA: Harvard University Press.

Dworkin, R. (1984), Rights as Trumps, in Waldron (1984).

Dworkin, R. (1990), *A Bill of Rights for Britain*, London: Chatto & Windus.

East Asian Pastoral Institute (1994), Report of a Human Rights Workshop, Manila, Philippines.

Etzioni, A. (1993), *The Spirit of Community: Rights, Responsibilities and the Communitarian Agenda*, New York: Crown.

Feinberg, J. (1980), *Rights, Justice and the Bounds of Liberty: Essays in Social Philosophy*, Princeton, NJ: Princeton University Press.

Fergusson, D. (1998), *Community, Liberalism and Christian Ethics*, Cambridge: Cambridge University Press.

Finnis, J. (1980), *Natural Law and Natural Rights*, Oxford: Clarendon Press.

Freeden, M. (1991), *Rights*, Milton Keynes: Open University Press.

Gewirth, A. (1993), Common Morality and the Community of Rights, in G. Outka and J. P. Reeder (eds.), *Prospects for a Common Morality*, Princeton, NJ: Princeton University Press.

Glendon, M. A. (1991), *Rights Talk: The Impoverishment of Political Discourse*, New York: Free Press.

Glendon, M. A. (2001), *A World Made New: Eleanor Roosevelt and the Universal Declaration of Human Rights*, New York: Random House.

Gorecki, J. (1996), *Justifying Ethics: Human Rights and Human Nature*, New Brunswick, NJ and London: Transaction Publishers.
Habermas, J. (1993), *Justification and Application: Remarks on Discourse Ethics*, Cambridge, MA: MIT Press.
Habgood, J. (1993), *Making Sense*, London: SPCK.
Harries, R. (1993), Human Rights in Theological Perspective, in R. Blackburn and J. Taylor (eds.), *Human Rights for the 1990s*, London: Mansell.
Harrison, R. (1983), *Bentham*, London: Routledge & Kegan Paul.
Hart, H. L. A. (1982), *Essays on Bentham: Jurisprudence and Political Theory*, Oxford: Clarendon Press.
Hawke, D. F. (1974), *Paine*, New York: W. W. Norton.
Henkin, L. (1990), *The Age of Rights*, New York: Columbia University Press.
Herbert, G. B. (2002), *A Philosophical History of Rights*, New Brunswick, NJ: Transaction Publishers.
Hoffman, D., and Rowe, J. (2003), *Human Rights in the UK: An Introduction to the Human Rights Act 1998*, Harlow: Pearson Longman.
Hohfeld, W. N. (1919), *Fundamental Legal Conceptions as Applied in Judicial Reasoning*, New Haven, CT: Yale University Press.
Human Rights Watch, World Report 1998, available from <http://www.hrw.org/research/worldreport.html> accessed Feb. 2006.
Jones, P. (1994), *Rights*, London: Macmillan.
Kearney, R. (1994) (ed.), *Continental Philosophy in the Twentieth Century*, London: Routledge.
Keeley, M. (1996), Community, the Joyful Sound, *Business Ethics Quarterly*, 6 (4).
Klug, F. (1996), A Bill of Rights as Secular Ethics, in Richard Gordon and Richard Wilmot-Smith (eds.), *Human Rights in the United Kingdom*, Oxford: Clarendon Press.
Klug, F. (2000), *Values for a Godless Age: The Story of the UK's New Bill of Rights*, London: Penguin.
MacIntyre, A. (1981), *After Virtue*, London: Duckworth.
Macmurray, J. (1995), *Persons in Relation*, new edn., intro. by Frank G. Fitzpatrick, London: Faber & Faber.
Mahoney, J. (1990), The Basis of Human Rights, in Charles E. Curran (ed.), *Moral Theology: Challenges for the Future*, New York: Paulist Press.
Mahoney, K. E., and Mahoney, P. (1993), *Human Rights in the Twenty-First Century: A Global Challenge*, Dordrecht: Martinus Nijhoff.
Maritain, J. (1940), *Scholasticism and Politics*, London: Bles.
Moltmann, J. (1990), Human Rights, the Rights of Humanity and the Rights of Nature, in Hans Küng and Jürgen Moltmann (eds.), *The Ethics of World Religions and Human Rights*, Concilium 1990/2, London: SCM Press.
Mulgan, G. (1995), Beyond the Lure of Off-the-Shelf Ethics, *The Independent* (Jan. 30).
Novak, Michael (1999), Human Dignity, Human Rights, *First Things*, 97 (Nov. 1999), 39–42.

Nussbaum, M., and Sen, A. (eds.) (1993), *The Quality of Life*, Oxford: Clarendon Press.

O'Hear, A. (1991), *What Philosophy Is*, London: Penguin.

O'Neill, O. (1986), *Faces of Hunger: An Essay on Poverty, Justice and Development*, London: Allen & Unwin.

O'Neill, O. (1996), *Towards Justice and Virtue: A Constructive Account of Practical Reasoning.*

O'Neill, O. (2000), *Bounds of Justice*, Cambridge: Cambridge University Press.

O'Neill, O. (2002), *A Question of Trust: The BBC Reith Lectures 2002*, Cambridge: Cambridge University Press.

Orend, B. (2002), *Human Rights: Concept and Context*, Peterborough, Ont.: Broadview Press.

Paine, L. S. (1996), Moral Thinking in Management: an Essential Capability, *Business Ethics Quarterly*, 6 (4).

Paine, T. (1984), *Rights of Man*, London: Penguin.

Phillips, D. R. (1993), *Looking Backward: A Critical Appraisal of Communitarian Thought*, Princeton, NJ: Princeton University Press.

Pogge, T. W. (2002), *World Poverty and Human Rights: Cosmopolitan Responsibilities and Reforms*, Cambridge: Polity Press.

Preston, R. H. (1983), *Church and Society in the Late Twentieth Century: The Economic and Political Task*, London: SCM.

Raes, K. (2002), The Philosophical Basis of Social, Economic and Cultural Rights, in P. Van der Auweraert, T. De Pelsmaeker, J. Sarkin, and J. Vande Lanotte (2002) (eds.), *Social, Economic and Cultural Rights: An Appraisal of Current European and International Developments*, Antwerp: Maklu, pp. 43–53.

Rawls, J. (1971), *A Theory of Justice*, Cambridge, MA: Harvard University Press.

Rawls, J. (1993), The Law of Peoples, in Shute and Hurley (1993).

Rawls, J. (1999), *The Law of Peoples*, Cambridge, MA: Harvard University Press.

Sassen, S. (2005), Global Civil Society and Human Rights, in Smith and van den Anker (2005).

Selbourne, D. (1997), *The Principle of Duty*, London: Abacus.

Sen, A. (1988), *On Ethics and Economics*, Oxford: Blackwell.

Sen, A. (1997), Economics, Business Principles and Moral Sentiments, *Business Ethics Quarterly*, 7 (3).

Sen, A. (1999), *Development as Freedom*, Oxford: Oxford University Press.

Sen, A. (1993), Capability and Well-being, in Nussbaum and Sen (1993).

Shue, H. (1996), *Basic Rights: Subsistence, Affluence, and U.S. Foreign Policy*, 2nd rev. edn., Princeton, NJ: Princeton University Press.

Shute, S., and Hurley, S. (1993) (eds.), *On Human Rights: The Oxford Amnesty Lectures 1993*, New York: Basic Books.

Singer, P. (2004), *One World: The Ethics of Globalization*, 2nd edn., New Haven, CT: Yale University Press.

Smith, R. K. M., and van den Anker, C. (2005) (eds.), *The Essentials of Human Rights*, London: Hodder Arnold.

Stirk, P. M. R., and Weigall, D. (1995), *An Introduction to Political Ideas*, London: Pinter, Cassell.

Sullivan, L. H. (1998), *Moving Mountains: The Principles and Purposes of Leon Sullivan*, Valley Forge, PA: Judson Press, Baptist Church of America.

Sumner, L. W. (2000), Rights, in H. LaFollette (2000) (ed.), *The Blackwell Guide to Ethical Theory*, Oxford: Blackwell.

Teilhard de Chardin (1975), *The Phenomenon of Man*, intro. by Sir Julian Huxley Collins, London: Collins Fontana.

Temple, W. (1987), *Christianity and Social Order*, London: Shepheard-Walwyn and SPCK.

Tierney, B. (1997), *The Idea of Natural Rights: Studies on Natural Rights, Natural Law and Church Law 1150–1625*, Atlanta, GA: Emory University.

Twiss, S. B. (1998), Religion and Human Rights: A Comparative Perspective, in Twiss and B. Grelle (eds.), *Explorations in Global Ethics: Comparative Religious Ethics and Interreligious Dialogue*, Oxford: Westview Press.

The United Nations and Human Rights 1945–1995 (1995), intro. by Boutros Boutros-Ghali, Secretary-General of the United Nations, New York: Department of Public Information, United Nations.

United Nations, Charter of the (1995), New York: Department of Public Information, United Nations.

UN Commission on Human Rights (1985), *Right and Responsibility of Individuals to Promote and Protect Human Rights*, New York: United Nations.

United Nations Records (1948), Official Records of the Third Session of the General Assembly, Part I, Third Committee, vol. IIIA (6).

Vardy, P., and Grosch, P. (1994), *The Puzzle of Ethics*, London: Fount, Harper Collins.

Waldron, J. (1984) (ed.), *Theories of Rights*, Oxford: Oxford University Press.

Waldron, J. (1987) (ed.), *Nonsense upon Stilts*, London: Methuen.

Walker, S. (1998), *The Rights Revolution: Rights and Community in Modern America*, New York and Oxford: Oxford University Press.

White, A. R. (1985), *Rights*, Oxford: Clarendon Press.

Chapter ④

Establishing Human Rights

In the previous chapter we have aimed to clarify various aspects of human rights and to consider the major criticisms which have been and are raised against them, and we have also identified the positive advantages of the theory. In this chapter we aim to consider what basis might be advanced for claiming that such human rights actually exist, and to examine the major approaches which have been pursued or can be proposed to provide a philosophical or rational basis for them.

A Matter of Belief

How are human rights to be understood today? From our historical analysis and contemporary perceptions it can be proposed that human rights have the characteristic of being personal entitlements, or qualities, or more accurately what Grotius and Suarez described as powers (whether legal or moral, or both) possessed by a human person which justifies that person in making certain claims, again legal or moral or both, on others. If this is accepted as an adequate description of what a human right is, then the question unavoidably arises of what reason or reasons can be advanced to establish the existence of these personal entitlements ascribed by definition to all human beings.

Historically, it is clear that human rights are considered to spring from two sources, human nature and, behind nature, a divine creator. Much of ancient Greek thought, and Roman after it, was permeated by the idea of a divine force controlling human events, as we have seen in our consideration of Stoicism. As Copleston (1944: 395) observed, "the ethical end . . . according to the Stoics, consists essentially in submission to the divinely appointed order of the world." More broadly, Gadamer has observed that "the magnificence of Greek metaphysics was that it

sought reason in the cosmos; it sought the *nous*, which is at work order-
ing and distinguishing in all the formations of nature" (Gadamer 1981:
35). But this cosmic *nous* was concerned not just with the material, but
also with the moral. Writing of the combination of morality with theology, Kitto notes (1991: 197) that among the Greeks "certain offences
which human law could not punish or men detect were placed under
divine sanction . . . The powers . . . that rule the physical universe must
also rule the moral universe." It is within this context of overarching
divine power that we can better understand not only the appeal of
Antigone to laws higher than the mere human dictates of Creon (see
above, p. 2), but also the recognition by Aristotle and those who came
after him of a form of cosmic "natural justice" superior to all purely
social agreements (see above, p. 2). In Cicero, too, one can identify the
presence of a divine power underlying morality and "natural law," and
this was taken up by early Christian thinkers, beginning with St Paul
and developed especially through Aquinas, up to the Reformation and
beyond (see above, pp. 3–5).

Thus, it was quite natural for the founders and exponents of the
classical natural rights movement of the eighteenth century to develop
their thinking within a more or less explicit religious context, and
to base their arguments for natural rights ultimately on a belief in a
creator god. Since God creates all human beings and wants them to
behave freely in such a way as to achieve their ultimate divinely planned
destiny, it follows that God equips every human creature with all the
necessary means to fulfill that destiny, including the ability to make
appropriate moral demands on their fellow human beings to enable
each human creature to attain in time and in eternity to their destined
fulfillment.

For Locke, as we have seen, the rules made by human beings in
society must be conformable to "the law of nature, that is, to the will
of God, of which that is a declaration" (above, p. 20). As we have also
seen Laslett observe (1963: 95), for Locke natural law "was at one and
the same time a command of God, a rule of reason, and a law in the
very nature of things as they are." Moreover, as Jeremy Waldron has
gone to considerable lengths to establish, Locke based his belief in basic
human equality, a central component of the idea of natural rights, ultimately on his Christian belief in creation (Waldron 2002). It was his
religious beliefs, then, acting in parallel with his drawing on the Aristotelian, medieval, and scholastic thinking on natural law, like others
before him, which provided Locke with the resources to address the
contemporary political and social situation in England, and in the
process to combine the traditional idea that the natural law enjoins

certain morally right actions with the portentous development that it also confers certain moral rights.

Belief in a creative deity also undergirded the thinking of Tom Paine in his impassioned defense of human rights, justifying the verdict on him as "a deist who insisted on the sovereignty of reason and on the equal rights of all men" (Copleston 1966: 260). As we noted, Paine took up Burke's incautious claims that social structures found their origin in tradition by insisting on logically pursuing this quest of tradition "till we come to the divine origin of the rights of man at the creation" (above, p. 28). And, of course, the formal appeal to a divine origin of human rights forms an eloquent strand in the Jeffersonian cadences of the American Declaration of Independence, in which the entitlement of Britain's colonies to seize self-rule is firmly based, in the Declaration's preamble, on "the Laws of Nature and of Nature's God"; and its most famous sentence affirms, as an opening foundation, "we hold these truths to be self-evident, that all men are created equal, that they are endowed by their Creator with certain unalienable rights . . ." (see above, p. 23).

On the influence of religion on Jefferson's argument in the Declaration, Max Beloff comments that he was by this time "emancipated" from the Christianity of his youth and was, even "if a deist rather than the atheist which his political enemies were later to see in him, disposed in the political as in the moral field to seek a sanction for his beliefs in the unaided operations of the human reason alone" (Bellof 1948: 67). Beloff appears to be seeking in these and other ways to diminish the influence which religion exercised on the mind of Jefferson in constructing his argument to justify human rights, but he is less than successful in this attempt. One indication that religion was a central factor in Jefferson's thinking is evident from the fact that the final text was changed in certain respects from the stronger religious draft which had been first produced by Jefferson and which had included reference to "the *Christian* king" of Great Britain violating nature's "most sacred rights of life and liberty" by engaging in an African slave trade which was "the opprobrium of *Infidel* powers," a charge dropped out of deference to some of the American states which supported the slave trade (Koch 1964: 133). Stronger confirmation that religious arguments played an important part in Jefferson's thought on human rights is provided by the passage in his earlier *Summary View of the Rights of British America* in which he had delivered himself of the religious affirmation that "The God who gave us life, gave us liberty at the same time" (pp. 135–6).

To modern readers of the Jeffersonian Declaration there is a further consideration to be taken to mind, not just the ascribing of rights to a divine creator but also the claim that the truths enunciated are "self-evident." As Beloff observes (1948: 69), "The reader of the Declaration of Independence must even now be on his guard against the compelling qualities of Jefferson's literary style. The truths which he calls self-evident were not self-evident at all either to his contemporaries or to later generations." Perhaps, the claim that the truths affirmed in the Declaration are "self-evident" may be evidence of Jefferson's adherence to the "common sense" theory of ethics which postulated a special moral faculty or "moral sense" enabling one simply to intuit without argumentation how one ought to behave in various situations (Koch 1964: 15). As Koch points out (p. 18), Jefferson wrote on one occasion of "that moral sense of right and wrong, which, like the sense of tasting and feeling in every man, makes a part of his nature." On another occasion he wrote of natural rights that "for the reality of these principles I appeal to the true fountain of evidence, the head and heart of every rational and honest man. It is there nature has written her moral laws, and where every man may read them for himself" (p. 145).

The philosophical drawbacks of such moral intuitionism have been well rehearsed in modern times, as we shall consider later; and added to this vulnerability of intuitionism as a means of moral knowledge, there is in the case of the Jeffersonian Declaration the further particular problem of identifying precisely what it is about "these truths" that makes them self-evident, and therefore in no need of rational argument to justify them. It does not seem sufficient simply to accept them as self-justifying claims in the way in which Susan Shell explains that "the Declaration of Independence explicitly presents itself as deriving from universal and self-evident principles of justice and, hence, as constituting a potential model to the world" (Shell 1990: 259). However, as Shell herself concludes (p. 283), "In an intellectual climate like our own, in which it has become easy to dismiss the liberal rights doctrine as an expression of cultural imperialism or bourgeois ideology or democratic decadence, the appeal to self-evidence may no longer be enough."

If what is self evident is the fact that all men are born equal, understanding "created" in a weak sense of coming into existence, as Beloff does (1948: 69), such a statement is manifestly not true, far less obviously true, in the face of the physical, mental, and social disparities and inequalities with which individual human beings do as a matter of fact begin their lives. On the other hand, if the proposition is understood in the strong sense that all human beings are actually created equal by God and this requires no proof, then this might be thought to imply that the existence of a creator god is itself self-evident and in no need of any justification, a position which is difficult to sustain. Perhaps, however, it is to be understood in the sense that, if a divine creator exists, or if one believes in the existence of God, which is not in itself necessarily self-evident, it obviously follows that God will create all members of the human family as basically equal in certain fundamental respects which can be identified as natural rights. Such appears to be the most plausible interpretation of the opening claim of the American Declaration of Independence, which we have just seen Jefferson describe as the "expression of the American mind," and which was uttered among a people by whom the Christian religion was by and large taken for granted. Copleston notes that "Jefferson himself simply assumed that the statement that all men are endowed by their Creator with certain inalienable rights is a matter of common sense. That is to say, common reason sees that it must be true, without any need of proof, though, once its truth has been recognized, moral and social conclusions can be drawn from it" (Copleston 1966: 261).

Religious sentiments also lay behind the French Declaration of the Rights of Man and of the Citizen, which followed in the wake of the American Declaration of Independence in expressing its claims for "natural, imprescriptible and inalienable rights" in a religious context and in basing them on a religious premise: "The National Assembly recognizes and declares, in the presence of the Supreme Being, and with the hope of his blessing and favour the following sacred rights of men and of citizens . . ." (Melden 1970: 140). It is surprising, then, to find Trigg describe the French Declaration as an "atheist creed" refusing to appeal to a creator to underwrite the equality and intrinsic worth of human beings (Trigg 2005: 161). We can question, of course, how sincerely held at the time, or respected in the aftermath, were such religious sentiments invoking the divine presence and witness on the Assembly's actions and characterizing natural rights as sacred, implying their origin in the divine work of creation. Yet our concern here is not with sincerity nor with consistency of behavior, but with the types and force of arguments which are proposed in justification of a doctrine of human rights.

There is no doubt, we can conclude, that one major strand of thought common to the succession of various claims for natural justice and natural rights, from ancient Greece to the eighteenth century, was a more or less explicitly religious one. What is perhaps not generally appreciated as following from this is that the traditional concept of natural law, viewed as the moral requirements entailed by human nature, as distinct from international law deriving its force from general consensus, is originally, and basically, not a philosophical, but a theological, concept. Bentham had a point when he expostulated, in rejecting natural law, that a law stipulating ways of behaving needs a lawgiver behind it.

Starting thus from a religious belief in a creating deity, it is simple to construct a logical argument in favor of human rights. The question has to be considered, however, to what extent human rights can be established without recourse to such a religious form of argument (see Bucar and Barnett 2005). As Shestack (2000: 36) observed, "When human beings are not visualized in God's image then their basic rights may well lose their metaphysical *raison d'être*." In this connection it is interesting to trace through the minutes of the meetings of the Human Rights Commission and of the Economic and Social Council of the United Nations as it debated whether or not human rights should be explicitly and formally recognized in the Universal Declaration as deriving from a divine creation of human nature (for example, UN Records 1948: 109–17). After prolonged discussion it was finally agreed to exclude all reference to a divine origin of human rights from the Declaration's opening article, which finally ran, "All human beings are born free and equal in dignity and rights. They are endowed with reason and conscience, and should act towards one another in a spirit of brotherhood" (UN Universal Declaration 1948, art. 1).

An Essential Requirement

In the event, then, the Human Rights Commission decided not to go down the religious or theological road, any more than the opening of the UN Charter had done, recognizing that this would not be universally acceptable, and preferring to look for alternative ways of introducing and validating the subject of human rights which would have more general, indeed, universal, acceptance. In point of fact, they chose to argue the case for human rights by seeming to present them as the indispensable means of bringing about and maintaining world peace. Thus, the founding Charter of the United Nations (*UN Charter* 1995), which clearly manifests that human rights are going to be central to the entire United Nations project, sets out its four ends of avoiding any further war, of reaffirming faith in fundamental human rights, of establishing conditions for justice and respect for treaties, and of producing a better society.

The expressed determination to "reaffirm faith" in human rights is striking and significant. The paragraph is not formally an argument for human rights, nor even an act of simply proclaiming its faith in them. It *reaffirms* faith in human rights, that is, a faith in human rights which was previously held but which now needs reaffirming because of, or better, in spite of, the dispiriting events of recent history. It expresses a human act of joint faith, a shared conviction of their indispensable importance for the future of humanity if history is not tragically to repeat itself. Falk (2000: 37) makes the interesting remark that the reason for the UN's focusing such attention on human rights was not solely because of the shocking revelations which emerged towards the end of the war of the atrocities which had been inflicted on innocent millions of people by the Nazi regime. The attention also arose, he suggests, from "the surfacing of a vague aura of guilt hovering over Western liberal democracies. This guilt was associated with their prolonged forbearance in relation to Nazi Germany so long as Hitler's atrocious crimes were directed at his own citizenry." If Falk is correct, then any sense of remorse for things left undone by the other Western powers could well have added fervor to their claim now that they were "reaffirming" their faith in human rights.

In this opening section of the initial UN Charter there might appear to be conviction more than argument concerning human rights. However, there is also an indication of an argument that acceptance of human rights is the only means to secure justice and create a better world. And this argument for human rights in terms of the results hoped for appears to be borne out in the Universal Declaration itself, where the preamble contends not only that barbarisms in the past have been the result of disregard and contempt for human rights, but also that for the future, "recognition of the inherent dignity and of the equal and inalienable rights of all members of the human family is the foundation of freedom, justice and peace in the world." It may appear, then, that the Universal Declaration's argument for human rights is based on the favorable consequences which their observance will bring about, a line of reasoning which appears to be not far from a rule-utilitarian expression of the argument by which John Stuart Mill justified the existence of rights claims on the ground of their utility (Mill 1973: 309; see above, pp. 31–3). If this is the case, then such a rule-utilitarian, or consequentialist, argument for human rights must suffer from the weaknesses generally ascribed to utilitarianism and to the broader theory of consequentialism of which utilitarianism is the best-known instance (see Crisp 1997: 181).

In defense, however, of the case for human rights used in the UN Universal Declaration against a charge of rule-utilitarianism, counter-considerations can be advanced. One of these is that consequentialism, of which utilitarianism is one type, allows for more than one way of considering an action whose morality is allegedly determined purely by its consequences. It can proceed by including the deed itself among all the consequences which follow from it, rather than postulating a discontinuity between the deed and what comes next. This is what enables Sen, for example, to note the possibility of "seeing consequences in very broad terms, including the value of actions performed" (Sen 1988: 75), an inclusive view of consequences which follows from Sen's earlier stipulation that consequentialism requires that every choice "be ultimately determined by the goodness of the consequent state of affairs" (p. 39), a state of affairs which includes the choice itself as well as its results.

Sen elsewhere (1988a: 196–7) invokes this expanded view of consequentialism and applies it to human rights in a manner pertinent to our consideration of the case for human rights proposed by the United Nations. He refers to the possibility of introducing "fulfilment and non-realization of rights in the evaluation of states of affairs" and remarks that incorporating realization of rights into such an evaluation is "perfectly natural" in various contexts, exemplifying this by recalling the judgment that the stage of Emergency Rule in India was a bad one because many people had their rights violated. As he comments, "this is a statement about a state of affairs, and it does include the violation of rights directly in the evaluation of the state. Statements like this can be used in a consequential analysis of actions, and this will translate the importance of fulfilment and violation of rights from the evaluation of states of affairs to that of actions."

A further consideration which can strengthen this expanded view of including a specific action within the overall scenario of the whole resulting situation emerges from considering the nature of the link between the action and its distinct consequences. In the case of respecting human rights what might be regarded as the "consequences" of justice and peace are intrinsically connected with the action itself, to such an extent that it is, in fact, difficult to separate the respect for human rights from the "resulting" justice and peace. Similarly, Sen's description of the state of affairs during the stage of Emergency Rule in India, as "a bad one because so many rights of so many people were violated" (1988: 197) obviously includes an intrinsic relation between the violation of rights and the bad state of affairs, to such an extent as to make distinguishing between them very difficult. In fact, it may now be suggested, in this example offered by Sen, as in the UN case for the existence of human rights, the argument is actually *not* a consequentialist one, even in the expanded sense of consequentialism described by Sen.

In his classic theologico-political study of the Roman empire, *The City of God*, Augustine of Hippo (354–430) explored the order to be found existing in various things, including the human individual, nature, and society, and he identified an aspect of that order, its settled nature or its serenity, as peace, concluding with the inductive definition that "peace is the tranquillity of order" (*pax omnium rerum tranquillitas ordinis*) (Augustine 1972; bk. 19, ch. 13, p. 870). In so doing, Augustine was not asserting that peace is the consequence of the order to be found in society, or that preserving the social order leads to peace as one of its results. He was in fact *identifying* peace with social order looked at from a particular point of view: its tranquillity, its calmness, its lack of agitation or absence of dis-order.

In a similar manner, it seems possible to consider respect for human rights to be not an action which results in justice and peace, but an action which is actually one of justice and peace; just as in Sen's Indian example the violation of human rights would not be an action which led to a bad state of affairs: it would *be* the bad state of affairs. This appears to be the approach of the United Nations in its statement on human rights. It may or may not be significant that it does not describe respect for human rights as the cause of "freedom, justice and peace," or that this desirable state of affairs is identified as the result of respect for human rights. It states that such recognition "is the foundation of freedom, justice and peace in the world," which could be interpreted as observing that the aggregation of individual acts of respect for human rights throughout the world in itself constitutes a situation of worldly freedom, justice, and peace. If so, then the UN case for human rights cannot be described, or faulted, as a consequentialist one, far less a utilitarian one, and it becomes unnecessary to argue that it is possible to reconcile human rights with consequentialism, as Sumner claims to do (1987). It appears accurate to describe the UN statement as what linguistic philosophy would term an "ostensive" statement, pointing to human rights as an instance and an essential requirement of what is meant by world freedom, justice, and peace. Just as peace, according to Augustine, is one way of looking at order, likewise universal respect for human rights is simply one way of looking at universal freedom, justice, and peace.

The Nature of Persons

As one considers other lines of argument which have been, and are, invoked to establish human rights, the traditional one, based on natural law and on a shared human nature, has had a long and distinguished history and is not without its supporters today, even in its secularized post-Grotian form of prescinding totally from its religious origin. The most distinguished exponent of this line of argument was Jacques Maritain, whose reflections on the nature of persons we have considered in the previous chapter (pp. 99–100), and who remarked that, quite apart from any Christian considerations, "belief in human nature and in the freedom of the human being . . . is in itself sufficient to convince us that there is an unwritten law, and to assure us that natural law is something as real in the moral realm as the laws of growth and senescence in the physical" (Maritain 1986: 141–2). Moreover, "natural law and the light of moral conscience within us do not prescribe merely things to be done and not to be done; they also recognize rights, in particular rights linked to the very nature of man" (Maritain 1986: 144).

However, not everyone has what Maritain termed "belief in human nature," and it seems fairly obvious that, in spite of his attempt to abstract here from his theology, his remarks on natural law and human rights are in fact offered against a backdrop of a religious belief in creation. The same idea of divine creation, and especially the creation of a single human nature for a purpose, or creation with a design, underlies his contention (1986: 140–1) that "possessed of a nature, being constituted in a given, determinate fashion, man obviously possesses ends which correspond to his natural constitution and which are the same for all – as all pianos, for instance, whatever their particular type and in whatever spot they may be, have as their end the production of certain attuned sounds."

The analogy with a piano and its built-in purpose, which Maritain uses to illustrate the force of the argument about the end of nature, in fact betrays certain religious presuppositions in his position, notably that of cosmic finality, which MacDonald was not slow to point out and to reject:

> Men do not share a fixed nature, nor, therefore, are there any ends which they must necessarily pursue in fulfilment of such nature. There is no definition of "man." There is a more or less vague set of properties which characterize in varying degrees and proportions those creatures which are called "human" . . . There is no end set for the human race by an abstraction called "human nature." There are only ends which individuals choose, or are forced by circumstances to accept. There are none which they *must* accept. Men are not created for a purpose as a piano is built to produce certain sounds. Or if they are, we have no idea of the purpose.   (MacDonald 1984: 30)

MacDonald expressed forcefully the dilemma facing natural law theorists with the demise of a belief that the universe possesses a divinely instilled purpose and destiny. Stout explains that natural law theory in its traditional form . . . seemed plausible so long as natural philosophy conceived of the cosmos in a moralized, teleological fashion. But when the teleological cosmos gave way to the impersonal and infinite universe of modern science, scientific and ethical realism tended to break apart, and ethical theorists predisposed towards realism had to work hard at finding something suitably real and natural for moral sentences to correspond to. (Stout 1992: 95)

The consequence, as he rightly saw, is that "traditional natural law theory becomes increasingly nostalgic in tone and quixotic in performance" (p. 95).

Quite apart from an explicit or implicit theological approach to the subject, other attempts to appeal to nature as a basis for human rights equally lack plausibility. One of the most respected exponents of human rights in the last century, Maurice Cranston, was well aware of the difficulties of justifying human rights, yet he does not seem sensitive to any difficulty in expounding Locke's claims for natural rights to life, liberty, and property. He explains:

natural rights begin as a claim which everyone naturally makes. Nobody wants to die a violent death, or to suffer an injury. These aversions are so universally and so intensely felt that we speak of them as natural. Man has a natural desire to survive, a natural impulse to defend himself from death and injury. . . . there is no denying that the desire to stay alive is, generally speaking, man's paramount wish, and the one that demands from others their most unfailing respect. To say that man has a right to life is to convert that demand into a kind of moral imperative, that is, to impose on all men a reciprocal duty to abstain from injuring their neighbours. (Cranston 1973: 25)

As so stated by Cranston, the argument for everyone's having a natural "right to life" begins from the alleged fact that every human being has a profound "natural" aversion to dying. No doubt Sir Thomas Browne was not alone in expressing a distaste for death when he commented, "I am not so much afraid of death, as ashamed thereof. 'Tis the very disgrace and ignominy of our natures" (Browne 1909: 40). It does not follow, however, as Cranston claims, that such a deep desire in every individual, or what Aristotle and Aquinas would have called such a basic "natural inclination," automatically creates in others a corresponding moral duty to respect that desire. We appear to have here an instance of what has been termed Hume's law, or the "naturalistic" fallacy, which moves effortlessly from a description of how things regularly are to a moral claim that this is how things ought to be. As

Waldron explains it (1984: 3), "the idea of *natural* rights is seen as a particularly glaring example of the 'Naturalistic Fallacy,' purporting to derive certain norms or evaluations from descriptive premises about human nature." The reasoning proposed here by Cranston can be logically saved only if we understand that it contains a latent minor premise which would disclose it as a theological argument, to the effect that: this is how things are; *this is how the creator wills them to be*; therefore, this is how they ought to be. In then examining the Lockean right to liberty Cranston (1973: 31) succumbs to the naturalistic fallacy in a similar manner, and he then argues for a natural right to property from its being a necessary means to observing the natural right to life (pp. 48–50), so that its fortunes stand or fall with the latter.

Among contemporary writers Roger Trigg offers an uncompromising, yet ultimately dissatisfying, case for basing human rights on human nature and natural law. He shows awareness of the ambiguities of the term "natural," of objections raised against the idea of any fixed, or shared, human nature, and of the naturalistic fallacy of moving from the way things are to prescribing that this is how they should be or should remain (Trigg 2005: 9–14). He is also aware that "the concept of natural law is as ambiguous as any other use of the term 'natural'" (p. 14), and that the physical laws of nature describe regularities, whereas natural law is used prescriptively, "telling us what we ought to be doing, rather than just what usually happens" (p. 21).

One may regard with sympathy Trigg's epistemological claim that "without a common humanity there would be no basic standard to which we could appeal to enable us to understand each other, whether within the confines of our own society or across cultures and societies" (Trigg 2005: 27). Yet one may wonder how he establishes that such a "common humanity" has a metaphysical basis and is morally normative, as it must be for natural law to have any meaning. Trigg's answer is invariably in terms of what is good for humans and what is bad (pp. 28–30): "we cannot pretend . . . that going against the grain of nature will not carry its costs. There are norms for living a properly functioning human life" (p. 32). However, his argument proceeds well beyond the realm of harmful consequences and begs a multitude of questions when he explains that

> many would feel that there is something intrinsically wrong with doing something unnatural, and that there is an intrinsic danger in going against the grain of nature. It is not just that bad consequences tend to happen sometimes. The very act, whatever it may be, disrupts natural processes in ways that may well be harmful, but may be unforeseeable.

As such it involves a level of risk that cannot be assessed by utilitarian criteria, but should itself be a warning. (p. 36)

Trigg (2005: 43) is clear that any idea of universal human rights "has to be linked to the very idea of being human," but his way of proceeding appears to be more that of offering reflections around salient ideas regarding human rights or of repeating broad claims about them than of establishing by argument just what they are, and how they derive, as he claims, from natural law. In the later chapters of his work he contrasts the competing claims for Christianity and for reason as providing sure ground for the universality of human nature and for nature and human rights acting as guides to moral action (pp. 154–7). It is not surprising to discover then that he finds Christianity more congenial as a source of moral knowledge, but it is revealing when he further asks "does it then follow that human rights must be grounded in theistic belief?" (p. 156), a question which he appears inclined to answer in the affirmative, although he does not really provide a clear reply in his subsequent reflections (pp. 156–9, 161–2).

Another approach to educing human rights from human nature seems to be latent in *The Realm of Rights*, in which Thomson (1990: 32–3) argues that we possess "natural" claims, whose source "has to consist in some feature of *us*, and we need to know what it is." Her eventual identification of this peculiarly human feature is that we each have "inherently individual interests, and that is a deep fact about us" (p. 221). In so far as Thomson, then, identifies the source of what she calls natural rights, such as life and liberty, this appears to be a deep constitutive feature of being human. In particular it appears for her to be the feature of being a human individual: that is, similar to others yet significantly distinct from others, not just a member of a beehive or an ant heap. As such, one is capable of having "inherently individual interests" which are capable of generating natural rights and moral claims upon others (pp. 219–23).

Commenting on Thomson's approach to human rights, Sumner describes it not so much as proceeding from the human constitution, as her argument has been summarized here, as being "intuitionist or casuistical" (Sumner 2000: 299), that is, assuming that there are principles underlying the kinds of rights we recognize, yet appealing to our "considered moral judgements" about particular cases. "Because she expects general agreement with these judgments, she makes no attempt to show that they are true" (p. 300), but is happy to draw from them implications for people's rights. The basic problem of her approach, Sumner concludes, is that "the argumentative structure she erects is clearly only as secure as its foundations, and those foundations consist of particular moral judgments whose truth is taken for granted" (p. 300). This judgment by Sumner, however, appears to concentrate only on Thomson's procedure, and does not take account of her attempts to establish a more metaphysical, "nature"-based, ground for rights based on the human individuality she comes to identify. Even given that in her support, however, it is not made clear, any more than in the arguments proposed by Cranston, why one's deep individual interests should constitute a basis for one's being morally justified in calling for appropriate action on the part of others.

Explicitly humanist writings, it might be thought, should provide a fruitful source for assessing the possibility of establishing human rights in a non-religious context, and it is interesting to find that a standard work on anti-religious humanism makes much of the central importance of human rights within the humanist ethical position. As Fowler writes,

> underpinning Humanist values is the ethic of support for the individual rights of all human beings. Every human being has a right to personal security, to adequate food and health care, to a home that provides sufficient warmth and economic comfort and to personal freedom – particularly the freedom to pursue the goals that are personally important in life, and which develop individual potential and promote individual progress. These are the kinds of ethical principles that inform Humanism's vision of a moral, equitable and stable society.　(1999: 214)

The work, however, is disappointing in that it does not appear to be aware that the establishing of human rights is a particular problem; and it offers no attempt to provide any justification for them.

A social approach to providing a basis for human rights is to be found in the work of MacDonald (1984: 34–40), whom we have already met criticizing Maritain. So far as concerns her own view, she concludes that " 'natural rights' are the conditions of a good society. But what those conditions are is not given by nature or mystically bound up with the essence of man and his inevitable goal, but is determined by human decisions." In fact, she maintains, propositions about human rights are actually instances of value utterances "which are more like records of *decisions* than propositions." Of course, one can ask, and MacDonald does, what reasons or grounds one might have for taking such decisions. What is involved, she suggests, is not strict proof or evidence, but something more like a form of advocacy, aiming to impress and convince, but not to prove. She concludes, "there are no certainties in the field of values. For there are no true or false beliefs about values, but only better or worse decisions and choices. And to encourage the better decisions we need to employ devices which are artistic rather than scientific."

MacDonald, then, is in agreement that some element of objectivity is relevant to human rights, as a basis for a proposition expressing them, or in her view leading to a "decision" to favor them. However, while she is clear that "whatever its emotional causes and effects, an articulate utterance . . . says something," and, where human rights are concerned, says something with an objective base, she is at a loss to account for what this would be, and why it would give credence to interpreting an objective situation in one way rather than another to justify one's moral decisions.

Very much of a mind with MacDonald, whom he quotes approvingly, Herbert claims in a typically sweeping generalization that "the rights issue addressed by philosophy today concerns not so much the *nature* of rights as it concerns what we *mean* when we *assert* that someone has a *human* right. The ontology of rights has been dissolved into the logic of rights talk" (Herbert 2002: 324). Expressing his sympathy for MacDonald's view at a late stage in his history of human rights, which then helps to explain his own agenda, Herbert explains that "the term 'natural was not so much descriptive as it was exclamatory . . . It was all word play, even then." So much so, notes Herbert, that, given that "the philosophical community" has accepted MacDonald's linguistic interpretation, "the current practical, philosophical viewpoint that dominates rights theory today . . . is that we need to employ moral terms and rights language in order to persuade the world of the 'truth' (moral importance) of our moral ideals." In other words, "the current debate . . . is primarily concerned with which linguistic usages best serve the moral needs of the world" (p. 325).

That is, one has to reply, if one belongs to the "analytical and post-modern segments" of the philosophical community (Herbert 2002: 341), which Herbert appears to identify as a majority which includes most human rights philosophers. Otherwise one might beg to differ, to maintain that the whole human rights project campaigning for a better world is considerably more than "word play," and that perhaps more philosophers than Herbert realizes are committed to this real and cognitivist interpretation of human rights. In the circumstances the observation might be permitted that, as the post-World War II development of nuclear weaponry and of technological advances in modern medicine helped to coax Anglo-Saxon philosophers out of their linguistic fastness and "the narrowly language-oriented agenda of analytical metaethics" (Darwall et al. 1992: 123), to make important and valuable contributions to the analysis and discussion of public policies on modern war and on modern health care, likewise the urgent modern concern for human rights, aroused by their blatant abuse and the continuous need to remedy human sufferings, has called the verbal bluff – and, especially in a post-Rawlsian universe, is in process of outdating it – that human rights is all about, or is nothing but, matters of linguistic usage.

Another at first sight traditional approach to finding a justification for human rights is offered by Mackie when he impressively constructs a fundamental right of all persons to choose progressively how they shall live. However, this turns out to be what might be called an "adoptive" approach to rights, when he explains, "I am not claiming that it is objectively valid, or that its validity can be found out by reason: I am merely adopting it and recommending it for general adoption as a moral principle" (Mackie 1984: 176). In fact, such an approach is consistent with the position taken by Mackie in his systematic work, *Ethics* (1977), to which he gave the revealing subtitle *Inventing Right and Wrong*, in which he maintains that there are no objective moral values. As he argues there (1977: 173), "although most people in making moral judgements implicitly claim, among other things, to be pointing to something objectively prescriptive, these claims are all false." This then strangely involves him (p. 173) in observing, on the one hand, that the notion of rights is "valuable and indeed vital" to the good life, but then concluding that "my rejection of objective values carries with it the denial that there are any self-subsistent rights."

A similar subjective approach is to be found in the writings of John Charvet, who explained that rights are the collective construct of society concerned to "express the equal value of the members . . . expressing the equal respect of each member for the others as free or autonomous beings" (Charvet 1995: 193). He denied, however, that "the idea of the respect owed to persons as free beings can be demanded on the basis of their inherent worth," or that there is "an objective value inhering in human beings that has the property of calling forth our respect," while nevertheless giving significance to the idea of human rights as resulting from "a special existential commitment to subordinate our self-interest to the idea of equality" (Charvet 2001: 13).

One does not, however, have to subscribe to a subjectivist approach to ethics to take an adoptive approach to human rights. One might be quite clear that there are objective moral values, that some types of behavior are right and others wrong irrespective of how we think of them, and that there may well be such things as human rights; and yet find it difficult to establish their existence as a matter of fact. What appears to be a similar adoptive approach to that of Mackie, although not one based on ethical subjectivism, is described by Paul Sieghart in his commentary on the International Legal Code on Human Rights, where he explains that

> philosophers and others have debated for many centuries about the concept of "rights" . . . Those debates still continue; indeed, they can have no final conclusion, since different starting points and different paths of reasoning will necessarily lead to different results – including those of Hitler and Stalin. It was precisely to overcome this uncertainty that the international community established its agreed legal code – much as scientists and engineers have established internationally agreed standards of measurement such as the metre and the gram, in order to short-circuit further disputes about miles, leagues, ells, pounds, ounces, and grains. (Sieghart 1985: pp. ix–x)

What this line of approach amounts to is an agreement, or a stipulation, among various parties that, given a state of uncertainty about human rights, certain things shall exist henceforth as a class of human rights which apply to all human individuals by virtue of their belonging to the human race. In itself such an agreement provides no indication of why it is these things that are chosen as rights rather than any others. The point, at least as indicated by Sieghart's analogy, is simply to fix on some settled norm in order to remove confusion and secure agreement in various situations of potential conflict. It is not a matter of reaching a shared recognition that such human rights do exist; it is a matter of agreeing to stipulate that such human rights shall exist from now on.

A professedly "dialectical" approach to establishing human rights has been developed by Gewirth by way of logical analysis of the conditions for acting in a free and purposive manner. These conditions comprise the agent's freedom and well-being: freedom as the procedural condition of action (or the efficient cause of the action); and well-being as providing a reason for acting, as the substantive condition of the action (or its final cause) (Gewirth 1996: 13–15). Having identified these features Gewirth maintains that (p. 18) "Every agent logically must hold or accept that he has rights to the necessary conditions of action and successful action in general." Again, he repeats, "persons must have and claim [human] rights because their objects are needed for the very possibility of action and generally successful action" (p. 16). Then once one has logically accepted that one has one's own rights to freedom and well-being, one can argue by way of universalizability, using the term popularized by R. M. Hare, that all other similar agents also have these rights equally with one's own (Gewirth 1996: 108; see Hare 1981: 108).

Once one has established the existence of rights, or moral claims, for oneself, it is not difficult in terms of logic and fairness to generalize to the possession of similar rights by other people like one's self. The difficulty for Gewirth's argument, however, here and later in its more developed form, appears to be his attempt to establish that one does have personal rights as a matter of fact and not just as a result of claiming that one logically should have them (Gewirth 1983: 1–24). He seems to argue, in an elusive or tantalizing way, that one must logically have freedom and purpose to be able to act, and that as a consequence one is morally entitled to require that others do not deprive one of that freedom or purpose. Yet, moving out from the subjective circle of logic to the objective circle of human relationships does not appear to be so effortless. As John Rawls (1975: 553–4) noted, "strong feelings and zealous aspirations for certain goals do not, as such, give people a claim upon social [or any other] resources." In other words, because I need freedom and purpose as necessary conditions for acting, and can claim from others respect for such freedom and purpose, it does not follow that I actually have a right to require others to respect or facilitate my freedom and purpose; it seems to follow only that if others do not respect my freedom or well-being I shall not be able to act as I want.

Nickel's main approach to establishing human rights appears to have some similarity to Gewirth's analysis of the necessary conditions for free and purposive behavior, a "stipulatory" characteristic like that of Sieghart, with pragmatic touches of Hobbes, as he notes. He develops what he terms "prudential reasons" for people reaching agreement on various human rights (Nickel 1987: 84–90). Like a number of other writers, however, he has no difficulty in identifying various human interests which everyone can judge central to their survival and flourishing; the problem, as ever, is how to transmute such personal interests into moral claims rather than just agree to them.

Intuitionist Approaches

Quite a different line of reflection aimed at establishing the existence of human rights is that known as intuitionism, or the argument from self-evidence which we have noted above (pp. 121–3) and which is often referred to in the field of human rights only to be dismissed. Thus, in the context of human rights Bobbio explained that one way of "demonstrating values" is "their consideration as self-evident truths"; but he recognizes that the appeal to self-evidence, has the defect of putting itself beyond the requirement of proof and rejects all rational argument: in reality, as soon as we put values which are proclaimed to be self-evident to the historical test, we realize that that which was considered evident by some people at a given time was not considered evident by others in another time. (Bobbio 1996: 13)

Again, Sieghart locates intuitionism in his list of the various lines of arguments for the existence of human rights and their difficulties:

so long as one needs to base one's support for human rights on God, or nature, or moral principle, or self-evidence, one is bound to be on tenuous ground if one is debating with someone who does not believe in God, has found no rights of Man embedded in the natural world, bases his morality on a different set of principles, and denies the self-evidence of any propositions that are not either tautological or trivial. (Sieghart 1985: 31)

And MacIntyre comments sardonically on arguments for human rights that "one of the things that we ought to have learned from the history of moral philosophy is that the introduction of the word 'intuition' by a moral philosopher is always a signal that something has gone badly wrong with an argument" (MacIntyre 1981: 72).

As an ethical theory intuitionism claims that there can be some instances of moral knowledge which are not inferred by reason (as, for instance, are logical deductions of natural law) but which are self-evident or immediately known, or "intuited," that is, directly "seen into" by the individual. Intuitionism as a modern sophisticated ethical theory was elaborated by G. E. Moore (1873–1958) for the purpose of refuting utilitarianism by claiming that certain moral situations or phenomena do not require to be proved, and are, indeed, "incapable of proof": they are simply "seen" to possess the quality of moral goodness (Moore 1965: p. x). However, from a philosophical point of view the idea of some situations or statements possessing a simple quality, or property, of moral goodness, as Moore maintained, is difficult to sustain or, indeed, to understand (see Frankena 1973: 102–5). Moral sentences, such as "almsgiving is good" or "killing innocent people is wrong," are not necessarily to be understood as simply applying or denying a moral property to a particular class of actions. Moreover, claimed moral intuitions are notoriously subject to dispute, and yet by definition appeals to such intuitions can be neither proved nor disproved rationally. "Well, either you see it or you don't" is a rather despairing abandonment of a moral argument. And it is difficult to grasp what it *means* to classify some action or situation as being simply good, or bad, morally, rather than explaining it in other terms, such as whether or not it contributes to human well-being, whether or not it accords with reason or with human nature, whether it is religiously commended or forbidden, and whether it is conducive or offensive to human dignity.

So far as concerns appealing to intuitionism as a basis for moral knowledge, Little (1993: 83) acknowledges that "intuitionists have usually gone too far both in the number and range of basic moral intuitions they claim," but he claims a much more modest strategy, suspecting that the list of what he calls "primary intuitions" is actually quite small, and that "the notion of intuition, or whatever synonym we may identify, is relevant only in respect to them" (p. 85). So far as specifically concerns human rights, he observes (p. 86) that "the rapidly growing international consensus on human rights rests upon a few incontrovertible intuitions concerning some fundamental taboos, such as the taboo against torture." In cases of moral revulsion he considers that moral theories claiming to explain why such actions are wrong "are little more than pompous distractions" (pp. 80–1). Not, he concludes, that the appealing to intuition disparages ethical reflection; "but it does understand such reflection to be after the fact, rather than before it" (p. 87).

In the light of the standard objections against intuitionism the questions have to be asked, what is one, or for that matter, what is Little, to make of those who would claim simply that they do not share his conviction of the undoubted existence of "a few incontrovertible intuitions concerning some fundamental taboos"? How is one to adjudicate between disputants in such cases, and on what criteria? Is torture of prisoners of war to be *absolutely*, and in all cases rejected as *self-evidently*, wrong? Can one not ask, or is one not compelled to ask, just what is it about torture which makes it so horrendous as a way of treating human beings? It is surely gratuitous to reject such genuine questioning as a "pompous distraction."

A modern approach to human rights by way of natural law combined with a form of intuitionism is developed by Finnis, who identifies seven basic aspects of human well-being, or "good" (life, knowledge, etc.), which he claims are self-evidently worthwhile activities, and, as such, values "to be pursued," in the terminology of Aquinas. So far as this relates to natural, or human, rights (which Finnis considers synonymous) he has valuable points to make about the advantages of a rights approach to morality, as we have already noted (above, pp. 112–13). However, although he refers (Finnis 1980: 198) to "an explanatory *justification* of claims of right," he does not provide one. In addition, his appeal to the seven basic aspects of human well-being as being self-evidently worthwhile, that is, valuable, or worth pursuing, draws from one commentator the charge of intuitionist *"ipsedixitism"* ("just because I say so") (MacCormick 1992: 128), as well as seeming to glide naturalistically from the statement that they are worth pursuing into the conclusion that therefore they ought to be pursued. In Finnis's later work, *Fundamentals of Ethics* (1983), the subject of rights finds no place.

In general, then, appeal to intuition and unmediated moral convictions appears to be problematic, so that one can only agree with so apparently sympathetic a thinker as Frankena (1973: 105), so far as human rights are concerned, that "the belief in self-evident ethical truths, and all that goes with it, is so difficult to defend that it seems best to look for some other answer to the problem of justification."

A related approach to that of moral intuitionism to explain the cogency of human rights can be taken through the idea of collective conviction rather than simply the idea of individual intuition, or intuitions; that is, by appealing to the impressive consensus which is to be found on the existence and significance of human rights. Drinan observed of the UN documents on human rights, that "while a discussion or a debate about the moral or metaphysical assumptions of the Charter of the United Nations and the Declaration of Human Rights might be useful, there appears to be a relatively settled feeling that the broad acceptance of the idea of human rights as universal is adequate to continue to make human rights enforceable" (Drinan 2001: 9–10). Such a line of argument is similar to that of Gillon, who could write more technically of "a powerful and widespread moral intuition that people simply have certain basic moral rights, certain intrinsic entitlements, that they can pit against any tendency of others who are stronger either individually or collectively to wrong them" (Gillon 1995: 55).

Bobbio (1996: 13–14) appeared to confirm this line of reflection when he wrote of the Universal Declaration of Human Rights that "the proof is in the general consensus over its validity. Advocates of natural law would have spoken of *consensus omnium gentium* [the consensus of all peoples] or *humani generis* [of the human race]." What he judged the inadequacy of appealing to human nature and to intuitionism as a ground for human rights thus led him (p. 14) to elect for this third line of proof, that "of showing that they are supported by consensus, whereby a value has greater validity the more it is agreed to." As he explains:

> the consensus argument replaces the test of objectivity which is considered impossible or at least extremely uncertain, with the test of intersubjectivity. Of course this is a historical and therefore not an absolute basis, but the historical basis of consent is the only one which can be

factually proved. The Universal Declaration of Human Rights can therefore be considered the greatest historical test of the *consensus omnium
gentium* [consensus of all peoples] in relation to a given value
system.   (Bobbio 1996: 14)

Impressive although Bobbio's rhetoric is, and possibly influenced by
the famous phrase of Augustine of Hippo when writing about beliefs in
Christian dogmas that "the judgement of the whole world is conclusive"
(*securus judicat orbis terrarum*), the argument from consensus is just
as precarious in the twenty-first century as it was in the fifth (Augustine
*c.*1860: bk. 3, ch. 24; *PL* vol. 43, col. 101). It has a note of historical
complacency about it, with little indication of wishing to recall the
moral blind spots from which whole civilizations and societies have
suffered, even though they may well also have had impressive – albeit
selective – consensus on some other expressions of human behavior.
Orend (2002: 79) alerts us to the realization that "raw consensus may
not be enough to justify important moral claims." The paragon of democracy, the Athens of the fifth century BCE, was founded on slavery
and xenophobia; Israelite society, the matrix of the Hebrew and
Christian Bibles, accepted slavery, favored genocide, and systematically
subordinated women; medieval Christian societies took for granted
physical torture and the atrocities of the Crusades; the Reformation era
in Europe was riddled on all sides with religious wars and discriminatory persecutions and executions; other cultures in history have prac-
ticed human sacrifice and ritual mutilation; the much vaunted American
Declaration of Independence ignored black men, and women; and European colonial land-grabbing in Africa, India, and Asia kept Kipling's
"lesser breeds" for long in exploitative subjection.

It is therefore a legitimate and salutary attitude for society in the
twenty-first century to be soberly alert to the human propensity to
morally complacent consensus, and to examine its conscience on what
may be its own present moral blind spots, on pain of claiming exemp-
tion from the human fallible condition. For consensus is a relative term,
suffering from the same handicap as the utilitarian criterion of the
"greatest number": it implies simply agreement, but it does not specify
how large, or how extensive, or how long-lasting that agreement must
be to provide a guarantee that it refers to objective truth. Truth is not
necessarily to be found in numbers, however large they may be.

It can be argued, of course, that the Universal Declaration of Human
Rights is quite uniquely impressive in its worldwide ethical consensus
that such rights do exist and are to be respected; and Bobbio made much
of this. As he emphasized,

I do not know whether people are aware of just how much the Universal Declaration represents an unprecedented historical event, given that for the first time in history a system of fundamental principles for human behaviour has been freely and expressly accepted by the majority of the people living on this planet through their governments. Through this declaration, a system of values is *universal* (for the first time in history) not in principle, but *de facto*, in that the consensus over its validity and suitability to govern the destiny of the future community has been expressly declared . . . Only after the Declaration, can we obtain the historical certainty that humanity in its entirety shares some common values, and finally believe in the universality of these values in a way which is historically legitimate, i.e., that by "universal" we mean, not an objective reality, but subjectively accepted by the universe of humanity. (Bobbio 1996: 14–15)

Still, however, Bobbio does not actually prove that human rights exist, but only that untold millions agree that they should be respected. And just as it is not possible to argue directly from the way nature is to the way it ought to be, it is similarly fallacious to argue from the fact that very many people agree on a certain state of affairs to the conclusion that they are correct in so doing.

Yet this also appears to be the view for which Donnelly (2003: 13) eventually seems to settle in seeking what he terms "the source of human rights." Considering various possible candidates from which to produce human rights he finds the idea of the satisfaction of needs obscure and controversial; and although he seems attracted to a "forward-looking moral vision of human nature" (p. 15), he recognizes that "few issues in moral or political philosophy are more contentious or intractable than theories of human nature" (p. 16), a consideration which he judges would make defending a particular theory proposing human nature as a source of human rights "a serious shortcoming" (p. 16). Indeed, he continues, not only can human nature not be a philosophical foundation for human rights; "there is no other foundation either" (p. 18). As he explains:

we can reasonably ask for good grounds for accepting, for example, the rights in the Universal Declaration of Human Rights. But such grounds – for example, their desirable consequences, their coherence with other moral ideals or practices, or the supporting authority of a revealed religious text – are not unassailable. They operate within rather than across communities or traditions. And we must recognize that there are other good grounds not only for these principles and practices but also for different, even "competing," practices. (p. 21)

Faced with what he considers a variety of equally unsatisfactory grounds for recognizing human rights Donnelly goes on (2003: 17), however, "fortunately, there is a remarkable international normative consensus on the list of rights contained in the Universal Declaration and the International Human Rights Covenants," a consensus which he comes to regard as providing the only practically adequate source of human rights. His final word, then, appears to have similarities with the views of Bobbio in appealing to a remarkable international consensus rooted in the Universal Declaration of Human Rights, but to this he appears to add the approach of Sieghart that such human rights are stipulated rather than proved.

> Human rights ultimately rest on a social decision to act as though such "things" existed – and then, through social action directed by these rights to make real the world that they envision . . . Like all social practices, human rights come with, and in an important sense require, justifications. But those justifications appeal to "foundations" that are ultimately a matter of agreement or assumption rather than proof.   (p. 21)

Later he explains his conclusion less technically in contending that "most leading elements in almost all contemporary societies endorse the idea that every human being has certain equal and inalienable rights and is thus entitled to equal concern and respect from the state" (p. 51).

Simply accepting the existence of human rights today is an approach which appears also to be the one favored by Richard Rorty, who agrees with human rights but in his 1993 Amnesty Lecture, entitled "Human Rights, Rationality and Sentimentality," expressed a deep skepticism about how they are arrived at. In fact, he rejects not only any "ahistoric" concept of human nature but also the foundationalism ranging from Plato to Kant which is aimed at establishing a rational basis for acting morally towards one's fellow humans; and he opts, it appears, simply to accept that we are currently living in a human rights culture. As he remarks:

> We are much less inclined than our ancestors were to take "theories of human nature" seriously, much less inclined to take ontology or history as a guide to life. We have come to see that the only lesson of either history or anthropology is our extraordinary malleability. We are coming to think of ourselves as the flexible, protean, self-shaping, animal rather than as the rational animal or the cruel animal. One of the shapes we have recently assumed is that of a human rights culture.   (Rorty 1993: 115)

His approach to this culture is summarized:

> We pragmatists argue from the fact that the emergence of the human rights culture seems *to owe nothing to increased moral knowledge, and everything to hearing sad and sentimental stories*, to the conclusion that there is probably no knowledge of the sort Plato envisaged. We go on to argue: Since no useful work seems to be done by insisting on a purportedly ahistorical human nature, there probably is no such nature, or at least nothing in that nature that is relevant to our moral choices. In short, my doubts about the effectiveness of appeals to moral knowledge are doubts about causal efficacy, not about epistemic status. (pp. 118–19; emphasis added)

Aligning him with communitarianism (on which, see above, pp. 91–5), Macedo describes Rorty's main purpose as "to debunk philosophical theories that claim to adjudicate in advance what counts as reliable knowledge" (Macedo 1990: 25). He continues, "Rorty assumes rather easily that democracies are at their 'best' when telling anecdotes. He implies that moral reasons and arguments really do not, in practice, 'pay their way' or have much 'cash value'" (p. 32). Certainly this general (and communitarian) characterization of Rorty's approach by way of "telling sad stories" seems borne out by what we have seen of his Amnesty Lecture on human rights. Moreover, light is thrown on Rorty's approach to human rights if one appreciates that as an avowed Deweyist pragmatist he is deeply disappointed at the extent of the disregard for human rights which is to be encountered, and that he is concerned about understanding why this should be the case and about what ways can be found to remedy it. Moral education, in the sense of Platonic or Kantian appeals to reason or knowledge or idealized pictures of moral human beings, evidently do not work in many cases, he contends, and no amount of constructing or promoting an "ahistorical" notion of human nature will improve the situation. As shown in the horrendous instances of human rights abuse related by Rorty, some people just persist in behaving as if most others simply do not count as "fellow" human beings. Surely, then, he argues, the answer must be to get at their feelings, to concentrate on what he appeals to as "sentimental education," that is, helping people on the one hand not to feel threatened by differences and on the other hand to feel a personal empathy with the unfortunate (see Macedo 1990: 128). To which the sad answer must surely be, not with any marked degree of improvement here either. And if that is the case, then Rorty's pragmatic appeal above to "causal efficacy not epistemic status" as his reason for dismissing moral knowledge must apply also to the sentimental awareness which he aims to inculcate in its place.

In fact, the root problem in such cases is not the intellectual power of universal human rights, nor the force of truth or reason or moral knowledge, nor a paradigmatic picture of what it is to be human, nor even an induced fellow feeling to create a sense of solidarity with unfortunate members of one's species. The root problem is getting some people to be moral at all. If that is the case, then the preferred approach must be to deny Rorty's dismissal of Plato's rationalism and to return to the latter's foundational question "why should I be moral?" as a basis for constructing a theory of human rights. Meantime, the pragmatic question arises what to do in situations where people simply disregard any idea of human rights, if only until they can be rendered, as Rorty envisions, more "sentimentally" aware and thus, hopefully, more morally sensitive. How can human rights be protected from moral solipsism, or the view that one is the only person who counts? It appears that if the effective answer is not to be found in educating people somehow, whether by reason or by sentiment, to help them break out of their egoistic universe, it can only be by others breaking into it, by some form of coercion. Hence the regrettable social necessity recognized by Orend (2002: 26–7) that "the contemporary human rights movement has, as probably its main goal, the effective translation of the moral values inherent in human rights theory into meaningful and concrete legal rights." In other words, if the moral power of rights does not prevail in protecting human beings, then recourse has to be had to legal power and the force of legal instruments, whether at national or at international levels.

One positive advantage of the arguments from consensus on the existence of human rights or from their simple acceptance, is that it concentrates attention on the rights themselves on which consensus or acceptance is claimed to exist. Yet, inevitably this approach raises once again the fundamental question, just what is it about human beings which in this line of argument forms the basis for such an impressive and unparalleled consensus? One part of an answer appears to lie in the increased attention given to the idea of human dignity as providing the basis, or the ground, for various claimed fundamental human rights.

Human Dignity

In celebrating the fiftieth anniversary of the Universal Declaration of Human Rights the UN High Commissioner for Human Rights, Mary Robinson (1998: 253, 257), described that document as "the international keystone of human dignity" and commented that its "universal vocation to protect the dignity of every human being has captured the imagination of humanity." Indeed, in the Universal Declaration itself, as Klug points out, "almost as a statement of defiance, the drafters chose to underline their belief that human dignity is an essential value by including the concept in the very first line of the Preamble: 'Whereas recognition of the inherent dignity and of the equal and inalienable rights . . .'" (Klug 2000: 100). This theme is pursued in the preamble in paragraph 5's reference to the "dignity and worth of the human person," and article 1 of the Declaration begins with a resounding affirmation of the central place of human dignity: "All human beings are born free and equal in dignity and rights. They are endowed with reason and conscience and should act towards each other in a spirit of brotherhood." As Klug concludes, "The message appears to be that human beings, endowed with 'reason' and 'conscience,' have a 'personality' whose 'free and full development' are essential elements of human dignity" (2000: 100–1; see Klug 1996: 29). Shestack notes (2000: 53) that from a religious viewpoint dignity is "the inherent quality of the sacredness of human beings," but Klug observes that in the modern era

> the concept of dignity replaced the idea of god or nature as the foundation of "inalienable rights." This completed the transition from "natural rights" to "human rights"; a term which did not come into common usage until this time . . . No longer was a higher being or pre-existing state of nature cited as the source of fundamental rights. Rights were to be accorded to all human beings without distinction because of the essential dignity of all humanity.   (Klug 2000: 101)

Human dignity, then, it is claimed, can stand on its own two feet as the acknowledged foundation of human rights. In his study *Taking Rights Seriously*, Dworkin (1978: 198) referred to "the vague but powerful idea of human dignity," and continued, "this idea, associated with Kant, but defended by philosophers of different schools, supposes that there are ways of treating a man that are inconsistent with recognizing him as a full member of the human community, and holds that such treatment is profoundly unjust." As Philip Alston commented (1998: 30), human dignity "is probably the single most important principle which underpins the Universal Declaration." Indeed, the UNESCO Symposium, which was aimed at informing the Human Rights Commission in the latter's work on the Universal Declaration, highlighted the central significance of human dignity in commenting that the UN's faith in freedom and democracy is founded on the faith in the inherent dignity of men and women. The United Nations cannot succeed in the great purposes to which it is committed unless it so acts that this dignity is given increasing recognition, and unless steps are taken to create the conditions under which this dignity may be achieved more fully and at constantly higher levels.   (UNESCO 1949: 259)

Nor is human dignity as the basis for human rights to be seen simply as a high-flown free-floating idea exemplifying Waldron's jibe (1984: 20) of "pious lip-service to slogans about human dignity." For instance, writing from a background of international health care, Jonathan Mann (1998: 176) highlighted the day-to-day significance of human dignity when he pointed out that "when dignity is violated, people suffer. Situations in which personal dignity is violated evoke strong emotions – of shame, humiliation, disgust, anger, powerlessness and sadness – which persist." At the same time, its universal and overriding significance was well brought out by Dworkin in his comment that "the essence of liberty is not agreement over particular hard cases, however, but an attitude: that the traditional liberties are so crucial to human dignity that hard questions should be decided in their favour as far as possible" (Dworkin 1990: 11).

The basic significance, then, of human dignity is that it is now claimed to underlie all objective approaches to how human beings are to be regarded and treated by each other. As Klug (2000: 12) expressed it, "the idea of human rights is relatively simple . . . It is based on an appreciation of the inherent dignity of each individual." In this context the question of establishing a basis for human rights now becomes the question of how one is to establish that human beings actually possess such a dignity and what it is. All references to human dignity in the context of human rights appear to agree in implying that all human beings are to be treated with something like a profound moral respect approaching awe or even natural reverence. But why should this be? Moreover, the idea of individual human dignity as an ultimate justification for human rights raises issues about what Orend describes as "the substantial vagueness surrounding the concept of human dignity . . . [It] is too large, vague and contested a concept to serve as a solid starting point for justifying human rights" (Orend 2002: 87–8). It is in an attempt to meet this requirement of a clearer understanding of what it is that underlies the whole idea of human dignity that the following section proposes that the answer lies in the intrinsic wonder of the thinking human person.

"The Wonder of Our Being"

The prime questions of life noted by many philosophers are "Why is there anything?", "Why is there something rather than nothing?" Sheer existence, the fact that any things exist, is not only something to wonder about, but also something to wonder at. And among the things that exist none appears to be more a cause for wonder than the human being. In the midst of all our mundane concerns it is easy to forget or to ignore what the Hebrew psalmist described as "the wonder of my being" (Psalms 139: 14; Grail version). It is this realization, of course, which has impelled countless millions of people to conjecture and worship a divine explanation for the wonder-full phenomenon of human beings. Quite regardless of this religious reaction, however, the emergence of the human being even as a matter of chance in a blind cosmos is a genuine cause for wonder; and the product of the human species in the course of evolution is something to be wondered at with something approaching awe, or natural reverence. The renaissance humanism of Shakespeare (*Hamlet* act 2, sc. 2) caught something of such wonder in Hamlet's reflections, even though they served only to increase his dejection at his personal fate: "What a piece of work is a man! How noble in reason! How infinite in faculty! in form, in moving, how express and admirable! in action how like an angel! in apprehension how like a god! the beauty of the world! the paragon of animals!"

In the light of such observations it does not appear fanciful to use the poetic term "wondrous" to describe human beings; for indeed the apprehension of such reality and the appreciation of such richness of being is kin to, if not identical with, the aesthetic experience. And as in all such experiences of awe, Cottingham notes (2003: 101–2): "the beauty is not 'projected' onto it by the observer, but is inescapably real, calling forth an irresistible response in our hearts. We *respond* to beauty, as we respond to truth and goodness: as objective realities beyond ourselves, that have the power to inspire us and draw us forward into the light." In other words, Cottingham concludes, "our aesthetic experience gives us intimations of a world of value outside our own urgent self-oriented concerns."

Considering this unique phenomenon of humanity more closely, may one then go further, and ask, Is there anything in particular in which it and its dignity consist? Blaise Pascal (1623–62) was in no doubt: for him the greatness of humankind lies precisely in the human power to think: "Thought constitutes the greatness of humanity." In a famous passage he explained (1956: 97), "The human being is just a reed, the weakest thing in nature; but it is a thinking reed . . . So our whole dignity consists in thought." The immense significance of human thought is dramatically brought out in Pascal's paradox, "by space the universe encompasses and swallows me up like a dot; but by thought I encompass the world." So, he concludes, "it is not in space that I should seek my dignity, but in the regulating of my thought." Other thinkers, notably Kant, would prefer to locate the unique characteristic of human beings in the will, in the power to choose, in individual autonomy (see above, pp. 34–5). Yet there appears much to commend Pascal's centering of human dignity on the power of human thought, if one can include in that rich concept the various human attributes of intelligence, reasoning, reflection, imagination, consciousness, and self-consciousness, as well as the human power of rational choice.

The same awareness of the significance of thought, and especially of self-consciousness, as the ground for the unique status and dignity of human beings, was developed more scientifically in recent times by another French thinker, the paleontologist Pierre Teilhard de Chardin (1881–1955). In his study *The Phenomenon of Man*, he identified three consecutive stages of evolution in the world: first the pre-life of matter; then the life of organisms; and finally the thought of human beings. As he commented in a chapter devoted to "The Birth of Thought": "from a purely positivist point of view man is the most mysterious and disconcerting of all the objects met with in science" (Teilhard de Chardin 1975: 181). And central to this striking feature of humanity is the power of human reflection, "the power acquired by a consciousness to turn in upon itself, to take possession of itself *as of an object* endowed with its own particular consistence and value: no longer merely to know oneself; no longer merely to know, but to know that one knows" (p. 183). For Teilhard the consequence of humanity's crossing "the threshold of thought" is immense:

> the being who is the object of his own reflection, in consequence of that very doubling back upon himself, becomes in a flash able to raise himself into a new sphere. In reality, another world is born. Abstraction, logic, reasoned choice and inventions, mathematics, art, calculation of space and time, anxieties and dreams of love – all these activities of *inner life* are nothing else than the effervescence of the newly formed centre as it explodes onto itself.   (Teilhard de Chardin 1975: 182–3)

As Teilhard's friend and admirer Julian Huxley commented:

a developed human being, as he rightly pointed out, is not merely a more highly individualized individual. He has crossed the threshold of self-consciousness to a new mode of thought, and as a result has achieved some degree of conscious integration – integration of the self with the outer world of men and nature, integration of the separate elements of the self with each other. He is a person, an organism which has transcended individuality in personality. This attainment of personality was an essential element in man's past and present evolutionary success. (Teilhard de Chardin 1975: 20)

For Teilhard the matter is summed up in the progressive triad of reality, "after the grain of matter, the grain of life; and now at last we see constituted the *grain of thought*"; so that with humanity we now have a phylum of "thinking centres" (pp. 192–3). Cottingham (2003: 61) captures the same idea in viewing the human race as composed of "millions of centres of individual consciousness, each informed with rationality, each yearning for truth, beauty and love."

In the face of these impressive expositions of the unique power of human thought, how is one to react to the encounter with complex human beings possessed of such astonishing ability? For the morally aware person, it seems this can only be with an attitude of respect, of reverence, and, indeed, of concern which may be summed up as a recognition of its inherent dignity and yet its vulnerability. As Pascal expressed it, humanity is no more than a flimsy reed, even although a reed which thinks. In his essay on human love C. S. Lewis (1960: 19–20) identified several types of pleasure: some which arise from the satisfaction of a need or desire, which he calls need-pleasures; some which are experienced in the act of giving, which he calls gift-pleasures; and others which can be unsought or unexpected, such as an encounter with beauty or aesthetic pleasures, which he calls pleasures in their own right, or pleasures of appreciation. The pleasure of appreciation, he explains (p. 22), makes us feel that "something has not merely gratified our sense in fact but claimed our appreciation by right." These three types of pleasure, according to Lewis, foreshadow different types of love, need-love, gift-love, and appreciative-love. Of the third he explains that "appreciative love gazes and holds its breath and is silent, rejoices that such a wonder should exist . . ." (p. 26). This pleasure of appreciation, he explains (p. 22), makes us feel that "something has not merely gratified our sense in fact but claimed our appreciation by right."

In other words, to develop Lewis's thought, such an object not only claims our admiration and appreciation; it elicits a reaction from us to value and cherish the object which is inspiring such appreciative love in us. Indeed, if there is anything to be said for the wonder and appreciation which we have proposed as being appropriate in encountering the grandeur of an ordinary thinking human being, then it seems less than a step for this wonder to become a moral respect for such a wondrous phenomenon and its interests, and a moral response to its promise and its needs. Cottingham identifies these well when he explains:

> we are talking about *human* lives – the lives of a very special kind of animal, subject to an array of interlinked imperatives – biological imperatives (for food, warmth, shelter, procreation), social imperatives (the need to cooperate, the drive to communicate), emotional imperatives (the need for such things as mutual recognition and affection), and lastly and just as importantly what might be called "rational" imperatives. Uniquely among known living things we are capable of standing back from our environment, questioning the way things are, challenging the actions of our fellows, entering into dialogues of criticism and justification.　(Cottingham 2003: 26–7)

It does not take much effort to view Cottingham's list of human "imperatives" and "needs" as a basis for human rights. More broadly, it is suggested that the encounter with human beings not only evokes awed wonder at their existence; it also elicits an appreciation of the value and inherent worth of such beings, impelling us to respect them. Herein is the ground of that inherent dignity of human persons which justifies them to direct moral demands towards other humans, forwarding to them and sharing with them all the "imperatives" which have been identified by Cottingham and which we have good reason to describe as human rights. To sum up, the Latin adjective *dignus*, which is the root of the English noun "dignity," means "worthy" or "deserving." What we have proposed as "the wonder of our being" seems well suited to explain why human beings possess an intrinsic dignity, and are therefore worthy, or deserving, of the deepest moral respect, as bearers of moral human rights.

Major Opponents

Consideration of the various approaches which can be examined in order to establish the existence and validity of human rights would not be complete without taking account of the fundamental and influential arguments which have been raised against the whole idea of human rights, notably by Jeremy Bentham and by Alasdair MacIntyre.

As we have already granted (above, p. 123), Bentham was justified in protesting against deriving natural rights from a natural law or a prescriptive law of nature if this was, as he considered, "imaginary" (Waldron 1987: 69). For the idea of a moral law emerging from human nature, or of a natural law which prescribes certain types of human behavior, is in fact a theological idea, presuming a divine lawgiver, for which Bentham had no time or concern. In recalling in our opening chapter the rational explanation of human rights which was offered by the disillusioned Christian jurist, Grotius, and his passing remark that this would apply even if God did not exist, we foresaw that, as belief in the existence of God came to be rejected, as it was by Bentham, there would certainly arise formidable intellectual difficulties for a secular idea of natural law which does not have a creating deity to support it (see above, pp. 10–11). In maintaining, then, that without a creating legislator there can be no law of creation, or law within human nature, possessing moral binding force Bentham was correct. Where he erred, however, was in linking rights inextricably with laws and in refusing to conceive of rights which were not the offspring of law. As he asserted gratuitously, "Right is with me the child of law: from different operations of the law result different sorts of rights. A natural right is a son that never had a father" (Waldron 1987: 73). His deep distaste for the French Revolution and its championing of the rights of man made it undesirable for him to go beyond the positivist idea of legal rights and venture into the realm of moral rights, while his predilection to resolve every moral question through his felicific calculus made any alternative moral resource quite unnecessary. As a consequence he was not able to envisage the possibility of there being also rights of another kind guiding behavior and was content vehemently to deny them any validity.

The other major opponent of human rights has been Alasdair MacIntyre who claims that there are no good reasons for alleging their existence (MacIntyre 1981: 72). This position appears to be influenced by his general thesis that ethics today is in a state of total confusion and incoherence, consisting, as it does, for the most part of disjointed relics of past ethical theories. As he explained,

> The language – and therefore also to some large degree the practice – of morality today is in a state of grave disorder. That disorder arises from the prevailing cultural power of an idiom in which ill-assorted conceptual fragments from various parts of our past are deployed together in private and public debates which are notable chiefly for the unsettlable character of the controversies thus carried on and the apparent arbitrariness of each of the contending parties. (MacIntyre 1981: 238)

For MacIntyre (1981: 60) the whole demise of moral converse today is due to the failure of "the Enlightenment Project," or the doomed claim to identify universal moral principles on new grounds in place of the ideas of cosmic purpose or, ultimately, of divine law.

In expounding this position in his highly influential work *After Virtue* (1981), MacIntyre has acquired something of a cult status among moral pessimists and communitarian thinkers. His thought has proved particularly congenial to the many Christians who welcome his confirmation and justification of their gloomy view of "fallen and sinful" human nature, and who follow him in advocating the rediscovery of sustainable communities which will keep out the worst of the contemporary moral malaise (see Mahoney 1992: 669–71). All this is summed up in his now famous, and alarmist, rallying call (1981: 245): "What matters at this stage is the construction of local forms of community within which civility and the intellectual and moral life can be sustained through the new dark ages which are already upon us . . . This time however the barbarians are not waiting beyond the frontiers; they have already been governing us for quite some time."

In propounding such a program based on hand-wringing moral nostalgia MacIntyre may not entirely deserve the disdain of Francis Wheen's criticism (2004: 187) that he is seeking sanctuary from reality in twelfth-century monasteries. However, his position is susceptible to the criticisms which we have already directed against neo-communitarianism in general (above, pp. 93–5). More precisely in our present context, it can be counter-argued that his thesis that there is no commonality of moral understanding and discourse to be found in society today is too bad to be true, for a number of reasons, meriting at least the moderate comment of Little that "the 'fragmentariness' of moral discourse which certainly does exist in our world, is a more structured affair than MacIntyre and Hauerwas [a similar spirit] seem to understand" (Little 1993: 744–5; see Macedo 1990: 13–16).

One weakness of MacIntyre's position concerns his methodological approach, since his explanatory diagnosis that it was the failure of the Enlightenment project "whose breakdown led to the chaos of moral values in contemporary culture," has been dismantled and rejected by Wokler (1994: 111), who concluded that "readers of McIntyre's philosophy of history are too often tempted with richly appetising food for thought, but then denied the required sustenance" (p. 120). In fact, Wokler is more concerned with the actual reasons which MacIntyre adduces to explain why modern moral discourse is chaotic than to what extent his unwarranted claim is true. He concludes, paradoxically, in defense of the Enlightenment, "The moral chaos of the modern world stems not from the failure of the Enlightenment Project but from its neglect and abandonment" (Wokler 1994: 126).

Moving beyond MacIntyre's method to consider his actual conclusions leads one to concur with Jeffrey Stout's diagnosis of "communitarian wistfulness" to be found in the writings of MacIntyre and those of his ilk (Stout 1988: 231). In fact, it seems important to make the point that he and many others who bewail what they consider moral confusion widespread in today's society do not distinguish sufficiently between moral chaos and moral pluralism, that is, a sustainable variety of moral views which may be held, often with equal sincerity, on contemporary issues. Moreover, it is remarkable that MacIntyre and those who echo his longing to restore a golden moral past consider it feasible to distinguish between on the one hand a modern society allegedly scattered in moral disarray and on the other hand harmoniously united communities and enclaves, especially Christian ones. To do so is blithely to ignore the serious moral disputes and divisions which today disturb and disrupt religious bodies themselves at least as readily as any others, in such areas as sexual behavior and practice, abortion, capitalism, politics, globalization, warfare, applications of modern medical technology, and the like. As we have written elsewhere, "To ignore or turn a blind eye to this modern Christian pluralism and diversity is the fatal flaw in viewing Christian communities today as the faithful moral remnant in society and the custodian of rejected values" (Mahoney 1992: 671–2).

Stout judges that MacIntyre and others, like Norman Bellah and his fellow authors of the equally widely influential *Habits of the Heart* (1985), "play the role of Jeremiah to modern society" (Stout 1988: 16). As such they may be identified as suffering from the occupational hazard of all prophets, of oversimplifying their case in order to make an impact (Mahoney 1987: 16). In response Stout (1988: p. xii) calls for "a picture of our society both more complicated and less dismal than MacIntyre's." For, he maintains, not only are the gloomy conclusions of MacIntyre and Bellah not borne out by their arguments, or by the research on which they base those arguments. To the contrary, Stout argues, "even though we no longer share a single theory of human nature (when did we exactly?) and despite the fact that Aristotelian teleology has long since passed out of philosophical fashion, most of us do agree on the essentials of what might be called the provisional *telos* of our society." In other words, he counter-maintains that there is a "relatively limited but nonetheless real and significant agreement on the good." There is no lack of controversies, Stout freely concedes, of course, but to draw conclusions only from these is to ignore the fact that "public discourse, at least under conditions of relative freedom, tends to concentrate on controversial matters, the better to resolve them, leaving platitudes to one side" (Stout 1988: 210–15). In other words, to adapt a phrase of

Richard Rorty's (1992: 63), we do agree on "an enormous number of platitudes."

In support of this assertion we may recall our earlier point on competing moral values (above, pp. 108–9) and suggest that a great deal of modern moral controversy in the public arena is not so much an argument which rejects certain values outright and champions others; it is more a matter of prioritizing the same values in different orders of importance. It would not be difficult to establish that many of the most impassioned ethical controversies in society are not about the importance of peace rather than justice, of freedom rather than responsibility, of human development rather than planetary integrity, of the inviolability of human life rather than the quality of that life or the significance of human choice, of the importance of the individual rather than of the community. All of these values are widely accepted singly in the abstract. Where controversy enters in is at the level of public policy and practical decision and action, when not all such values can be realized, and when choices have to be made between what are now perceived to be in the circumstances competing moral values. Then public moral debate differs little from private moral reflection in facing a necessary choice between what Stout terms "conflicting considerations." Yet it remains true, as he maintains (1988: 215), that there are vast regions of the moral terrain over which we do not spend much time and effort in battle and in which we can identify a quite substantial "overlapping consensus."

Today, of course, this "overlapping consensus" on moral matters which Stout rightly invoked against MacIntyre has become undeniable. It becomes increasingly difficult to reconcile MacIntyre's general thesis of modern moral incoherence, and his particular derision aimed at human rights, with the phenomenon of the increasingly worldwide agreement on human rights and on their moral demands, even if those demands are regrettably very far from being satisfied. Nor is it true to assert sweepingly, as MacIntyre does (1981: 67), that "in the United Nations declaration on human rights of 1949 [*sic*] what has since become the normal UN practice of not giving good reasons for *any* assertions whatsoever is followed with great rigour." As we saw at the beginning of this chapter, the Universal Declaration of Human Rights opened with a carefully constructed statement referring back to the argument of the initial Charter of the UN on behalf of human rights.

How conclusive such or any reasons to establish human rights are is matter for debate and has been the topic of this chapter; but it is debate which is possible precisely because of a shared, even if contested, moral discourse very far from the broad-brushed and allegedly widespread disarray and incoherence, allegedly resulting from the failure of the Enlightenment project, which lies at the base of MacIntyre's whole project. Considering the privileged position which enables some philosophers to reject the very idea of human rights inclines one to sympathize with Jones's remark that "outside the cocooned world of the academy, people are still victims of torture, still subjected to genocide, still deprived of basic freedoms and still dying through starvation. We should remember these people before we decide to forget about rights" (Jones 1994: 227).

Conclusion

Although the claim is not infrequently heard at a popular level that there is no proof for the existence of human rights, yet, from what we have been considering, it is clear that there is no shortage of arguments aiming to establish their existence, arguments ranging from divine creation to natural law and human nature, to personal individuality, to intuition and consensus, to social stipulation and cultural convention, and to human dignity, including its being grounded on "the wonder of our being." The question arises whether any of these arguments may be considered successful in proving their case and in compelling assent. It may be worth bearing in mind Orend's (2002: 69–70) remark that often there can be more than one good reason for a particular conclusion, and there is no necessity for there being only one successful argument, comparing such a process of reasoning to the work of a lawyer marshaling all possible evidence to support a legal claim in court. Applying this to human rights, Orend concludes, "it seems compelling to observe that different people can support human rights for a variety of reasons, and there is probably more than one good reason that provides powerful support for the existence of human rights and the force of their claim on our behaviour" (p. 70).

This may well be the case, but one reaction to Orend's proposal is to consider it somewhat evasive in claiming that there is "probably more than one good reason" for human rights, and to maintain that it does not meet the basic question, which comes down to whether there is *any* good reason to accept them. In part support of his position, however, it might be possible to invoke the evidence of John Henry Newman and his theory of using "the convergence of probabilities" to establish certitude. Writing in 1864, admittedly in a religious context, Newman argued that certainty can arise not just from one compelling reason, but also from "the accumulative force of certain given reasons which, taken one by one, were only probabilities" (Newman 1967: ch. 4, sect. 2; pp. 180–1; cf. ch. 1, p. 31). If this proposal is generally acceptable, then it could be possible to argue that, even if there is no single compelling argument for the existence of human rights, nevertheless at least some of the proposed, and possibly impressive, arguments which we have been reviewing can accumulate or coalesce to result in a degree of certainty which would be greater than that provided by just any one such argument, thus forming at least a very persuasive case for human rights, which is perhaps the most one could hope for, in the spirit of Orend's suggestion above.

Failing that approach, of all the arguments which we have been examining which claim to establish human rights, it might be worth asking now if there is, or are, any in particular which might appear to be more likely to be accorded general assent. Prescinding from the theological line of argument, which, although comparatively unproblematic in itself, is specific in its inherent dependence on religious belief and so cannot be proposed for universal approval, it appears that little general credence would be given today to arguments from "natural law," this being, as we have argued, historically and logically an extension of the religious argument from a divine creator. Even the simple idea of human nature, however, considered in any normative sense as a source for "natural" and then "human" rights, is greeted with considerable skepticism by many today, no doubt nervous of any hint of the metaphysical, and particularly of Aristotelian teleology. The argument from intuition would be greeted with similar reserve for different reasons, although the notion of a growing worldwide consensus might be thought to have its appeal, especially if this is considered uniquely extensive and impressive, as it is regarding human rights. The idea that human rights are the result simply of social stipulation or of cultural or linguistic convention strictly does not call for a proof that they exist, but only for a proof that this is an adequate way of accounting for them.

Perhaps the most impressive approach to establish the existence of human rights, and one with the widest appeal, could be considered that adopted by the United Nations. For one thing, this approach was the one finally accepted after prolonged argument and discussion by the combined representatives of the United Nations, and it carries with it the authority of that international body. Of course, claims to authority in support of this, or any, particular argument are no substitute for the intrinsic force of reason; yet it might nevertheless be seen as providing at least ground for caution against rejecting the UN approach without very good cause. When to the UN line of reasoning which we described above as "ostensive," that is, pointing to respect for human rights as the essential "foundation" of justice and peace, one adds the appeal by the United Nations, and others, to human dignity as that in humans which is the basis of universal respect for their moral rights, then the UN case for human rights gathers added weight. And this may receive further momentum and persuasiveness from our suggestion that it is the wonder of human rational existence which provides welcome precision to that intrinsic dignity and renders humans worthy of the deepest moral respect as bearers of human rights.

At this stage of a study which has traced the origin and growth of the idea of natural rights from the classical, biblical, and medieval worlds through the revolutionary ages of Europe and America and recovering from the ideological attacks of Marxism to gain new strength in the human rights movement of modern times and the international convergence on their recognition, and which has attempted to clarify our understanding of these moral claims and to assess the various arguments which have been called in their support as well as the objections of their opponents, we can reasonably project that the future of these moral instruments of human development is immensely promising as well as challenging. Such a future is well described in words of Conor Gearty which concluded his editorial introduction to a collection of papers entitled *Understanding Human Rights*:

> What unites all the essays in this volume is a pride in the potential for justice and fairness in the language of human rights. The eclipse of Marxist and broadly socialist political ideology may or may not be permanent. It is clear, however, that the undoubted decline of these essentially idealistic philosophies has given human rights thinking a new opportunity to rediscover its radical roots. The simple notions of individual human dignity and of equal rights for all were revolutionary when they first gained common currency in eighteenth-century Europe. They continued to terrify the wealthy and powerful until they were submerged by the misleading spell cast by universal enfranchisement and by the supposed danger posed by Marx-inspired thought. The door is now open for the idea of human rights to break free of establishment opinion and to rediscover itself as the agent of change on behalf of the poor, the marginalized and the dispossessed; on behalf, in other words, of those many people whose human rights are continuously mocked by their inhuman daily predicaments. (Gearty and Tomkins 1999: p. xvi)

It is in sympathy with these sentiments and with a view to considering some of these "inhuman daily predicaments" that we propose now to conclude our study by considering some aspects of the application of human rights today.

References

Alston, P. (1998), The Universal Declaration in an Era of Globalization, in van der Heijden and Tahzib-Lie (1998).

Augustine of Hippo (*c.*1860), *Contra Epistolam Parmeniani*, Migne, *Patres Latini*, vol. 43: 33–107.

Augustine of Hippo (1972), *De Civitate Dei*, trans. E. Bettenson, Harmondsworth: Penguin.

Bellah, R. N., et al. (1985), *Habits of the Heart: Individualism and Commitment in American Life*, New York: Harper & Row.

Bellof, M. (1948), *Thomas Jefferson and American Democracy*, London: Hodder & Stoughton.

Berlin, I. (1969), *Four Essays on Liberty*, Oxford: Oxford University Press.

Bobbio, N. (1996), *The Age of Rights*, Cambridge: Polity Press.

Browne, Sir T. (1909), *Browne's "Religio Medici"* [1643], Oxford: Clarendon Press.

Bucar, E. M., and Barnett, B. (2005) (eds.), *Does Human Rights Need God?* Grand Rapids, MI: Eerdmans.

Charvet, J. (1995), *The Idea of an Ethical Community*, Ithaca, NY: Cornell University Press.

Charvet, J. (2001), The Possibility of a Cosmopolitan Ethical Order Based on the Idea of Universal Human Rights, in Hakan Seckinelgin and Hideaki Shinoda (eds.), *Ethics and International Relations*, Basingstoke: Palgrave Macmillan.

Copleston, F. C. (1944), *A History of Philosophy*, vol. 1, London: Burns, Oates & Washbourne.

Copleston, F. C. (1966), *A History of Philosophy*, vol. 8, London: Burns & Oates.

Cottingham, J. (2003), *On the Meaning of Life*, London: Routledge.

Cranston, M. (1973), *What are Human Rights?* London: Bodley Head.

Crisp, R. (1997), *Routledge Philosophy Guidebook to Mill on Utilitarianism*, London: Routledge.

Darwall, S., Gibbard, A., and Railton, T. (1992), Towards *Fin-de-Siècle* Ethics: Some Trends, *Philosophical Review*, 101 (1992), 115–89.

Donnelly, J. (2003), *Universal Human Rights in Theory and Practice*, 2nd rev. edn., Ithaca, NY: Cornell University Press.

Drinan, R. F. (2001), *The Mobilization of Shame: A World View of Human Rights*, New Haven, CT: Yale University Press.

Dworkin, R. (1978), *Taking Rights Seriously*, Cambridge, MA: Harvard University Press.

Dworkin, R. (1990), *A Bill of Rights for Britain*, London: Chatto & Windus.

Falk, Richard A. (2000), *Human Rights Horizons: The Pursuit of Justice in a Globalizing World*, London: Routledge.

Finnis, J. (1980), *Natural Law and Natural Rights*, Oxford: Clarendon Press.

Finnis, J. (1983), *Fundamentals of Ethics*, Oxford: Clarendon Press.

Fowler, J. (1999), *Humanism, Beliefs and Practices*, Brighton: Sussex Academic Press.
Frankena, W. K. (1973), *Ethics*, 2nd edn., Englewood Cliffs, NJ: Prentice-Hall.
Gadamer, H.-G. (1981), *Reason in the Age of Science*, Cambridge, MA: MIT Press.
Gearty, C., and Tomkins, A. (1999) (eds.), *Understanding Human Rights*, London: Pinter, Cassell.
Gewirth, A. (1983), The Epistemology of Human Rights, *Social Philosophy and Policy*, 1 (2) (1983–4).
Gewirth, A. (1996), *The Community of Rights*, Chicago: University of Chicago Press.
Gillon, R. (1995), *Philosophical Medical Ethics*, New York: John Wiley & Sons.
Glendon, M. A. (2001), *A World Made New: Eleanor Roosevelt and the Universal Declaration of Human Rights*, New York: Random House.
Hare, R. M. (1981), *Moral Thinking: Its Levels, Method, and Point*, Oxford: Clarendon Press.
Herbert, G. B. (2002), *A Philosophical History of Rights*, New Brunswick, NJ: Transaction Publishers.
Jones, P. (1994), *Rights*, London: Macmillan.
Kitto, H. D. F. (1991), *The Greeks*, London: Penguin.
Klug, F. (1996), A Bill of Rights as Secular Ethics, in Richard Gordon and Richard Wilmot-Smith (eds.), *Human Rights in the United Kingdom*, Oxford: Oxford University Press.
Klug, F. (2000), *Values for a Godless Age: The Story of the UK's New Bill of Rights*, London: Penguin.
Koch, A. (1964), *The Philosophy of Thomas Jefferson*, Chicago: Quadrangle Books.
Laslett, P. (1963) (ed.), *John Locke: Two Treatises of Government*, Cambridge: Cambridge University Press.
Lewis, C. S. (1960), *The Four Loves*, London: Geoffrey Bles.
Little, D. (1993), The Nature and Basis of Human Rights, in G. Outka and J. Reeder, Jr. (eds.), *Prospects for a Common Morality*, Princeton, NJ: Princeton University Press.
MacCormick, N. (1992), Natural Law and the Separation of Law and Morals, in R. P. George (ed.), *Natural Law Theory: Contemporary Essays*, Oxford: Clarendon Press.
MacDonald, M. (1984), Natural Rights, in Waldron (1984).
Macedo, S. (1990), *Liberal Virtues: Citizenship, Virtue, and Community in Liberal Constitutionalism*, Oxford: Clarendon Press.
MacIntyre, A. (1981), *After Virtue*, London: Duckworth.
Mackie, J. L. (1977), *Ethics: Inventing Right and Wrong*, London: Penguin.
Mackie, J. L. (1984), Can There be a Right-Based Moral Theory? in Waldron (1984).

Mahoney, J. (1987), *The Ways of Wisdom*, London: King's College.

Mahoney, J. (1992), The Challenge of Moral Distinctions, *Theological Studies*, 53 (4), 663–82.

Mann, J. (1998), Health and Human Rights, in van der Heijden and Tahzib-Lie (1998).

Maritain, J. (1986), *"Christianity and Democracy" and "The Rights of Man and Natural Law,"* San Francisco, CA: Ignatius Press.

Melden, A. I. (1970) (ed.), *Human Rights*, Belmont, CA: Wadsworth.

Mill, J. S. (1973), *Utilitarianism*, ed. Mary Warnock, London: Collins Fontana.

Moore, G. E. (1965), *Principia Ethica*, Cambridge: Cambridge University Press.

Newman, J. H. (1967), *Apologia Pro Vita Sua: Being a History of His Religious Opinions*, Oxford: Clarendon Press.

Nickel, J. W. (1987), *Making Sense of Human Rights: Philosophical Reflections on the Universal Declaration of Human Rights*, Berkeley, CA: University of California Press, new rev. edn. (forthcoming), Oxford: Blackwell.

O'Neill, O. (2000), *Bounds of Justice*, Cambridge: Cambridge University Press.

Orend, B. (2002), *Human Rights: Concept and Context*, Peterborough, Ont.: Broadview Press.

Pascal, B. (1956), *Pascal's Pensées*, London: Everyman's Library.

Rawls, J. (1975), Fairness as Goodness, *Philosophical Review*, 84 (4) (Oct.).

Robinson, M. (1998), The Universal Declaration of Human Rights: The International Keystone of Human Dignity, in van der Heijden and Tahzib-Lie (1998).

Rorty, R. (1992), Cosmopolitanism without Emancipation: a Response to Lyotard, in S. Lash and J. Friedman (eds.), *Modernity and Identity*, Oxford: Blackwell.

Rorty, R. (1993), Human Rights, Rationality and Sentimentality, in S. Shute and S. Hurley (eds.), *On Human Rights: The Oxford Amnesty Lectures 1993*, New York: Basic Books.

Sen, A. (1988), *On Ethics and Economics*, Oxford: Blackwell.

Sen, A. (1988a), Rights and Agency, in S. Scheffler (ed.), *Consequentialism and Its Critics*, Oxford: Oxford University Press, pp. 187–223.

Shell, S. (1990), Idealism, in Allan Bloom (ed.), *Confronting the Constitution*, Washington, DC: AEI Press.

Shestack, J. J. (2000), The Philosophical Foundations of Human Rights, in Symonides (2000), pp. 31–66.

Sieghart, P. (1985), *The Lawful Rights of Mankind: An Introduction to the International Legal Code of Human Rights*, Oxford: Oxford University Press.

Stout, J. (1988), *Ethics After Babel: The Languages of Morals and Their Discontents*, Boston, MA: Beacon Press.

Stout, J. (1992), Truth, Natural Law, and Ethical Theory, in R. P. George (ed.), *Natural Law Theory: Contemporary Essays*, Oxford: Clarendon Press.

Sumner, L. W. (1987), *The Moral Foundation of Rights*, Oxford: Clarendon Press.

Sumner, L. W. (2000), Rights, in H. LaFollette (ed.), *The Blackwell Guide to Ethical Theory*, Oxford: Blackwell, pp. 288–305.

Symonides, J. (2000) (ed.), *Human Rights: Concept and Standards*, Aldershot: Ashgate.

Teilhard de Chardin, P. (1975), *The Phenomenon of Man*, intro. by Sir Julian Huxley, London. Collins Fontana.

Thomson, J. J. (1990), *The Realm of Rights*, Cambridge, MA: Harvard University Press.

Trigg, R. (2005), *Morality Matters*, Oxford: Blackwell.

United Nations Educational, Scientific and Cultural Organisation (UNESCO) (1949), *Human Rights: Comments and Interpretations*, London and New York: Allan Wingate.

United Nations Records (1948), Official Records of the Third Session of the General Assembly, Part I, Third Committee, vol. IIIA (6).

United Nations, Charter of the (1995), New York: Department of Public Information, United Nations.

United Nations *Universal Declaration of Human Rights* (1948), New York: United Nations.

van der Heijden, Barend, and Tahzib-Lie, Bahiaq (1998) (eds.), *Reflections on the Universal Declaration of Human Rights: A Fiftieth Anniversary Anthology*, The Hague: Martin Nijhoff.

Waldron, J. (1984) (ed.), *Theories of Rights*, Oxford: Oxford University Press.

Waldron, J. (1987) (ed.), *Nonsense upon Stilts*, London: Methuen.

Waldron, J. (2002), *God, Locke, and Equality: Christian Foundations in Locke's Political Thought*, Cambridge: Cambridge University Press.

Wheen, F. (2004), *How Mumbo-Jumbo Conquered the World: A Short History of Modern Delusions*, London: Collins, Fourth Estate.

Wokler, R. (1994), Projecting the Enlightenment, in J. Horton and S. Mendus (eds.), *After MacIntyre: Critical Perspectives on the Work of Alasdair MacIntyre*, Cambridge: Polity Press.

Chapter ⑤

The Globalizing of Human Rights

Of the many areas in life in which human rights have an important part to play, one of the most extensive and significant, and even crucial, must be the modern phenomenon of globalization. As a general term, "globalization" refers to the expansion of the scale of human events, activities, and interactions from a local to a worldwide, or global, level. In the 1960s the communications guru, Marshall McLuhan (1968), was popularizing the new description of the earth as a "global village," a single human community linked by telecommunications. Then a morning in July 1969 provided dramatic witness to the reality of globalization, when the world woke up to find blazoned across the front pages of its newspapers the first astonishing photographs taken by astronauts of the earth hovering in space.

Global Expansion

In many respects, in fact, the world has been "shrinking," feeling significantly smaller and coming increasingly together in numerous ways. Distances have diminished and travel expanded through jet transport; communications have accelerated and multiplied through new information technology, satellite networks, and the worldwide web, revolutionizing the transfer of knowledge as well as of capital; geographical and cultural differences are being shared and becoming domesticated and commonplace; and through satellite video-links events and happenings in every quarter of the world are becoming instantly experienced first-hand worldwide as they occur, often enabling distant spectators to become participants. There are no longer any "remote" quarters of the globe. In addition, the growing worldwide sense of forming one interdependent community has been intensified by the need to find planetary solutions to environmental crises which are mounting on a continental and global scale, well expressed as early as Barbara Ward's 1972 study entitled *Only One Earth*, as well as by the fear since the September 2001 air attack on the New York World Trade Center, and bombings in other continents, of what is becoming recognized as global terrorism.

The most pervasive manifestation of globalization has been the worldwide expansion of opportunities for trade, involving faster and cheaper transport of goods, services, and facilities to global markets, the removal of various trade barriers, the growth and spread of e-commerce, movements towards global economic and financial integration, and the development of a world economy (see Crane and Matten 2004: 436–7). Steiner observed that "Since the end of the cold war ... businesses are now playing a role in economic development once reserved to states," a role which "has both stemmed from and strengthened the contemporary process of globalization with its stress on developing market economies, deregulating business activities, privatizing state enterprises, lowering national barriers, and expanding world trade and investment" (Harvard 1999: 9). Nor is it just the lives of individuals and communities of people which are affected and changed by globalization. Social structures, including states and national governments, are involved in the networking which is being set in place and in the new interrelationships and interdependence which are created in the process. So much so, Symonides concluded (1998: 28), that "the autonomy and policy-making capability of states is being undermined by economic and cultural internationalization." Within a wider focus, as Evans (1998: 12) observed, "the literature on globalization suggests a new global order concerned with powerful processes of cultural, social, economic and political change, which challenge past beliefs about the nature of sovereignty, society and the wider international political community."

Moral attitudes and reactions to globalization vary widely, even extremely, and there is no sign of the stream of literature on both its negative and positive consequences dwindling. One study by Stiglitz (2002), a committed opponent, surveys the perceived disadvantages of globalization and argues that, among other ills, it worsens poverty, extends or entrenches the use of child labor, worsens the plight of women in developing countries, erodes democracy, imperils local cultures, and despoils the environment. Other charges are that increased multinational mobility around the world is leading to a lack of commitment by businesses to local societies which results in insecurity in labor markets, and has the destabilizing effect of encouraging social disengagement which is manifested in family and personal rootlessness, short-term perspectives, and a taste for novelty and trivialities. In addition, it is claimed that global markets and global branding manipulate market choices, erode local individualist choices, and impoverish cultures by homogenizing them. Regular comment on the harmful effects of globalization appears on the website of the World Development Movement (WDM 2005); and attacks, which often appear to be as much against capitalism as such as against globalization, take the form of rallies and often violent demonstrations, planned on the internet, which originated at the meeting of the World Trade Organization in Seattle in 1999 and have continued to accompany and disturb meetings of the World Economic Forum and other international financial and economic bodies.

By contrast, writing in defense of globalization Jagdish Bhagwati (2004) portrays it as driving liberal trade, as preventing short-sighted trade protection which leaves the poor worse off, and as raising incomes and improving the longer-term development prospects of the world's poor. Similar strong argumentation is provided by Philippe Legrain (2002: 10) in a detailed rebuttal of the charges against globalization, which begins by observing that "it has become a convenient scapegoat for all manner of real and perceived ills that have little or nothing to do with it." Likewise, the British Labour Party Member of Parliament and former Secretary of State for International Development, Clare Short (2004), has argued that what has made for the greatest progress in combating global poverty has been "the opening up of markets, facilitating the investment of multinational companies and production of manufactured goods, clothing, toys and now even services, such as call centres, based in the poorest countries and serving our desires and consumption patterns." In brief, she maintained, "the engine of economic growth necessary to reduce poverty, on a large scale, has been investment generated by the increasingly integrated global economy"; and she concludes that the obvious needs to ensure effective regulation and control, and to spread the gains of globalization much more widely, should not be allowed to gainsay this basic fact. Indeed, Wolf (2004: 95) opined, "the pity is not that there has been too much globalization, but that there is too little." In a wider-lens view, globalization has also provided valuable channels of transnational communication, enabling people, countries, and NGOs to learn from each other, to witness and to call attention to violations of human rights in previously obscure areas of the globe, and to mobilize collective reactions and remedial proposals (see McGrew 1998: 198–201).

Seeking a Global Ethic

Awareness of the global dimension of so many human activities today, and sensitivity to their potential global impact for good or ill on millions of individuals, as we have just noted, has led to various attempts to identify a system of ethics which would be global in its applicability (see Twiss and Grelle 1998). Indeed, as globalization expands and individual countries are disposed to lose their economic, political, and even legislative autonomy, there appears a particular need to find some unified system of normative behavior, whether it be legal or moral or both, which can give some measure of protection worldwide to the interests of states and nations and their citizens. One of the leading exponents of such a so-called "global ethic," Hans Küng, explained:

> Globalisation of the economy, technology and the media has also meant globalisation of problems (from financial and labour markets to the environment and organized crime). What is therefore also needed is globalisation of ethics: not a uniform ethical system, but a necessary minimum of shared ethical values, basic attitudes and standards to which all regions, nations and interest groups can subscribe – in other words, a shared basic ethic for mankind.   (1998: 165–6)

The point is made from a geopolitical viewpoint by Evans that "with the realization that the global rather than the national economy exercises the greater influence on economic well-being, the state loses its significance as a centre of authority through which people can express their preferences and claim their rights . . . Although national governments continue to engage in international politics, governance is conducted by . . . a group of formal and informal organizations without democratic pretensions," including the World Bank, the World Trade Organization, the Trilateral Commission, and the Group of Eight (Evans 1998: 14).

In addition, of equal concern must be the potential relevance of such a global ethic to deal with unregulated global capitalism, since a striking, sometimes alarming, feature of the market operating at a global level is the way in which companies can transcend the territorial boundaries, and therefore the regulatory control, of individual states as they move around the world in order to minimize their labor, tax, environmental, and other local costs.

United Nations reference to the idea of a global ethic was introduced in the 1995 Report *Our Global Neighbourhood* produced by the Commission on Global Governance which the United Nations set up in 1992.

The Report called for "broad acceptance of a global civic ethic" which would acknowledge the core values of respect for life, liberty, justice and equity, mutual respect, caring, and integrity; and it continued:

> the realities of the emerging global neighbourhood require that, in addition to promoting the values just described, we should develop a global ethic that applies equally to all those involved in world affairs. Its efficacy will depend on the ability of people and governments to transcend narrow self-interests and agree that the interests of humanity as a whole will be best served by acceptance of a set of common rights and responsibilities.   (UN Commission on Global Governance 1995: ch. 2)

As the Commission concluded, "We therefore urge the international community to·unite in support of a global ethic of common rights and shared responsibilities. In our view, such an ethic – reinforcing the fundamental rights that are already part of the fabric of international norms – would provide the moral foundation for constructing a more effective system of global governance."

Other international bodies which have worked to promote the idea of a global ethic have been the Parliament of World Religions in its 1993 Chicago Declaration *on The Principles of a Global Ethic*, and the Inter-Action Council of former heads of state and governments in its 1997 *Universal Declaration on Human Responsibilities* (Küng and Schmidt 1998). Both documents addressed their appeal to the world's moral sentiments on human grounds without making any exclusive claim for religion, and both explicitly reaffirmed the Universal Declaration of Human Rights, while feeling a need to supplement it by putting it within a wider ethical context of shared values and by stressing the need for a recognition of the central significance of responsibilities parallel to that of rights.

Cultural Relativism

In various quarters of modern society there is thus an impressive convergence of moves to recognize that, in response to the increasing phenomenon of globalization, human rights can apply as a universal ethical norm affecting all human behavior in this new context. There is a widespread conviction not only that they can, but indeed that they must. The point is made succinctly by Orend (2002: 161): "Now that our interconnections are genuinely international, we need core ground-rules to govern our interactions and our shared institutions," which he maintains would importantly involve human rights.

There is also, however, widespread acknowledgment that applying human rights as a global ethic incurs serious difficulties, above all that of questioning the very possibility of elaborating one set of universal ethical norms or standards which will apply worldwide in every society and culture. McGrew (1998: 205) notes "the growing salience of inter-civilizational conflicts over universal human rights," thus drawing attention to the whole phenomenon of cultural relativism, with which human rights, or any universal system of morality, needs to come to terms.

It is important to be clear that what is at issue here is the claim for ethical relativism among cultures. Obvious differing ways of behavior in different lands, relating to dress, diet, customs, social conventions, and the like, do not necessarily have ethical implications, although they can create social pitfalls for the unwary foreigner (see Carte and Fox 2004). Nor in principle do differences in legislation involving such areas as tax structures, traffic or alcohol regulations, etc. indicate ethical relativism. The critical area in which we are interested is whether, and to what extent, moral behavior and expectations, as distinct from social and legal, take strikingly different forms across cultures.

Nickel (1987: 61–8) provides a useful analysis of cultural diversity around the world against which to consider human rights, and he distinguishes several meanings which can be given to the term "moral relativism" (pp. 68–81), focusing in on what he calls "strong prescriptive relativism" (p. 77), which endorses "normative diversity" and which provides the strongest case for cultural relativism against human rights, although it is an approach by which Nickel himself is not particularly impressed. "One may see the value of preserving, say, the cultural and religious traditions of India without concluding that the Indian caste system should be preserved" (p. 79).

Nickel (1987: 74) observes that "the strongest form of prescriptive relativism holds that the only valid universal norm is one requiring tolerance," a remark which leads one to recognize the importance of distinguishing between ethical imperialism, ethical tolerance, and ethical relativism. Ethical imperialism signifies that one is enforcing one's own values and ethical views on other people regardless of their wishes to the contrary; and the West is routinely accused of this by its opponents. Ethical tolerance, by contrast, involves respecting other people's ethical views which differ from one's own. Tolerance does not wish to impose one's own different views on others, yet it is important to note that tolerance does not involve approving or accepting other people's views in preference to one's own; in fact, it presumes there is a difference, which it respects.

In fact, morally speaking ethical tolerance is worlds apart from both ethical imperialism and ethical relativism; paradoxically, it is in its own right, in the words of Thomas Donaldson (1993: 69), "a universalizable moral value . . . a far cry from relativism." In contrast, then, to ethical imperialism and to ethical tolerance, ethical relativism entails accepting that the ethical views which individuals or groups profess on particular matters may differ and yet be all equally valid, or equally right for those who maintain them. As Speake sums up (1979: 281), "to be a relativist about value is to maintain that there are no universal standards of good and bad, right and wrong."

What globalization and the bid to fashion a global ethic bring into prominence, then, is that what McGrew (1998) has pointed to as "inter-civilizational conflicts over universal human rights" need to be countered. Glendon put the contrary position disarmingly when she referred to the Human Rights Commission's ability "to give the lie to claims that peoples with drastically opposed worldviews cannot agree upon a few common standards of decency" (Glendon 2001: p. xix).

More systematically, the response to the claim of ethical relativism to be found in different cultures can take two possible forms. One is to tackle head-on as a matter of principle whether cultural diversity must involve ethical relativism, or whether on the contrary one can establish basic ethical values and norms whose writ circles the globe. In other words, are there certain typical ways of behaving towards people which are to be judged totally and universally wrong, as being incompatible with the inherent dignity of the individual human person? The other approach to claims for justified cultural ethical relativism is to scrutinize specific examples of behavior where a different ethical verdict is claimed to be justified by local or regional custom or circumstances, and to examine these instances one by one. Jagger (2000: 366), for instance, makes a highly relevant point in an article on feminist ethics when she observes that the issue of universal ethical standards "has special poignancy for feminists . . . the dilemma of respecting cultural difference, on the one hand, while maintaining an unwavering opposition to male dominance, on the other."

On the whole, when the piecemeal and empirical approach is adopted, invariably the first candidate for justified ethical relativism is the practice of bribery, which is claimed by many people as ethically inevitable and widely acceptable in certain societies which are considered more or less endemically corrupt. Apart from bribery, however, there is little agreement on other claimants for ethical acceptability in certain regions but not necessarily in others. Few, if any, people would argue in principle to accept ethically such cultural phenomena as discrimination against women or lower castes; physical mutilation either as a female cultural tradition or as a method of criminal punishment for men; the honor killing of "disgraced" female family members; the practice of suttee, or self-immolation of widows; child labor; genocide or "ethnic cleansing"; xenophobia or routine exploitation of outsiders; or environmental spoliation. The consequence is that if one is able to handle the issue of bribery, invariably the bribing of officials, without appealing to ethical relativism, then the case for ethical relativism peculiar to different cultures as a general principle tends to collapse.

Bribery is a complex social and moral phenomenon which in its most flagrant forms many societies are at least officially struggling to outlaw as harmful to their long-term international interests. It is the petty everyday form prevalent in some societies, the so-called "facilitating payments," which can create ethical fatalism in foreigners and result in a resigned relativist acceptance that "when in Rome one should do as the Romans do" (Argandoña 2005). In analysing the ethics of bribery, however, it is helpful to make some distinctions. There is a significant difference between on the one hand offering an official a bribe to do something which is morally wrong, and on the other hand paying an official a bribe just to do their proper job, or provide normal service, the arrangement which many authorities, including the International Chamber of Commerce (ICC 1977), consider constitutes the vast majority of reported cases of bribery. However, this latter everyday practice of bribery is more accurately to be described as the reluctant paying of extortion, or as the price exacted to enable one to conduct one's normal, and ethical, affairs. It is similar to being compelled to pay blackmail or "protection money" or to suffer a "shakedown," as an unfair imposition levied for getting on with one's life and honest activities. Some powerful multinational companies are in a position simply to refuse to pay outright bribes or extortions, even including petty "facilitating payments" to oil the wheels of day-to-day transactions. And the *New York Times*, for instance (July 3, 2005), provided evidence that local cultures in Africa are by no means complaisant with bribery when it commended "brave governmental forays against corruption in places like Nigeria." Consequently, when a company or an individual does not have resources for resistance, then paying up unwillingly in such situations is much more a case of choosing a lesser evil than an instance of engaging in a practice to be approved of as ethically desirable and commendable in any particular society (see Mahoney 1995).

The more general and principled line of response to the claim of ethical relativism which denies any universal ethical norms or principles is to confront it with the major objections: that in principle absolutely any behavior could therefore be morally acceptable somewhere; that it entails that there are no universal moral principles at all; that moral debates and attempts at persuasion are ultimately pointless; and that there is absolutely no role in any society for moral rebels or moral reformers, no moral fulcrum with which one can, Archimedes-like, move the world. Relativism denies that there are any legitimate basic moral convictions, in such areas as trust, truthfulness, property, loyalty, and arbitrary killing. Glendon makes the point plainly:

> No one has yet improved on the answer of the UNESCO philosophers: Where basic human values are concerned, cultural diversity has been exaggerated. The group found, after consulting with Confucian, Hindu, Muslim, and European thinkers, that a core of fundamental principles was widely shared in countries that had not yet adopted rights instruments and in cultures that had not embraced the language of rights. Their survey persuaded them that basic human rights rest on "common convictions" even though these convictions "are stated in terms of different philosophic principles and on the background of divergent political and economic systems." (Glendon 2001: 222; see Maritain 1949: 258–9)

Moreover, the claim to justify cultural moral relativism suffers from a major fallacy: it presumes that all cultures are ethically sacrosanct and are above ethical critique. As Donaldson and Dunfee comment (1999: 22), "to believe that no ethical view held by an individual or culture is better than any other view is equivalent to believing child rapists are as worthy as child educators." In the course of the UN Vienna Conference on Human Rights, the US Secretary of State, Warren Christopher, argued: "We respect the religious, social and cultural characteristics that make each country unique. But we cannot let cultural relativism become the last refuge of repression" (see Drinan 2001: 54).

Clearly both human rights and diverse cultures have to be respected, but only when they are compatible. For instance, clitoridectomy, whatever the tribal mores or cultural gloss which can be invoked to commend or to countenance it as a form of female initiation, is still gross bodily mutilation; and as such, like punitive amputation of any other parts of the body, it is an intrusion completely alien to the physical integrity and human dignity of the individual involved, in addition to condemning its object to an impaired sexual future. It is stark instances such as this and others which we have identified above which put in question bland generalizations that all cultures are to be equally respected ethically, and which justify the point made by Jones that the human rights theorist should not be "too readily cowed by the invocation of cultural diversity," and should be prepared for "the possibility of conflict between human rights and cultural traditions." In such cases, as he concludes roundly, "unless it is morally neutered, a doctrine of human rights cannot give its blessing to practices that it identifies as morally grotesque and inhuman merely because those practices are shrouded in the mantle of culture" (Jones 1994: 218–20).

Part of the function of human rights, then, as expressing a globally effective ethic is to act as a continuing critique not only on individuals but also on whole societies and cultures, North and South, East and West. In the past the history of the abolition of slavery is probably the most telling example of cultures being painfully challenged by the emergence of new ethical insights. The struggle for women's rights today, which encounters more entrenched cultural opposition in some areas of the globe than in others, is another striking instance of all cultures being ethically challenged almost as part of their evolution. We are accustomed to individuals having what might be called ethical blind spots and of their moral vision being impaired in some areas of behavior, such as respect for the truth, for others' feelings or reputations, or for other people's property. Likewise, it is entirely possible for cultures, and not only individuals, to be what Little (1993: 85) describes as "morally handicapped," and to suffer from such handicap not only historically, but also in the modern world. After all, it was in Europe, the cradle of natural rights, that in the 1930s the greatest onslaught in history on human rights took place.

By definition, then, the doctrine of universal human rights sits in ethical judgment on all societies and cultures and it de-absolutizes in the name of human dignity all political, social, and economic structures or regimes. Its purpose may even be described as to diagnose moral blind spots and to prescribe for them, wherever societies suffer from such blind spots, or Little's "moral handicap," around the globe. The intriguing corollary is for any society to ask itself, on pain of ethical complacency, the uncomfortable question, What are its current moral blind spots in contravention of human rights, even though by definition such blind spots are unknown, at least to the general mass of people. Sensitivity such as this provides a new context and confirmation for the observation of Habgood (1993: 108), already noted above (p. 95) that "assertions of rights represent the leading edge of moral insight." Today, for example, we may be in the painful process of slowly removing the scales from our eyes which have concealed the ways in which various societies have systematically abused indigenous peoples, on which the UN has begun to take some faltering steps (see Falk 2000: 50–1), and the extent to which we have all through environmental and ecological irresponsibility simply dismissed the interest of future generations from our consideration.

There is always the challenge, however, of recognizing and allowing for different ways, or even, degrees, of implementing human rights in various cultures. An Anglo-Chinese conference organized by Gresham College, London, in which the author took part some years ago included an intriguing paper entitled "Justice with a Chinese Face." The first generation of human rights deals mainly with individual personal liberty, and the aim is for these to be exercised in full against any excessive state intervention. The second generation of human rights – social, economic, and cultural rights – relate to living conditions in society, and, although protection of political and civil rights require some state provision and cost, nevertheless social, economic, and cultural rights depend much more on state resources and state intervention to ensure and monitor their enjoyment and their exercise. Here the practical feasibility of state guarantee for such rights is relative, being heavily dependent on the political, economic, and social context of each particular community and the international pressures to which it may be subject. The challenge is then for states to use their resources, including debt and aid resources – and to be permitted by others to use these resources – to create a culture which is congenial to human rights, which may take account of Sen's theory of "capabilities" (above, pp. 78–9) and which will vary in degree according to local need, with the right to housing, for instance, differing between favorable and hostile climates, the right to education being perceived differently in a developing African country and a sophisticated Western country, and the right to a living wage being obviously relative to the local cost of living.

The need in a globalized world is surely, therefore, to promote a culture of universal human rights based on a common humanity which at the same time respects different traditions where it is possible to allow moral space for them. As the UN Vienna Declaration proclaimed:

> All human rights are universal, indivisible and interdependent and inter-related. The international community must treat human rights globally in a fair and equal manner, on the same footing, and with the same emphasis. While the significance of national and regional particularities and various historical, cultural and religious backgrounds must be borne in mind, it is the duty of States, regardless of their political, economic and cultural systems, to promote and protect all human rights and fundamental freedoms.   (*The UN and Human Rights* 1995: p. 450)

As globalization continues, and intensifies, it will become an increasingly relevant task in every area of human activity to identify and deploy further applications of basic human rights, and to operate as a global monitor for them. Fergusson has observed that "the language of human rights is the only plausible candidate for a global moral language" (1998: 450); and this can only be because, as Clague concluded (2000: 140), "human rights serve an important transcultural and international purpose in expressing a set of universally applicable minimum standards for social living."

Global Human Rights

The growth of globalization in modern times has also had its effect on human rights, expanding their area of relevance also to a notably global scale. In particular there appear to be three human rights which are being significantly globalized in this way: economic justice in the face of global poverty, environmental justice in the face of global environmental disorders, and HIV/AIDS justice in the face of the worldwide pandemic.

A striking feature of the phenomenon of globalization is not only to increase and multiply human resources and market opportunities for many of the world's inhabitants, but also to show as on a giant cosmic screen the dire needs which increasingly affect large groups of the world's population, and in so doing, to expand to a global scale the moral claims of some human rights, notably economic rights. Nickel observes (1987: 149) that "the purpose of including economic rights among human rights is to identify areas within the economic sphere where powerful moral considerations provide fairly clear guidance for individual actions and social and political institutions." He goes on to provide an analysis of economic rights by distinguishing between production-related rights and consumption-related rights. Production-related rights cover the rights necessary for creating the means of human subsistence, including rights to personal property, to employment, to fair remuneration, to health and safety and other conditions at work and to participate in the market (pp. 149–60). By contrast, consumption-related rights are those which "serve to make possible the acquisition, use, and consumption of goods" (p. 160), all of these coming down to satisfying what Nickel describes as "the right to adequate nutrition," a right which he maintains falls to be satisfied, in default of personal resources, by state welfare provision (p. 161).

Enlightening as Nickel's analysis of economic rights is, it fails to consider the big-screen picture, that is, not just the global dimension of production-related rights within an international market, but also, even more urgently, the world scenario of consumption-related rights dominated by the phenomenon of global poverty and hunger. For, whatever its manifold economic and cultural advantages for the human family, especially long-term, there is no doubt that globalization in its many forms and manifestations contains much potential for harm, especially in terms of the economic inequalities and inequities which result between individuals and nations, as detailed in the 1998 UNESCO study on new dimensions and challenges for human rights (Symonides 1998). As Robinson noted in a work on international relations theory, the world of globalization is "a world that is not only increasingly interconnected, but is also characterized by massive and ever-widening disparities in levels of well-being and access to basic goods and resources" (Robinson 2001: 57).

This sobering realization is regularly acknowledged by the World Trade Organization and the International Monetary Fund in reviewing the conditions which they require developing governments to implement in return for aid. Ironically such WTO conditions can involve the cutting of food subsidies and the adoption of harmful labor practices (Leary 1998: 265). Global poverty and resulting global mortality exacerbated by international debt, corrupt governments, and discriminatory trade tariffs is a depressing aspect of globalization (see McGrew 1998: 196); and this, if basic human rights have any ethical purchase, must morally outweigh all of the present advantages of globalization for the inhabitants of the richer, more powerful nations, as well as its promised "no jam today, but jam tomorrow" dividends for millions of vulnerable individuals and countless groups spread throughout the developing world. The agenda of the Group of Eight's (G8) global summits of the wealthiest advanced industrialized nations regularly addresses, with no great marked success, the issues of debt relief packages, development aid, and, recently, ways of promoting integrity in recipient governments through combating corruption and seeking transparency in national budgets, procurement systems, and awards of concessions on natural resources sectors. However, sadly there is little indication that the most recent G8 meeting, in Scotland in 2005, did much to improve the situation of global poverty, in spite of the intense mobilization there of NGOs and numerous other parties and agencies determined to "make poverty history." In fact, whatever is effected in terms of providing aid and of canceling debt, and even of controlling local government corruption, it is to be feared that little lasting success is to be hoped for so long as no honest attention is given to the longstanding obstacle to international trade, especially south–north, caused by the protectionist rules, for example, in agriculture and textiles, which are rigged against poorer, less developed economies, and which are judged to constitute the single greatest cause of their continuing poverty. The much vaunted principle that market negotiations must take place on a "level playing field" is scandalously absent from the arena of international trade.

Writing of the appalling apparently intractable poverty in sub-Saharan Africa, for example, Linden charges that there is "a strong element of hypocrisy in the avowed commitment of the USA and the European Union to Africa's development. Their trade policies have blocked promising avenues for rural development amongst their weaker competitors" (Linden 2005: 149). The political reasons, Linden observes, are not far to seek for such obstinate persistence on the part of richer countries in maintaining subsidies which grossly favor home industries, especially agriculture, while crippling tariffs are levied on imports. "When push comes to shove, neo-liberalism gives way to protective tariffs designed to consolidate votes in key sections of the electorates of the North" (Linden pp. 149–50).

Taking a broad view, the 1993 Vienna Declaration of the UN World Conference on Human Rights, which applied to peoples as much as to individuals, identified the promotion and protecting of human rights as a "global task." It affirmed

> that extreme poverty and social exclusion constitute a violation of human dignity and that urgent steps are necessary to achieve better knowledge of extreme poverty and its causes, including those related to the problem of development, in order to promote the human rights of the poorest, and to put an end to extreme poverty and social exclusion and to promote the enjoyment of the fruits of social progress. (UN Vienna Declaration 1993)

Underlying and stimulating this Vienna statement on economic rights was the uncompromising report made to the Conference by the UN Committee on Economic, Social and Cultural Rights, which stated that

> the international community as a whole continues to tolerate all too often breaches of economic, social and cultural rights which, if they occurred in relation to civil and political rights, would provoke expressions of horror and outrage and would lead to concerted calls for immediate remedial action. In effect, despite the rhetoric, violations of civil and political rights continue to be treated as though they were far more serious, and more patently intolerable, than massive and direct denials of economic, social and cultural rights. (quoted in Eide 2000: 112)

Another human right which has all too clearly taken on a global dimension is the right to a safe environment. Anxiety for global ecology and the physical environment are of deep and growing concern today, at local, continental, and increasingly at world levels. From one point of view, a healthy environment has to be seen as part of the basic individual human right to subsistence (above, pp. 77–8). Nussbaum (1968: 23), for instance, is quite clear that "by minimal economic security, or subsistence, I mean unpolluted air, unpolluted water, adequate food, adequate clothing, adequate shelter, and minimal preventive public health care." However, increasing urgency about the quality of the air, as well as of the earth and its waters, has multiplied anxieties to bring human environmental interests and rights to the forefront of global concern, to become what Bobbio (1996: 69), among others, described as one of the new third generation of human rights (above, pp. 96–7) of which the first he was to identify was "the right to live in an unpolluted environment, which has been the basis for the ecological movements that have shaken both individual countries and the international system." Systematic deforestation and greenhouse gas emissions, the thinning of the earth's protecting ozone layer and global warming, are all being connected with environmental pollution, variations in ocean levels, and growing regional climatic fluctuations, to shape a highly volatile and worrying future for the world as a whole.

Singer (2004: 14) sums up the environmental prospect for the human species by observing that "there can be no clearer illustration of the need for human beings to act globally than the issues raised by the impact of human activity on our atmosphere"; and he provides a detailed assessment of what this impact will entail. In 1988 the United Nations General Assembly set up the Intergovernmental Panel on Climate Change, and the "Earth Summit" which was then held in Rio de Janeiro in 1992 agreed on a Convention which called on, but did not require, the powerful developed nations to take the initiative in tackling climate change and its harmful results. Subsequently, in 1997, the Kyoto Protocol, to which, notoriously, the United States administration declined to give its consent, agreed on setting varying targets for the developed nations to reduce their total emissions (Singer 2004: 21–3, 49–50).

Of course, respect for a country's and the world's environment can often appear to be in conflict with concern for economic development, especially of and in the Third World, as Hayden recognizes. At Rio, he noted, "while many of the industrialised nations argued for more stringent environmental protection along with continued economic growth, the majority of developing nations insisted that their precarious economic development – and thus the exploitation of their natural resources – could not be imperilled by an undue emphasis on environmental protection" (Hayden 2005: 123). One consequence was for the Conference to set up the UN Commission on Sustainable Development (CSD), in recognition of the emergence and growth of the human right to development which we noted earlier (pp. 55–6) and of the idea of "sustainable development" which the Bruntland Report in 1987 had defined as that which can "ensure that it meets the needs of the present without compromising the ability of future generations to meet their own needs" (Hayden 2005: 123).

In fact, one of the clearest instances of a potential conflict between human rights on a large scale is that to be found between the right to development of individual, and especially of developing, nations, and the right to a healthy environment of not just that nation's, but the whole world's inhabitants, the dilemma being how to satisfy the former without endangering the latter. What is quite evident, however, is that neither of these rights, to development and to environmental justice, can be effectively pursued within the confines of one country or nation state, or even a single region. Economic development, no less than environmental integrity, is now of its essence part of a network embracing the entire globe, the economic network of the market, and the environmental network of the climate, which are themselves intimately connected. Only if both are faced and negotiated realistically at an international, and ultimately global, level, well above the self-interest of individual countries, can justice be done to both rights. What Hayden has to say negatively about environmental rights can equally apply to development rights: "Thinking about justice – and particularly of environmental justice as an integral component of global justice – can no longer be confined within the boundaries of nation-states" (Hayden 2005: 133). Extending that view positively, Nussbaum (1968: 12) links both development and environment together in a hoped-for common future when she observes, "Any intelligent deliberation about ecology – as also, about the food supply and population – requires global planning, global knowledge, and the recognition of a shared future."

A third human rights issue which is especially topical and urgent today and which is assuming a global dimension concerns HIV/AIDS, which has expanded, as Keenan shows, from being a medical issue to constituting a socio-political issue, with concern moving from a focus on clinical health to a public health approach and then to issues of social policy (Keenan 2005). As this progressed from an individual ailment to take the shape of a spreading global pandemic, the invoking of human rights with reference to HIV/AIDS moved out from such standard rights as access to health care, autonomy, privacy, non-discrimination, and non-stigmatization to encompass wider social and group rights as these confront such issues as poverty, power disparity resulting from gender, and unavailability of affordable generic medical resources.

Fuller and Keenan (2004) show how the response to a global HIV/ AIDS pandemic has been greatly served by recourse to the language of human rights, and how this weapon has been increasingly deployed by the UN, for instance in its 2001 UN General Assembly Special Session on AIDS (UNGASS). There the Declaration of Commitment on HIV/ AIDS noted with deep concern that "the global HIV/AIDS epidemic, through its devastating scale and impact, constitutes a global emergency and one of the most formidable challenges to human life and dignity, as well as to the effective enjoyment of human rights, which undermines social and economic development throughout the world and affects all levels of society – national, community, family and individual." In response to this global situation the Declaration's first concern was naturally to affirm the right to physical and mental health, in the areas of prevention, care, support, and treatment, and to follow this by requiring "the full realization of human rights and fundamental freedoms for all" as essential to a global response to the HIV/AIDS pandemic. More recently UNAIDS has been set up by the United Nations as a Joint United Nations Programme to work for "accelerated, comprehensive and coordinated global action on the epidemic" (UNAIDS). Moreover, alongside the continuing concern of the United Nations through a variety of departments, similarly worthy of note is the unremitting work of Human Rights Watch in its HIV/AIDS campaign (<http://www.hrw. org>).

Towards Cosmopolitanism

The trajectory of human rights must logically culminate, it appears, in arriving at some form of cosmopolitanism. As Henkin (1990: p. xvii) commented, human rights are now "the idea of our time"; so much so that it appears that their inner dynamism and their momentum within the march of modern history are driving the human race gradually to the realization that, in the words of Boutros Boutros-Ghali, it constitutes "a single human community" (*The UN and Human Rights* 1995: p. 442).

Earlier in this study we examined the powerful current of communitarian thinking which has been running through Western society, partly in reaction to the popularity of human rights; and we noted the reserve, to say the least, which those who share that thinking have towards the notion of human rights (see above, pp. 93–5). We noted also the popularity of the idea, not of a variety of distinct, exclusive, communities, but of one single human community, which first achieved prominence in the claim of Diogenes to be a "citizen of the world" (above, p. 95). In fact, although the theme of cosmopolitanism is thus considerably older than the idea of human rights they both have an inherent drive towards universalism and an intrinsic aversion to any ideas of inequality, isolationism, separatism, or unwarranted privilege among human beings.

In his study, *Cosmopolitan Global Politics*, Patrick Hayden explains how the sentiment of Diogenes influenced not only his fellow members of the philosophical school of Cynics in Athens, but also, more significantly, the highly influential Stoic school and thinkers, so much so that, as Orend commented (2002: 195), "in a radical departure from earlier Greek isolationism and narrow ethnic nationalism, the Stoics were truly cosmopolitan in their outlook." This included the later Roman thinkers, Cicero, Seneca, and Marcus Aurelius, through whom the Stoic cosmopolitan sentiment flowed into the Enlightenment thought of Diderot, Paine, Locke, and especially of Kant (Hayden 2005: 12–22; see Nussbaum 1996: 6–11). Tom Paine (1948: 228) spoke characteristically for Enlightenment cosmopolitanism when he declared ringingly, "Independence is my happiness, and I view things as they are, without regard to place or person; my country is the world, and my religion is to do good." More systematically the thought was expressed in Kant's doctrine of "an ideal moral community called the 'kingdom of ends'," or what Martha Nussbaum (1996: 134) termed a "virtual commonwealth," one composed of individuals each of whom must be considered an end and never merely as a means in the calculations of others (Hayden 2005: 18; see pp. 21–2). In fact, in his essay on *Perpetual Peace* Kant went so far as to sketch a constitution for a cosmopolitan form of government which would comprise a federation of independent and democratic nation states committed to the maintenance of universal peace and treating strangers in such a way that, as he predicted, "continents distant from each other can enter into peaceful mutual relations which may eventually be regulated by public laws, thus bringing the human race nearer and nearer to a cosmopolitan constitution" (Reiss 1991: 106).

Summing up the whole tradition of cosmopolitanism, Hayden explained (2005: 3) that it refers to the view that "all human beings have equal moral standing within a single world community." Like other writers on the subject, he distinguishes between moral cosmopolitanism and institutional cosmopolitanism, the latter of which he also usefully terms "legal" cosmopolitanism, since it refers to the legal and other instruments which have the function of giving institutional expression to moral cosmopolitanism. "Legal cosmopolitanism contends that a global political order ought to be constructed, grounded on the equal legal rights and duties of all individuals" (p. 3). And he notes the important role of Kant's legal and political philosophy as well as his moral philosophy in his argument for cosmopolitanism when he comments that "undeniably this unification of the moral, legal and political in Kant's thought is what elevates the cosmopolitan tradition in the modern era from a basic ethical sensibility [that is, moral cosmopolitanism] to a genuinely global political project [i.e. institutional cosmopolitanism]" (p. 17).

The Inadequacies of States

Both forms of cosmopolitanism are also concerned to question in an increasingly globalized world the claimed competency of state powers and territorial boundaries over individual human beings to the extent that they provide grounds for division and differential treatment and for ignoring the welfare of "foreigners" wherever they may happen to live (Hayden 2005: 1–2). Hayden identifies the modern position as follows:

> In much of the current literature on globalization there is widespread agreement that the existing system of global governance is deficient in many fundamental respects . . . Of particular concern is the erosion of state power by the forces of globalization which has weakened the Westphalian form of international governance – the current "self-regulating" order of the states system leaving it poorly equipped to deal with global problems. (p. 23)

Not all cosmopolitan thinkers, however, consider that there inevitably must, or should, result a world state or a world government. Short of that, most agree that moral cosmopolitanism must find, or must aim to find, expression in some sort of transnational global governance, not necessarily nor exclusively between national governments but involving other actors, ranging from the United Nations and the International Monetary Fund and the World Bank to multinational corporations and internationally active non-government agencies.

Another influential writer on the subject, Onora O'Neill (2000: 168–85), provides a series of reflections opening up the inherent weakness of presuming in modern times that individual states are the obvious location for the exercise of power over individuals and for dealing with activities which are more transnational than international. In this way she pushes against the moral purpose of statehood which seemed apparently fixed in perpetuity when the Peace of Westphalia, agreed in 1648 among the major central European powers apart from England, brought to an end decades of internal European religious wars and recognized the full territorial sovereignty of the member states of the former Holy Roman Empire, with the princes becoming absolute sovereigns in their own dominions. Later it was respect for this agreement, and particularly concern for their own national sovereign independence, which led the major participants, Britain and Russia, in the United Nations discussions on human rights to express immense reservations and, indeed, fears at the prospect of any enthusiastic acceptance of universal civil and political human rights which could entail interference in the domestic affairs of sovereign member states (see above, pp. 44–5).

One problem which arises in handling the idea of cosmopolitanism is how to find the correct terminology to identify its desirable relationship to individual states and nations. Using the term "inter-national" implies activities taking place between states, and one is looking for something wider and higher than that. Some writers, including Haydn (2005: 35) and, with misgivings, O'Neill (2000: 115), use the term "transnational" in connection with "metropolitanism" to refer to its concerns crossing state boundaries, much as large commercial companies do. Perhaps, however, O'Neill has best captured the connection between metropolitanism and state boundaries (O'Neill 2000: 168–85), doing justice to the former and without abolishing the latter, when she describes such boundaries as being desirably "porous." It is characteristic of communitarians, including MacIntyre, she observes, to limit the application of justice within the boundaries of a community (p. 121), whereas "cosmopolitans think that boundaries should be (more) porous to persons and their activities" (p. 189). Introducing the idea of "porousness" confirms the argument of Hayden that states in themselves have lost any absolute or exclusive claims which they may once have had. As he writes, "while contemporary cosmopolitans are sceptical about ideas for a world government or world state they nevertheless challenge the traditional supremacy of the state system. The significance of state boundaries is increasingly unsettled as globalization provides for escalating public and private interactions and transnational flows of people, money, technology and culture, as well as disease, drugs, arms and pollution" (Hayden 2005: 99).

Additionally, introducing this concept of the desirable "porousness" of state boundaries enables O'Neill to meet the charges that moral, as contrasted with institutional, cosmopolitanism is both a feeble form of idealism, which has no practical implications, and a dangerous form of idealism, which points to a world state and "the dismantling of the institutions we take to protect our security." What she argues for, as a result, is what she calls an "approximate moral cosmopolitanism" encouraging attempts to introduce some measure of institutional cosmopolitanism by recognizing and encouraging "porous" boundaries to states, as experienced already in the flow of capital, trade, people, information, and ideas (O'Neill 2000: 201). As she concludes, moral cosmopolitanism points to "forms of institutional cosmopolitanism in which further boundaries become porous in further ways" (p. 202; see p. 189).

Going further towards polarizing the comparison between the claims of states and the claims of cosmopolitanism, and trying to force a choice between them, can lead to the situation encountered by Martha Nussbaum through her essay, "Patriotism and Cosmopolitanism," in which she set up national patriotism and supranational cosmopolitanism in unavoidable tension and claimed that "our highest allegiance must be to the community of humankind" (Cohen 1996: p. vii). Nussbaum's argument, it should be noted in her defense, had a practical point, in that she felt that American youth required "cosmopolitan education," one that would recognize that "while they happen to be situated in the United States, they have to share this world with the citizens of other countries" (Nussbaum 1996: 6). In response to Nussbaum, various critics took issue with her apparently disregarding the claims of kin or nation, particularly when these appeared to conflict with international needs (Cohen 1996: 39–41), or felt that both poles of national and cosmopolitan consciousness required closer critique (Cohen 1996: 58–9). Moreover, Trigg (2000: 118) felt that Nussbaum did not distinguish sufficiently between patriotism and nationalism, patriotism being a love of country that need not shut out the rest of the world and can recognize other patriotisms, whereas nationalists "will be more aggressive in pursuing the interests of their country above all others [and] would not allow their national pretensions to be held back by appeals to universal justice" (p. 117). The real problem, Trigg continued, is raised not by our loyalty but by the object of our loyalty: "Unless it is to become dangerous, patriotism must be harnessed to a country which itself encapsulates, and encourages, the very highest moral ideals" (Trigg 2005: 119).

More in support of Nussbaum's argument, Amartya Sen pointed out that "the demands of fundamental allegiance need not be identical to those of exclusive allegiance" (Cohen 1996: 112), and noted that we can "accept multiplicity of loyalties" (p. 113). In fact, however, he argues, what Nussbaum was at pains to correct was a serious neglect, "that of the interest of people who are not related to us through, say, kinship or community." Thus, "the assertion that one's fundamental allegiance is to humanity at large brings every other person into the domain of concern, without eliminating anyone" (p. 114).

In responding to her various critics Nussbaum stressed that her overall aim was "that we should view the equal worth of all human beings as a regulative constraint on our political actions and aspirations" (Cohen 1996: 133). She found attractive the idea which originated in early Stoic thought of a series of expanding concentric circles of moral concern for others, so that one starts at the center with one's self and expands out to encompass one's family, neighbors, and citizens, until "outside all these circles is the largest one, humanity as a whole" (Nussbaum 1996: 9). The moral implications of expanding circles are questioned, however, by Shue (1996: 131–52). In a critical exploration of the claimed limitations imposed by nationality upon international responsibilities he raised what many will consider counter-intuitive questions when he set out to explore just why, when the question arises of having a duty to provide aid to those in need in other societies, one's compatriots should be considered to have priority. He judges that an approach to morality by way of concentric circles so that responsibility for others appears to diminish as one moves from the center outwards raises crucial questions of what it is that people at the center presumably share more than those in outer circles which justifies giving the former greater moral consideration. He recognizes that presumably this factor is stronger kinship of some kind or a strong community of interest or of identity, but Shue persists in asking precisely why this should be considered morally relevant and should entail a deeper sense of responsibility. He concludes (1996: 139), "priority for compatriots as a moral theory is at best unproven, however widely assumed."

Shue also (1996: 174–5) appears to take up the claims of the wider community when he suggests as one plausible step to expanding cosmopolitanism the building of "a general global consensus that state sovereignty is conditioned upon the protection of at least basic rights and that the international community not only may but ought to step in when the failures of states to protect rights becomes egregious," adding that

> when a state utterly or egregiously fails to protect the rights of the people residing within its jurisdiction, the rest of humanity must have capacities to do more than sit idly by until the slaughter is finished or merely assist the victims after they are violated without resisting the violators . . . If the state cannot be eliminated, as one certainly might wish, the question becomes whether it can be civilized. (p. 174)

Thus, considering any sort of world government totally unlikely as well as dangerous, he advocates at least "conditional sovereignty, judged by minimal international standards, including the provision of protection for basic rights" (p. 175).

Others sympathetic to moral cosmopolitanism also see the need for some structural expression, and Pogge's study on *World Poverty and Human Rights*, for instance, contains a detailed exercise of applied institutional cosmopolitanism. Most, however, share misgivings at the prospect of a world government, and would prefer to see, not global government, but some form of global civil society developing. Thus, Falk recognizes that "we are in transition from a world of states to a globalized order assuming some as yet undetermined structure of authority and influence" (Falk 2000: 236 n. 7). It may be true, as Trigg comments (2005: 128), that "it is a mistake to assume that morality, even the morality of nations, is only real if it takes on a political guise." Yet Falk is surely correct in observing that "the overarching aim of normative commitment is to incorporate rights and justice into a framework of humane governance" (Falk 2000: 10), whatever structure that framework may take. However, Trigg (2005: 128) may be given the final word here: "Whether or not international institutions should be set up to enforce a 'cosmopolitan law,' governments ought to be answerable to the people they represent, and those people should never forget their moral responsibilities, any more than members of a government should" (p. 128).

"Principled" Cosmopolitanism

At the beginning of this section we observed that the movement of cosmopolitanism and the idea of human rights converge in possessing a common dynamism and momentum, and can take the form of moral cosmopolitanism and institutional cosmopolitanism. From the human rights point of view it remains important to keep this distinction in mind and in this way to view moral cosmopolitanism as exercising a continual goad to find or create practical expression in some forms of institution and to monitor those expressions, without losing its impetus of being primarily a moral phenomenon. Its essentially moral, rather than political or practical, characteristic may be the more difficult to keep to the fore because the first recorded reference to cosmopolitanism, its claim by Diogenes, occurred in ancient Athens, a culture in which politics saturated all other areas of life, including the ethical, as it is evident in the works of Plato and Aristotle. Perhaps, then, we can be alerted to the almost inseparable political ramifications of cosmopolitanism today by Michael Walzer's distancing observation that "I am not even aware that there is a world such that one could be a citizen of it" (Cohen 1996: 125).

Yet it does not appear totally accurate to describe all modern cosmopolitanism as essentially inspired by ethical considerations, human fellow feeling and concern for human rights, when at least institutional cosmopolitanism seems also to be driven by the pressures of globalization to find some way of managing these pressures. It could be helpful and enlightening, therefore, to introduce another distinction, that between pragmatic cosmopolitanism and principled cosmopolitanism. Pragmatic cosmopolitanism can be taken to describe the situation towards which we appear to be driven as we experience various features of globalization. For instance, in his study *One World: The Ethics of Globalization* (2004), Peter Singer illustrates successively in detail how we are increasingly aware of all sharing one deteriorating atmosphere, as we have noted earlier (pp. 175–6), how we are moving towards one global international market economy, how one body of law is emerging at a worldwide level to tackle various issues including genocide and the need for humanitarian intervention, and how we are becoming sensitive to the ethical issues of fairness and impartiality which would be involved in forming one human community worldwide which includes millions of abjectly poor people. Attempting to manage these characteristics of modern living demonstrates that the traditional dogma of sovereign states is becoming increasingly ineffective and outmoded, and that we are being required to move towards one form of regulatory governance for the whole world, for which Singer thinks a much improved United Nations Organization might form a basis. In this way, it appears, then, we are being driven for pragmatic reasons to find only in some form of cosmopolitanism the solution to the issues which are being created and exacerbated by globalization.

By contrast, the idea of principled cosmopolitanism arises less from our being driven by pragmatic pressures, and more from our being drawn by the moral consciousness of belonging to a single human race; and it strives to give expression to that awareness in a variety of ways. This need not extend as far as seeking or constructing a form of world government, with all the attendant risks which are not far to seek in today's climate of suspicion of powerful structures, if only because, as Trigg notes succinctly (2005: 133), "global governments will make global mistakes." Principled cosmopolitanism will, however, create and develop a variety of bodies, networks, movements, and enterprises which transcend national walls and which seek to give expression to the awareness of being part of a shared humanity. Such cosmopolitanism born of principle, which can obviously support the development of pragmatic cosmopolitanism, will invariably want to give pride of place to respect and concern for the whole panoply of human rights, whether at national or at international levels, as constant witness to the awareness that more than neighborhood is involved and that basic human kinship is being recognized in the single moral family to which all human beings belong. Hayden (2005: 65) expresses well the centrality of ethical concern for human rights worldwide, and the dynamic of what we have called principled cosmopolitanism, when he observes that "the globalization of human rights has become the cornerstone of the project of cosmopolitan global politics."

Human Solidarity

Perhaps, finally, we can highlight principled cosmopolitanism's essentially ethical core based on human rights, and avoid the almost inevitable political trappings stemming from its Greek origin, by invoking another famous statement in classical literature, the remark in the comedy *The Self-Tormenter* of the Roman playwright, Publius Terentius Afer, normally known as Terence (d. 158 BCE), in which the busybody character, Chremes, justifies his continuous meddling in other people's business, by claiming, "I'm a human being: I don't consider that anything human is foreign to me" (*homo sum: humani nil a me alienum puto*) (Barsby 2001: act 1, l. 77; p. 186). Sententious though it is in context, it may also be part of Terence's irony that the self-justifying sentiment uttered by such a fusspot as Chremes expresses in a clear, and unpolitical, manner the insight which is at the heart of moral cosmopolitanism and which can be seen as a corollary to the idea of human rights, that no human being is, or should be, foreign or alien to any other. It is interesting to note how O'Neill contrasts communitarianism and cosmopolitanism in terms of how they behave towards strangers (2000: 187), for that is precisely the point which cosmopolitanism can draw from Terence: humans are not aliens or strangers to one another. More technically, we can accept the point made by Hayden (2005: 67), applying it to what we have distinguished as principled, rather than pragmatic, cosmopolitanism, that "cosmopolitanism claims that we owe duties of justice to all the persons of the world and thus that normative theories of global politics should focus first on the interests or welfare of persons rather than states" (p. 67).

The final conclusion of this chapter on the global significance of human rights, and of our study as a whole, is that the uncovering and emergence of basic human rights has immeasurably enriched the human race's ethical resources, and with it our ability to identify and to confront, and even to remedy worldwide, what Robert Burns (1995) described feelingly as "man's inhumanity to man." For what the existence of human rights reveals is human solidarity, that human beings constitute, as Boutros Boutros-Ghali observed (*The UN and Human Rights* 1995: p. 442), "a single human community." More than that, we can now conclude, human rights constitute of the human race a single moral family, one in which every individual, whether child, woman, or man, has a call on their fellows as well as a duty to their fellows to treat one another only in accordance with their intrinsic dignity as human beings.

What the future holds for the pursuit of human rights and for their effective recognition must remain uncertain and problematic. Hayden's observation cannot be gainsaid when he concludes that it is "evident that the human rights regime has made astonishing progress in an incredibly short period of time and that the concept of human rights has been adopted as the universal moral-political discourse of our age" (Hayden 2005: 65). Nor can there be any doubt of either the truth or the continuing relevance of the conclusion offered by Smith and van den Anker in their study on *The Essentials of Human Rights* (2005: p. xi), that "the challenge for human rights is now to work towards more universal implementation worldwide." Accordingly, the aim not only of the United Nations, as observed by one Secretary-General (*The UN and Human Rights* 1995: p. 125), but of all concerned to meet the challenge of human rights must be to "continue to mobilize [our] efforts, so that human rights may one day emerge at last as the common language of humanity."

References

Argandoña, A. (2005), Corruption and Companies: the Use of Facilitating Payments, *Journal of Business Ethics*, 60 (Sept.), 251–64.

Barsby, J. (2001) (ed.), *Terence: Comedies*, Loeb Classical library, Cambridge, MA: Harvard University Press.

Bhagwati, J. (2004), *In Defense of Globalization*, Oxford: Oxford University Press.

Burns, R. (1995), Man was Made to Mourn, in *Complete Poems and Songs*, London: HarperCollins.

Carte, P., and Fox, C. (2004), *Bridging the Culture Gap: A Practical Guide to International Business Communication*, London: Kogan Page.

Clague, J. (2000), A Dubious Idiom and Rhetoric: How Problematic is the Language of Human Rights in Catholic Social Thought? In J. S. Boswell,

F. P. McHugh, and J. Verstraeten (eds.), *Catholic Social Thought: Twilight or Renaissance?* Leuven: Leuven University Press.

Cohen, J. (1996) (ed.), *For Love of Country: Debating the Limits of Patriotism*, Boston, MA: Beacon Press.

Copleston, F. C. (1944), *A History of Philosophy*, vol. 1, London: Burns, Oates & Washbourne.

Crane, A., and Matten, D. (2004), *Business Ethics, a European Perspective: Managing Corporate Citizenship and Sustainability in the Age of Globalization*, Oxford: Oxford University Press.

Donaldson, T. (1993), When in Rome, Do . . . What?, in Paul M. Minus (ed.), *The Ethics of Business in a Global Economy*, Amsterdam: Kluwer.

Donaldson, T., and Dunfee, T. W. (1999), *Ties that Bind: A Social Contracts Approach to Business Ethics*, Cambridge, MA: Harvard Business School Press.

Donnelly, J. (2003), *Universal Human Rights in Theory and Practice*, 2nd rev. edn., Ithaca, NY: Cornell University Press.

Drinan, R. F. (2001), *The Mobilization of Shame: A World View of Human Rights*, New Haven, CT: Yale University Press.

Eide, A. (2000), Economic and Social Rights, in Symonides (2000), pp. 109–74.

European Communities Official Journal (Dec. 18, 2000), Luxembourg: Publications Office.

Evans, T. (1998), Power, Hegemony and Human Rights, in Evans (ed.), *Human Rights Fifty Years On: A Reappraisal*, Manchester: Manchester University Press.

Falk, Richard, A. (2000), *Human Rights Horizons: The Pursuit of Justice in a Globalizing World*, London: Routledge.

Fergusson, D. (1998), *Community, Liberalism and Christian Ethics*, Cambridge: Cambridge University Press.

Fuller, J. D., and. Keenan, J. F. (2004), The Language of Human Rights and Social Justice in the Face of HIV/AIDS, *Budhi: A Journal of Ideas and Culture*, 8 (1–2), 211–33.

Glendon, M. A. (2001), *A World Made New: Eleanor Roosevelt and the Universal Declaration of Human Rights*, New York: Random House.

Habgood, J. (1993), Human Nature and Human Rights, in Habgood, *Making Sense*, London: SPCK.

Harvard (1999), *Business and Human Rights: An Interdisciplinary Discussion*, Cambridge, MA: Harvard University Press.

Hayden, P. (2005), *Cosmopolitan Global Politics*, Aldershot: Ashgate.

Henkin, L. (1990), *The Age of Rights*, New York: Columbia University Press.

Hoffman, D., and Rowe, J. (2003), *Human Rights in the UK: An Introduction to the Human Rights Act 1998*, Harlow: Pearson Longman.

International Chamber of Commerce (ICC) (1977), *Extortion and Bribery in Business Transactions*, Paris: ICC.

Jagger, A. M. (2000), Feminist Ethics, in H. LaFollette (2000) (ed.), *The Blackwell Guide to Ethical Theory*, Oxford: Blackwell.

Jones, P. (1994), *Rights*, London: Macmillan.

Keenan, J. F. (2005), Development in Bioethics from the Perspective of HIV/ AIDS, *Cambridge Quarterly of Health Care Ethics*, 14 (4), 416–23.

Küng, H. (1998), Human Responsibilities Reinforce Human Rights: The Global Ethic Project, in Barend van der Heijden and Bahiaq Tahzib-Lie (eds.), *Reflections on the Universal Declaration of Human Rights: A Fiftieth Anniversary Anthology*, The Hague: Martin Nijhoff.

Küng, H., and Schmidt, H. (1988) (eds.), *A Global Ethic and Global Responsibilities: Two Declarations*, London: SCM Press.

Leary, V. A. (1998), Globalization and Human Rights, in J. Symonides (ed.), *Human Rights: New Dimensions and Challenges*, Paris: UNESCO.

Legrain, P. (2002), *Open World: The Truth about Globalisation*, London: Abacus.

Lewis, J. R., and Skutsch, C. (2001) (eds.), *The Human Rights Encyclopedia*, Armonk, NY: Sharpe Reference; eBook version (2005), Thomson Gale.

Linden, I. (2005), A New Map of the World, *New Blackfriars*, 86 (1002) (Mar.).

Little, D. (1993), The Nature and Basis of Human Rights, in G. Outka and John P. Reeder (eds.), *Prospects for a Common Morality*, Princeton, NJ: Princeton University Press.

Locke, J. (1963), *Two Treatises of Government*, ed. Peter Laslett, Cambridge: Cambridge University Press.

Lomasky, L. E. (1987), *Persons, Rights, and the Moral Community*, Oxford: Oxford University Press.

Mahoney, J. (1995), Ethical Attitudes to Bribery and Extortion, in Sally Stewart and G. Donleavy (eds.), *Whose Business Values? Some Asian and Cross-Cultural Perspectives*, Hong Kong: Hong Kong University Press.

Maritain, Jacques (1949), *Human Rights: Comments and Interpretations*, London: Wingate.

McGrew, A. G. (1998), Human Rights in a Global Age: Coming to Terms with Globalization, in Tony Evans (ed.), *Human Rights Fifty Years On: A Reappraisal*, Manchester: Manchester University Press.

McLuhan, M. (1968), *War and Peace in the Global Village*, London: Bantam.

Nickel, J. W. (1987), *Making Sense of Human Rights: Philosophical Reflections on the Universal Declaration of Human Rights*, Berkeley: University of California Press, new rev. edn. (2007), Oxford: Blackwell.

Nussbaum, M. C. (1996), *For Love of Country: Debating the Limits of Patriotism*, ed. J. Cohen, Boston, MA: Beacon Press.

O'Neill, O. (2000), *Bounds of Justice*, Cambridge: Cambridge University Press.

Orend, B. (2002), *Human Rights: Concept and Context*, Peterborough, Ont.: Broadview Press.

Paine, T. (1984), *Rights of Man*, Harmondsworth: Penguin.

Pogge, T. W. (2002), *World Poverty and Human Rights: Cosmopolitan Responsibilities and Reforms*, Cambridge: Polity Press.

Reiss, H. (1991) (ed.), *Kant: Political Writings*, 2nd enlarged edn., Cambridge: Cambridge University Press.

Robinson, F. (2001), Exploring Social Relations, Understanding Power, and Valuing Care: the Role of Critical Feminist Ethics in International Relations Theory, in Hakan Seckinelgin and Hideaki Shinoda (eds.), *Ethics and International Relations*, Basingstoke: Palgrave Macmillan.

Short, C. (2004), Consume and Survive, *Tablet* (Jan. 17).

Shue, H. (1996), *Basic Rights: Subsistence, Affluence, and U.S. Foreign Policy*, 2nd rev. edn., Princeton, NJ: Princeton University Press.

Singer, P. (2004), *One World: The Ethics of Globalization*, 2nd edn., New Haven, CT: Yale University Press.

Smith, R. K. M., and van den Anker, C. (2005) (eds.), *The Essentials of Human Rights*, London: Hodder Arnold.

Speake, J. (1979) (ed.), *A Dictionary of Philosophy*, Basingstoke: Pan Reference.

Stiglitz, J. (2002), *Globalisation and its Discontents*, London: Penguin.

Sumner, L. W. (2000), Rights, in H. LaFollette (2000) (ed.), *The Blackwell Guide to Ethical Theory*, Oxford: Blackwell.

Symonides, J. (1998), New Human Rights Dimensions, Obstacles and Challenges: Introductory Remarks, in Symonides (ed.), *Human Rights: New Dimensions and Challenges*, Paris: UNESCO.

Trigg, R. (2005), *Morality Matters*, Oxford: Blackwell.

Twiss, Sumner B., and Grelle, B. (1998), *Explorations in Global Ethics: Comparative Religious Ethics and Interreligious Dialogue*, Oxford: Westview Press.

The United Nations and Human Rights 1945–1995 (1995), intro. by Boutros Boutros-Ghali, Secretary-General of the United Nations, New York: Department of Public Information, United Nations.

United Nations Commission on Global Governance (1995), *Our Global Neighbourhood*, Oxford: Oxford University Press.

United Nations General Secretary's Report (2001), available at <http://www. un.org/documents/secretariat.htm> accessed Feb. 2006.

United Nations Joint Commission on AIDS (UNAIDS), available at <http:// www.unaids.org> accessed Feb. 2006.

United Nations Vienna Declaration (1993), New York: United Nations.

Universal Declaration of Human Rights (1948), New York: United Nations Department of Public Information.

Ward, B., and Dubos, R. (1972), *Only One Earth: The Care and Maintenance of a Small Planet*, London: André Deutsch.

Wolf, M. (2004), *Why Globalization Works: The Case for the Global Market Economy*, New Haven, CT: Yale University Press.

World Development Movement (2005), available from <http://www.wdm.org. uk/> accessed Feb. 2006.

Bibliography

Almond, B. (1993), Rights, in Peter Singer (ed.), *A Companion to Ethics*, Oxford: Blackwell.

Alston, P. (1998), The Universal Declaration in an Era of Globalization, in van der Heijden and Tahzib-Lie (1998).

Amnesty International (2005), available from <http://www.amnesty.org> accessed Feb. 2006.

Annan, K. (1998), Message of the United Nations Secretary-General, in van der Heijden and Tahzib-Lie (1998).

Annan, K. (2005), *In Larger Freedom*, United Nations General Assembly, available from <http://www.un.org/largerfreedom/contents.htm> accessed Feb. 2006.

Archibugi, Daniele, and Koenig-Archibugi, Mathias (2003), Globalization, Democracy and Cosmopolis: a Bibliographical Essay, in Archibugi and Koenig-Archibugi (2003).

Argandoña, A. (2005), Corruption and Companies: the Use of Facilitating Payments, *Journal of Business Ethics*, 60 (Sept.), 251–64.

Aristotle, see Grant (1885).

Augustine of Hippo (c.1860), *Contra Epistolam Parmeniani*, Migne, *Patres Latini*, vol. 43.

Augustine of Hippo (1972), *De Civitate Dei*, trans. E. Bettenson, Harmondsworth: Penguin.

Aung San Suu Kyi (1992), In Quest of Democracy, *Journal of Democracy*, 2 (1).

Avineri, S., and de-Shalit, A. (1996) (eds.), *Communitarianism and Individualism*, Oxford: Oxford University Press.

Barsby, J. (2001) (ed.), *Terence: Comedies*, Loeb Classical library, Cambridge, MA: Harvard University Press.

Bellah, R. N., et al. (1985), *Habits of the Heart: Individualism and Commitment in American Life*, New York: Harper & Row.

Bellof, M. (1948), *Thomas Jefferson and American Democracy*, London: Hodder & Stoughton.

Bentham, J., see Hart (1982), Waldron (1987).
Berlin, I. (1969), *Four Essays on Liberty*, Oxford: Oxford University Press.
Bhagwati, J. (2004), *In Defense of Globalization*, Oxford: Oxford University Press.
Bloom, A. (1990) (ed.), *Confronting the Constitution*, Washington, DC: AEI Press.
Bloom, I., Martin, P. J., and Proudfoot, W. L. (1996) (eds.), *Religious Diversity and Human Rights*, New York: Columbia University Press.
Bobbio, N. (1996), *The Age of Rights*, trans. Allan Cameron, Cambridge: Polity Press.
British Institute of Human Rights, available from <http://www.bihr.org/> accessed Feb. 2006.
British Institute of Human Rights (2002), *Annual Review for 2002*, London: King's College.
Browne, Sir T. (1909), *Browne's "Religio Medici"* [1643], Oxford: Clarendon Press.
Browning, A. (1953) (ed.), *English Historical Documents VIII, 1660–1714*, London: Eyre & Spottiswoode.
Brownlie, I. (1997) (ed.), *Basic Documents on Human Rights*, 3rd edn., Oxford: Clarendon Press.
Bucar, E. M., and Barnett, B. (2005) (eds.), *Does Human Rights Need God?* Grand Rapids, MI: Eerdmans.
Buchanan, A. (1985), *Ethics, Efficiency, and the Market*, Totowa, NJ: Rowman & Allenheld.
Buckland, W. W. (1966), *A Text-Book of Roman Law from Augustus to Justinian*, 3rd edn., Cambridge: Cambridge University Press.
Burke, E. (1988), *Reflections on the Revolution in France*, ed. Conor Cruise O'Brien, London: Penguin.
Burns, R. (1995), Man was Made to Mourn, *Complete Poems and Songs*, London: HarperCollins.
Burns, R. I. (2001) (ed.), *Las Siete Partidas*, Philadelphia: University of Pennsylvania Press.
Carte, P., and Fox, C. (2004), *Bridging the Culture Gap: A Practical Guide to International Business Communication*, London: Kogan Page.
Charvet, J. (1995), *The Idea of an Ethical Community*, Ithaca, NY: Cornell University Press.
Charvet, J. (2001), The Possibility of a Cosmopolitan Ethical Order based on the Idea of Universal Human Rights, in Hakan Seckinelgin and Hideaki Shinoda (eds.), *Ethics and International Relations*, Basingstoke: Palgrave Macmillan.
Cicero (1928) *De re publica*, ed. T. E. Page, Loeb Classical Library, London: Heinemann.
Cicero (1960) *De inventione*, trans. H. M. Hubbell, Loeb Classical Library, London: Heinemann.
Clague, J. (2000), A Dubious Idiom and Rhetoric: How Problematic is the Language of Human Rights in Catholic Social Thought? In J. S. Boswell,

F. P. McHugh, and J. Verstraeten (eds.), *Catholic Social Thought: Twilight or Renaissance?* Leuven: Leuven University Press.

Cohen, G. A. (1993), Equality of What? On Welfare, Goods, and Capabilities, in Nussbaum and Sen (1993).

Cohen, J. (1996) (ed.), *For Love of Country: Debating the Limits of Patriotism*, Boston, MA: Beacon Press.

Cohler, A. M., et al. (1995) (trans.), Montesquieu, *The Spirit of the Laws*, Cambridge: Cambridge University Press.

Cooney, W. (1998), Rights Theory, in Ruth Chadwick (ed.), *Encyclopedia of Applied Ethics*, London: Academic Press.

Copleston, F. C. (1944), *A History of Philosophy*, vol. 1, London: Burns, Oates & Washbourne.

Copleston, F. C. (1960), *A History of Philosophy*, vol. 6, London: Burns & Oates.

Copleston, F. C. (1966), *A History of Philosophy*, vol. 8, London: Burns & Oates.

Costello, J. E. (2002), *John Macmurray: A Biography*, Edinburgh: Floris.

Cottingham, J. (2003), *On the Meaning of Life*, London: Routledge.

Craig, R. (1963), *Social Concern in the Thought of William Temple*, London: Victor Gollancz.

Crane, A., and Matten, D. (2004), *Business Ethics, a European Perspective: Managing Corporate Citizenship and Sustainability in the Age of Globalization*, Oxford: Oxford University Press.

Cranston, M. (1958), *John Locke*, Oxford: Oxford University Press.

Cranston, M. (1973), *What are Human Rights?* London: Bodley Head; New York: Taplinger.

Cranston, M. (1987), *Jean-Jacques: The Early Life and Work of Jean-Jacques Rousseau*, London: Penguin.

Cranston, M. (1991), *The Noble Savage: Jean-Jacques Rousseau*, London: Penguin.

Crisp, R. (1997), *Routledge Philosophy Guidebook to Mill on Utilitarianism*, London: Routledge.

Crocker, L. G. (1963), *Nature and Culture: Ethical Thought in the French Enlightenment*, Baltimore, MD: Johns Hopkins University Press.

Curran, C. E. (2003), *Catholic Social Teaching, 1891–Present: A Historical, Theological, and Ethical Analysis*, Washington, DC: Georgetown University.

Darwall, S., Gibbard, A., and Railton, T. (1992), Towards *Fin-de-Siècle* Ethics: Some Trends, *Philosophical Review*, 101 (1992), 115–89.

de George, R. T. (1999), *Business Ethics*, 5th edn., Upper Saddle River, NJ: Prentice Hall.

Documents of the United Nations Conference on International Organization (1945), vol. 1: Closing Plenary Session, June 26, 1945, Doc. 1209 P/16 June 27, 1945, San Francisco: United Nations.

Donaldson, T. (1993), When in Rome, Do . . . What?, in Paul M. Minus (ed.), *The Ethics of Business in a Global Economy*, Amsterdam: Kluwer.

Donaldson, T., and Dunfee, T. W. (1999), *Ties that Bind: A Social Contracts Approach to Business Ethics*, Cambridge, MA: Harvard Business School Press.

Donnelly, J. (2003), *Universal Human Rights in Theory and Practice*, 2nd rev. edn., Ithaca, NY: Cornell University Press.

Dowling, E. (2005), The Capability Approach and Human Rights, in Smith and van den Anker (2005).

Drinan, R. F. (2001), *The Mobilization of Shame: A World View of Human Rights*, New Haven, CT: Yale University Press.

Duncan-Jones, A. (1952), *Butler's Moral Philosophy*, Harmondsworth: Penguin.

Dworkin, R. (1978), *Taking Rights Seriously*, Cambridge, MA: Harvard University Press.

Dworkin, R. (1984), Rights as Trumps, in Waldron (1984).

Dworkin, R. (1990), *A Bill of Rights for Britain*, London: Chatto & Windus.

Dworkin, R. (1996), Does Britain Need a Bill of Rights?, in Gordon and Wilmot-Smith (1996).

East Asian Pastoral Institute (1994), *Report* of a Human Rights Workshop, Manila, Philippines.

Eide, A. (2000), Economic and Social Rights, in Symonides (2000), pp. 109–74.

Etzioni, A. (1993), *The Spirit of Community: Rights, Responsibilities and the Communitarian Agenda*, New York: Crown.

Europe Infos, Commission of the Bishops' Conferences of the European Community, Brussels.

European Communities Official Journal (Dec. 18, 2000), Luxembourg: Publications Office.

European Convention on Human Rights: Collected Texts (1995), Brussels: Council of Europe Press.

European Union Charter (2005), available from <http://www.federalunion.org.uk/europe/charter.shtml> accessed Feb. 2006.

Evans, T. (1998), Power, Hegemony and Human Rights, in Evans (ed.), *Human Rights Fifty Years On: A Reappraisal*, Manchester: Manchester University Press.

Falk, R. A. (2000), *Human Rights Horizons: The Pursuit of Justice in a Globalizing World*, London: Routledge.

Feinberg, J. (1980), *Rights, Justice and the Bounds of Liberty: Essays in Social Philosophy*, Princeton, NJ: Princeton University Press.

Fergusson, D. (1998), *Community, Liberalism and Christian Ethics*, Cambridge: Cambridge University Press.

Finnis, J. (1980), *Natural Law and Natural Rights*, Oxford: Clarendon Press.

Finnis, J. (1983), *Fundamentals of Ethics*, Oxford: Clarendon Press.

Foner, L., and Genovese, E. D. (1969) (eds.), *Slavery in the New World*, Englewood Cliffs, NJ: Prentice Hall.

Foreign and Commonwealth Office (2005), *Annual Report on Human Rights*, London: Foreign and Commonwealth Office.

Fowler, J. (1999), *Humanism, Beliefs and Practices*, Brighton: Sussex Academic Press.

Frankena, W. K. (1973), *Ethics*, 2nd edn., Englewood Cliffs, NJ: Prentice-Hall.

Freeden, M. (1991), *Rights*, Milton Keynes: Open University Press.

Fuller, J. D., and Keenan, J. F. (2004), The Language of Human Rights and Social Justice in the Face of HIV/AIDS, *Budhi: A Journal of Ideas and Culture*, 8 (1–2), 211–33.

Gadamer, H.-G. (1981), *Reason in the Age of Science*, Cambridge, MA: MIT Press.

Gearty, C., and Tomkins, A. (1999) (eds.), *Understanding Human Rights*, London: Pinter, Cassell.

Gewirth, A. (1983), The Epistemology of Human Rights, *Social Philosophy and Policy*, 1(2) (1983–4).

Gewirth, A. (1993), Common Morality and the Community of Rights, in G. Outka and J. P. Reeder (eds.), *Prospects for a Common Morality*, Princeton, NJ: Princeton University Press.

Gewirth, A. (1996), *The Community of Rights*, Chicago: University of Chicago Press.

Gillon, R. (1995), *Philosophical Medical Ethics*, New York: John Wiley.

Glendon, M. A. (1991), *Rights Talk: The Impoverishment of Political Discourse*, New York: Free Press.

Glendon, M. A. (2001), *A World Made New: Eleanor Roosevelt and the Universal Declaration of Human Rights*, New York: Random House.

Gordon, R., and Wilmot-Smith, R. (1996) (eds.), *Human Rights in the United Kingdom*, Oxford: Oxford University Press.

Gorecki, J. (1996), *Justifying Ethics: Human Rights and Human Nature*, New Brunswick, NJ and London: Transaction Publishers.

Grant, A. (1885), *The Ethics of Aristotle*, London: Longman's, Green.

Grant, M. (1971), *Cicero: On the Good Life*, London: Penguin.

Grosz, S., Beatson, J., and Duffy, P. (2000), *Human Rights: The 1998 Act and the European Convention*, London: Sweet & Maxwell.

Grotius, H. (1853), *De Jure Belli et Pacis*, ed. W. Whewell, London: University Press.

Habermas, J. (1993), *Justification and Application: Remarks on Discourse Ethics*, Cambridge, MA: MIT Press.

Habgood, J. (1993), Human Nature and Human Rights, in Habgood, *Making Sense*, London: SPCK.

Hampson, N. (1984), *The Enlightenment*, London: Penguin.

Harare Commonwealth Declaration on Democracy and Human Rights (1991), London: Commonwealth Secretariat.

Hare, R. M. (1981), *Moral Thinking: Its Levels, Method, and Point*, Oxford: Clarendon Press.

Harries, R. (1993), Human Rights in Theological Perspective, in R. Blackburn and J. Taylor (eds.), *Human Rights for the 1990s*, London: Mansell.

Harrison, R. (1983), *Bentham*, London: Routledge & Kegan Paul.

Hart, H. L. A. (1982), *Essays on Bentham: Jurisprudence and Political Theory*, Oxford: Clarendon Press.

Harvard (1999), *Business and Human Rights: An Interdisciplinary Discussion*, Cambridge, MA: Harvard University Press.

Hawke, D. F. (1974), *Paine*, New York: W. W. Norton.

Hayden, P. (2005), *Cosmopolitan Global Politics*, Aldershot: Ashgate.

Henkin, L. (1990), *The Age of Rights*, New York: Columbia University Press.

Herbert, G. B. (2002), *A Philosophical History of Rights*, Brunswick, NJ: Transaction Publishers.

Hill, C. (1965), *The Century of Revolution, 1603–1714*, London: Abacus, Sphere Books.

Hobbes, T. (1974), *Leviathan*, ed. C. B. Macpherson, London: Penguin.

Hoffman, D., and Rowe, J. (2003), *Human Rights in the UK: An Introduction to the Human Rights Act 1998*, Harlow: Pearson Longman.

Hohfeld, W. N. (1919), *Fundamental Legal Conceptions as Applied in Judicial Reasoning*, New Haven, CT: Yale University Press.

Hollenbach, D. (1979), *Claims in Conflict: Retrieving and Renewing the Catholic Human Rights Tradition*, New York: Paulist Press.

Holt, J. C. (1982) (ed.), *Magna Carta and the Idea of Liberty*, Malabar, FL: R. E. Krieger.

Horgan, J. (1997), *Mary Robinson: A Woman of Ireland and the World*, Dublin: O'Brien Press.

Human Rights Watch (2005), available from <http://www.hrw.org/> accessed Feb. 2006.

Human Rights Watch, World Report 1998, available from <http://www.hrw.org/research/worldreport.html> accessed Feb. 2006.

Humphrey, J. P. (1984), *Human Rights and the United Nations: A Great Adventure*, Dobbs Ferry, NY: Transnational Publishers.

International Chamber of Commerce (ICC) (1977), *Extortion and Bribery in Business Transactions*, Paris: ICC.

Jacobs, F. G., and White, R. A. C. (1996), *The European Convention on Human Rights*, Oxford: Clarendon Press.

Jagger, A. M. (2000), Feminist Ethics, in H. LaFollette (2000) (ed.), *The Blackwell Guide to Ethical Theory*, Oxford: Blackwell.

Jones, P. (1994), *Rights*, London: Macmillan.

Jover Zamora, J. M. (1998) (ed.), *Historia de España Menéndez Fidal*, Madrid: Espasa Calpe.

Kant, I. (1964), *Groundwork of the Metaphysics of Morals*, trans. H. J. Paton, New York: Harper.

Kant, I. (1991), *The Metaphysics of Morals*, trans. M. Gregor, Cambridge: Cambridge University Press.

Keane, J. (1995), *Tom Paine: A Political Life*, London: Bloomsbury.

Kearney, R. (1994) (ed.), *Continental Philosophy in the Twentieth Century*, London: Routledge.

Keeley, M. (1996), Community, the Joyful Sound, *Business Ethics Quarterly*, 6 (4).

Keenan, J. F. (2005), Development in Bioethics from the Perspective of HIV/ AIDS, *Cambridge Quarterly of Health Care Ethics*, 14 (4), 416–23.

King, A. (2001), *Does the UK Still Have a Constitution?* London: Sweet & Maxwell.

Kitto, H. D. F. (1991), *The Greeks*, London: Penguin.

Klein, H. S. (1969), Anglicanism, Catholicism, and the Negro Slave, in Foner and Genovese (1969).

Klug, F. (1996), A Bill of Rights as Secular Ethics, in Gordon and Wilmot-Smith (1996).

Klug, F. (2000), *Values for a Godless Age: The Story of the UK's New Bill of Rights*, London: Penguin.

Koch, A. (1964), *The Philosophy of Thomas Jefferson*, Chicago: Quadrangle Books.

Köhler, O. (1981), in H. Jedin and J. Dolan (eds.), *Handbook of Church History*, vol. 6, London: Burns & Oates.

Küng, H. (1998), Human Responsibilities Reinforce Human Rights: The Global Ethic Project, in van der Heijden and Tahzib-Lie (1998).

Küng, H., and Schmidt, H. (1988) (eds.), *A Global Ethic and Global Responsibilities: Two Declarations*, London: SCM Press.

Laslett, P. (1963) (ed.), *John Locke: Two Treatises of Government*, Cambridge: Cambridge University Press.

Leary, V. A. (1998), Globalization and Human Rights, in J. Symonides (ed.), *Human Rights: New Dimensions and Challenges*, Paris: UNESCO.

Legrain, P. (2002), *Open World: The Truth about Globalisation*, London: Abacus.

Lewis, C. S. (1960), *The Four Loves*, London: Geoffrey Bles.

Lewis, J. R., and Skutsch, C. (2001) (eds.), *The Human Rights Encyclopedia*, Armonk, NY: Sharpe Reference; eBook version (2005), Thomson Gale.

Linden, I. (2005), A New Map of the World, *New Blackfriars*, 86 (1002) (Mar.).

Little, D. (1993), The Nature and Basis of Human Rights, in G. Outka and John P. Reeder (eds.), *Prospects for a Common Morality*, Princeton, NJ: Princeton University Press.

Locke, J. (1963), *Two Treatises of Government*, ed. Peter Laslett, Cambridge: Cambridge University Press.

Lomasky, L. E. (1987), *Persons, Rights, and the Moral Community*, Oxford: Oxford University Press.

Lowe, E. J. (2005), *Locke*, London: Routledge.

Luard, E. (1982), A *History of the United Nations*, New York: St. Martin's Press.

Luther, M. (1964), Lecture on Galatians, in *Luther's Works*, ed. Jaroslav Pelikan, vol. 27, St. Louis, MI: Concordia Publishing House.

MacCormick, N. (1992), Natural Law and the Separation of Law and Morals, in R. P. George (ed.), *Natural Law Theory: Contemporary Essays*, Oxford: Clarendon Press.

MacDonald, M. (1970), Natural Rights, in Melden (1970).

MacDonald, M. (1984), Natural Rights, in Waldron (1984).

Macedo, S. (1990), *Liberal Virtues: Citizenship, Virtue, and Community in Liberal Constitutionalism*, Oxford: Clarendon Press.

MacIntyre, A. (1981), *After Virtue*, London: Duckworth.

Mack, M. P. (1962), *Jeremy Bentham: An Odyssey of Ideas 1748–1792*, London: Heinemann.

Mackie, J. L. (1977), *Ethics: Inventing Right and Wrong*, London: Penguin.

Mackie, J. L. (1984), Can There be a Right-Based Moral Theory?, in Waldron (1984).

Macmurray, J. (1995), *Persons in Relation*, new edn., intro. by Frank G. Fitzpatrick, London: Faber & Faber.

Macpherson, C. B. (1974) (ed.), Thomas Hobbes, *Leviathan*, London: Penguin.

Mahoney, J. (1987), *The Making of Moral Theology: A Study of the Roman Catholic Tradition*, Oxford: Clarendon Press.

Mahoney, J. (1987), *The Ways of Wisdom*, London: King's College.

Mahoney, J. (1990), The Basis of Human Rights, in Charles E. Curran (ed.), *Moral Theology: Challenges for the Future*, New York: Paulist Press.

Mahoney, J. (1992), The Challenge of Moral Distinctions, *Theological Studies*, 53 (4), 663–82.

Mahoney, J. (1995), Ethical Attitudes to Bribery and Extortion, in Sally Stewart and G. Donleavy (eds.), *Whose Business Values? Some Asian and Cross-Cultural Perspectives*, Hong Kong: Hong Kong University Press.

Mahoney, K. E., and Mahoney, P. (1993), *Human Rights in the Twenty-First Century: A Global Challenge*, Dordrecht: Martinus Nijhoff.

Malik, C. (1948), International Bill of Human Rights, *United Nations Bulletin*, 5 (July 1).

Malik, C. (1949), An International Achievement, *United Nations Bulletin*, 6 (Jan. 1).

Mann, J. (1998), Health and Human Rights, in van der Heijden and Tahzib-Lie (1998).

Marcus Aurelius (1961), *Meditations*, Everyman's Library, London: Dent.

Maritain, J. (1940), *Scholasticism and Politics*, London: Bles.

Maritain, J. (1949), *Human Rights: Comments and Interpretations*, London: Wingate.

Maritain, J. (1986), *"Christianity and Democracy" and "The Rights of Man and Natural Law,"* San Francisco: Ignatius Press.

Marx, K. (1992), On the Jewish Question, in Marx, *Early Writings*, ed. L. Colletti, London: Penguin.

McGrew, A. G. (1998), Human Rights in a Global Age: Coming to Terms with Globalization, in T. Evans (ed.), *Human Rights Fifty Years On: A Reappraisal*, Manchester: Manchester University Press.

McLuhan, M. (1968), *War and Peace in the Global Village*, London: Bantam.

Melden, A. I. (1970) (ed.), *Human Rights*, Belmont, CA: Wadsworth.

Mill, J. S. (1973a), *Utilitarianism*, ed. Mary Warnock, London: Collins Fontana.

Mill, J. S. (1973b), *On Liberty*, in Mill, *Utilitarianism*, ed. Mary Warnock, London: Collins Fontana.

Miller, F. D., Jr. (1995), *Nature, Justice, and Rights in Aristotle's Politics*, Oxford: Clarendon Press.

Moltmann, J. (1990), Human Rights, the Rights of Humanity and the Rights of Nature, in Hans Küng and Jürgen Moltmann (eds.), *The Ethics of World Religions and Human Rights*, *Concilium* 1990/2, London: SCM Press.

Montesquieu, Baron de (1995), *The Spirit of the Laws*, trans. A. M. Cohler et al., Cambridge: Cambridge University Press.

Moore, G. E. (1965), *Principia Ethica*, Cambridge: Cambridge University Press.

Morsink, J. (1999), *The Universal Declaration of Human Rights: Origins, Drafting and Intent*, Philadelphia: University of Pennsylvania Press.

Mulgan, G. (1995), Beyond the Lure of Off-the-Shelf Ethics, *The Independent* (Jan. 30).

Newell, W. R. (1990), Reflections on Marxism and America, in Bloom (1990).

Newman, J. H. (1967), *Apologia Pro Vita Sua: Being a History of His Religious Opinions*, Oxford: Clarendon Press.

Nickel, J. W. (1987), *Making Sense of Human Rights: Philosophical Reflections on the Universal Declaration of Human Rights*, Berkeley: University of California Press, new rev. edn. (forthcoming), Oxford: Blackwell.

Norman, R. (1983), *The Moral Philosophers*, Oxford: Clarendon Press.

Novak, Michael (1999), Human Dignity, Human Rights, *First Things*, 97 (Nov. 1999), 39–42.

Nussbaum, M. C. (1996), *For Love of Country: Debating the Limits of Patriotism*, ed. J. Cohen, Boston, MA: Beacon Press.

Nussbaum, M., and Sen, A. (eds.) (1993), *The Quality of Life*, Oxford: Clarendon Press.

O'Brien, C. C. (1988), Introduction, in Burke (1988).

O'Hear, A. (1991), *What Philosophy Is*, London: Penguin.

O'Neill, O. (1986), *Faces of Hunger: An Essay on Poverty, Justice and Development*, London: Allen & Unwin.

O'Neill, O. (1996), *Towards Justice and Virtue: A Constructive Account of Practical Reasoning*, Cambridge: Cambridge University Press.

O'Neill, O. (2000), *Bounds of Justice*, Cambridge: Cambridge University Press.

O'Neill, O. (2002), *A Question of Trust: The BBC Reith Lectures 2002*, Cambridge: Cambridge University Press.

Orend, B. (2002), *Human Rights: Concept and Context*, Peterborough, Ont.: Broadview Press.

Padover, S. K. (1942), *Jefferson*, London: Jonathan Cape.

Pagels, E. (1979), The Roots and Origins of Human Rights, in A. H. Henkin (ed.), *Human Dignity: The Internationalisation of Human Rights*, New York: Aspen Institute for Humanistic Studies.

Paine, L. S. (1996), Moral Thinking in Management: an Essential Capability, *Business Ethics Quarterly*, 6 (4).

Paine, T. (1984), *Rights of Man*, intro. by Eric Foner, Harmondsworth: Penguin.

Paine, T. (1989), *Common Sense*, in Paine, *Political Writings*, ed. Bruce Kuklick, Cambridge: Cambridge University Press.

Pascal, B. (1956), *Pascal's Pensées*, London: Everyman's Library.

Paton, H. J. (1964) (trans.), Immanuel Kant, *Groundwork of the Metaphysics of Morals*, New York, Harper.

Peffer, R. G. (1990), *Marxism, Morality and Social Justice*, Princeton, NJ: Princeton University Press.

Phillips, D. R. (1993), *Looking Backward: A Critical Appraisal of Communitarian Thought*, Princeton, NJ: Princeton University Press.

Pogge, T. W. (2002), *World Poverty and Human Rights: Cosmopolitan Responsibilities and Reforms*, Cambridge: Polity Press.

Pope John Paul II (1995), Address to the Fiftieth General Assembly of the United Nations Organization, *Origins*, Washington, DC: CNS Documentary Service, vol. 25.

Pope Paul VI (1965), Discours aux Nations Unies, *Acta apostolicae sedis*, vol. 57, Vatican City: Vatican Press, pp. 877–85.

Preston, R. H. (1983), *Church and Society in the Late Twentieth Century: The Economic and Political Task*, London: SCM.

Raes, K. (2002), The Philosophical Basis of Social, Economic and Cultural Rights, in P. Van der Auweraert, T. De Pelsmaeker, J. Sarkin, and J. Vande Lanotte (2002) (eds.), *Social, Economic and Cultural Rights: An Appraisal of Current European and International Developments*, Antwerp: Maklu, pp. 43–53.

Raphael, D. D. (1967), Human Rights, Old and New, in Raphael (ed.), *Political Theory and the Rights of Man*, Bloomington: Indiana University Press.

Rawls, J. (1971), *A Theory of Justice*, Cambridge, MA: Harvard University Press.

Rawls, J. (1975), Fairness as Goodness, *Philosophical Review*, 84 (4) (Oct.).

Rawls, J. (1993), The Law of Peoples, in Shute and Hurley (1993).

Rawls, J. (1999), *The Law of Peoples*, Cambridge, MA: Harvard University Press.

Reiss, H. (1991) (ed.), *Kant: Political Writings*, 2nd enlarged edn., Cambridge: Cambridge University Press.

Robertson, A. H., and Merrills, J. G. (1996), *Human Rights in the World*, Manchester: Manchester University Press.

Robinson, F. (2001), Exploring Social Relations, Understanding Power, and Valuing Care: the Role of Critical Feminist Ethics in International Relations Theory, in Hakan Seckinelgin and Hideaki Shinoda (eds.), *Ethics and International Relations*, Basingstoke: Palgrave Macmillan.

Robinson, M. (1998), The Universal Declaration of Human Rights: the International Keystone of Human Dignity, in van der Heijden and Tahzib-Lie (1998).

Roosevelt, E. (1992), *The Autobiography of Eleanor Roosevelt*, New York: Da Capo Press.

Roosevelt, F. D. (1941), *The Public Papers and Addresses of Franklin D. Roosevelt*, vol. 4: *1940 volume*, London: Macmillan.

Rorty, R. (1992), Cosmopolitanism without Emancipation: A Response to Lyotard, in S. Lash and J. Friedman (eds.), *Modernity and Identity*, Oxford: Blackwell.

Rorty, R. (1993), Human Rights, Rationality and Sentimentality, in Shute and Hurley (1993).

Rousseau, J.-J. (1984), *A Discourse on Equality*, trans. M. Cranston, London: Penguin.

Rousseau, J.-J. (1994), *The Social Contract*, in *"Discourse on Political Economy" and "The Social Contract,"* trans. C. Betts, World's Classics, Oxford: Oxford University Press.

Russell, R. B., assisted by Muther, J. E. (1958), *A History of the United Nations Charter: The Role of the United States 1940–45*, Washington, DC: Brookings Institute.

Ruston, R. (2004), *Human Rights and the Image of God*, London: SCM.

Sassen, S. (2005), Global Civil Society and Human Rights, in Smith and van den Anker (2005).

Scruton, R. (1991), *A Short History of Modern Philosophy*, London: Routledge.

Selbourne, D. (1997), *The Principle of Duty*, London: Abacus.

Sen, A. (1988), *On Ethics and Economics*, Oxford: Blackwell.

Sen, A. (1988), Rights and Agency, in S. Scheffler (ed.), *Consequentialism and Its Critics*, Oxford: Oxford University Press, pp. 187–223.

Sen, A. (1993), Capability and Well-being, in Nussbaum and Sen (1993).

Sen, A. (1997), Economics, Business Principles and Moral Sentiments, *Business Ethics Quarterly*, 7 (3).

Sen, A. (1999), *Development as Freedom*, Oxford: Oxford University Press.

Shell, S. (1990), Idealism, in Bloom (1990).

Shestack, J. J. (2000), The Philosophical Foundations of Human Rights, in Symonides (2000), pp. 31–66.

Short, C. (2004), Consume and Survive, *Tablet* (Jan. 17).

Shue, H. (1996), *Basic Rights: Subsistence, Affluence, and US Foreign Policy*, 2nd rev. edn., Princeton, NJ: Princeton University Press.

Shute, S., and Hurley, S. (1993) (eds.), *On Human Rights: The Oxford Amnesty Lectures 1993*, New York: Basic Books.

Sieghart, P. (1985), *The Lawful Rights of Mankind: An Introduction to the International Legal Code of Human Rights*, Oxford: Oxford University Press.

Simpson, A. W. B. (2001), *Human Rights and the End of Empire: Britain and the Genesis of the European Convention*, Oxford: Oxford University Press.

Singer, P. (2004), *One World: The Ethics of Globalization*, 2nd edn., New Haven, CT: Yale University Press.

Smith, R. K. M., and van den Anker, C. (2005) (eds.), *The Essentials of Human Rights*, London: Hodder Arnold.

Sophocles (1998), *Antigone*, ed. H. Lloyd-Jones, Loeb Classical Library, Cambridge, MA: Harvard University Press.

Speake, J. (1979) (ed.), *A Dictionary of Philosophy*, London: Pan Reference.

Stiglitz, J. (2002), *Globalisation and its Discontents*, London: Penguin.

Stirk, P. M. R., and Weigall, D. (1995), *An Introduction to Political Ideas*, London: Pinter, Cassell.

Stout, J. (1988), *Ethics After Babel: The Languages of Morals and Their Discontents*, Boston, MA: Beacon Press.

Stout, J. (1992), Truth, Natural Law, and Ethical Theory, in R. P. George (ed.), *Natural Law Theory: Contemporary Essays*, Oxford: Clarendon Press.

Sugden, C. (1996), *The Right to be Human: Biblical Studies in Human Rights*, Cambridge: Grove Books.

Sullivan, L. H. (1998), *Moving Mountains: The Principles and Purposes of Leon Sullivan*, Valley Forge, PA: Judson Press, Baptist Church of America.

Sumner, L. W. (1987), *The Moral Foundation of Rights*, Oxford: Clarendon Press.

Sumner, L. W. (2000), Rights, in H. LaFollette (2000) (ed.), *The Blackwell Guide to Ethical Theory*, Oxford: Blackwell, pp. 288–305.

Symonides, J. (1998), New Human Rights Dimensions, Obstacles and Challenges: Introductory Remarks, in Symonides (ed.), *Human Rights: New Dimensions and Challenges*, Paris: UNESCO.

Symonides, J. (2000) (ed.), *Human Rights: Concept and Standards*, Aldershot: Ashgate.

Tanner, N. P. (1990) (ed.), *Decrees of the Ecumenical Councils*, London: Sheed & Ward; Washington, DC: Georgetown University Press.

Teilhard de Chardin, P. (1975), *The Phenomenon of Man*, intro. by Sir Julian Huxley, London: Collins Fontana.

Temple, W. (1987), *Christianity and Social Order*, London: Shepheard-Walwyn and SPCK.

The United Nations and Human Rights 1945–1995 (1995), intro. by Boutros Boutros-Ghali, Secretary-General of the United Nations, New York: Department of Public Information, United Nations.

Thomson, J. J. (1990), *The Realm of Rights*, Cambridge, MA: Harvard University Press.

Tierney, B. (1997), *The Idea of Natural Rights: Studies on Natural Rights, Natural Law and Church Law 1150–1625*, Atlanta, GA: Emory University.

Trigg, R. (2005), *Morality Matters*, Oxford: Blackwell.

Tuck, R. (1993), *Natural Rights Theories: Their Origin and Development*, Cambridge: Cambridge University Press.

Twiss, S. B. (1998), Religion and Human Rights: A Comparative Perspective, in Twiss and B. Grelle (1998).

Twiss, S. B., and Grelle, B. (1998), *Explorations in Global Ethics: Comparative Religious Ethics and Interreligious Dialogue*, Oxford: Westview Press.

UN Commission on Human Rights (1985), *Right and Responsibility of Individuals to Promote and Protect Human Rights*, New York: United Nations.

UN News Service, <http://www.un.org/apps/news/printnews.asp?nid=18411>.

United Nations Action in the Field of Human Rights (1994), New York and Geneva: United Nations.

United Nations Bulletin, Lake Success, NY: United Nations Department of Public Information (ceased publication in June 1954).

United Nations, Charter of the (1995), New York: Department of Public Information, United Nations.

United Nations Commission on Global Governance (1995), *Our Global Neighbourhood*, Oxford: Oxford University Press.

United Nations Economic and Social Council Official Records, New York: United Nations.

United Nations Educational, Scientific and Cultural Organisation (UNESCO) (1949), *Human Rights: Comments and Interpretations*, London and New York: Allan Wingate.

United Nations General Secretary's Report (2001), available at <http://www.un.org/documents/secretariat.htm> accessed Feb. 2006.

United Nations Joint Commission on AIDS (UNAIDS), available at <http://www.unaids.org> accessed Feb. 2006.

United Nations Records (1948), Official Records of the Third Session of the General Assembly, Part I, Third Committee, vol. IIIA (6).

United Nations *Universal Declaration of Human Rights* (1948), New York: United Nations.

United Nations Vienna Declaration (1993), New York: United Nations.

United Nations Yearbook on Human Rights (various years), New York: United Nations.

Universal Declaration of Human Rights (1948), New York: United Nations Department of Public Information.

van der Heijden, Barend, and Tahzib-Lie, Bahiaq (1998) (eds.), *Reflections on the Universal Declaration of Human Rights: A Fiftieth Anniversary Anthology*, The Hague: Martin Nijhoff.

Vardy, P., and Grosch, P. (1994), *The Puzzle of Ethics*, London: Fount, HarperCollins.

Villey, M. (1962), *Leçons d'histoire de la philosophie du droit*, Paris: Dalloz.

Waldron, J. (1984) (ed.), *Theories of Rights*, Oxford: Oxford University Press.

Waldron, J. (1987) (ed.), *Nonsense upon Stilts*, London: Methuen.

Waldron, J. (2002), *God, Locke, and Equality: Christian Foundations in Locke's Political Thought*, Cambridge: Cambridge University Press.

Walker, S. (1998), *The Rights Revolution: Rights and Community in Modern America*, Oxford: Oxford University Press.

Ward, B., and Dubos, R. (1972), *Only One Earth: The Care and Maintenance of a Small Planet*, London: André Deutsch.

Warnock, M. (1998), *An Intelligent Person's Guide to Ethics*, London: Duckworth.

Weinreb, L. L. (1987), *Natural Law and Justice*, Cambridge, MA: Harvard University Press.

Weinreb, L. L. (1992), Natural Law and Rights, in Robert P. George (ed.), *Natural Law Theory: Contemporary Essays*, Oxford: Clarendon Press.

Wheen, F. (2004), *How Mumbo-Jumbo Conquered the World: A Short History of Modern Delusions*, London: Collins, Fourth Estate.

White, A. R. (1985), *Rights*, Oxford: Clarendon Press.

Williams, I. (2002), The Salon Interview: Mary Robinson, in the internet newsletter *Salon Premium* <http://www.salon.com/people/interview/> accessed Feb. 2006.

Wokler, R. (1994), Projecting the Enlightenment, in J. Horton and S. Mendus (eds.), *After MacIntyre: Critical Perspectives on the Work of Alasdair MacIntyre*, Cambridge: Polity Press.

Wolf, M. (2004), *Why Globalization Works: The Case for the Global Market Economy*, New Haven, CT: Yale University Press.

Wollstonecraft, M. (1995), *"A Vindication of the Rights of Men", with "A Vindication of the Rights of Women" and "Hints,"* ed. Sylvana Tomaselli, Cambridge: Cambridge University Press.

World Development Movement (2005), available from <http://www.wdm.org.uk/> accessed Feb. 2006.

Index